GIVE US THIS DAY

365 Daily Devotions for Today's Youth

Written by Carol Greene
Illustrated by Ted Bolte

Publishing House
St. Louis

For Carole and Dennis

The prayer on page 27 is reprinted from the book A CHILD'S GOODNIGHT BOOK by Margaret Wise Brown. Copyright © 1943, 1950. Used by permission of Addison-Wesley Publishing Company, Inc.

3558 South Jefferson Avenue, St. Louis, MO 63118

Printed in the United States of America

Library of Congress Cataloging in Publication Data

Greene, Carol.
Give us this day.

SUMMARY: Includes devotions based on an emotion, idea, or action for each day of the church year.
1. Children—Prayer-books and devotions—English.
2. Devotional calendars—Juvenile literature.
[1. Prayer books and devotions] I. Title.
BV4571.2.G73 242'.2 79-27813
ISBN 0-570-03496-5

CONTENTS

PREFACE

I wrote this book—me, Carol Greene, who on the outside is 37 years old at the time of writing. But time is a funny thing. Somewhere inside me is a Carol Greene who is still seven years old and wants to go on playing hopscotch for the rest of her life. And somewhere inside me is a Carol Greene who is 11 or 12 or 13. This Carol Greene goes to junior high and feels utterly miserable part of the time and in love with life and everything about it another part of the time. She is very curious about God, how she feels about Him and how He feels about her.

It is the junior high Carol Greene who wrote this book, and in order to make it speak to as many of you as possible, she used an old writer's trick. Hundreds of years ago, people used to write plays and tell stories about "everyman" and "everywoman". That was so everyone could find himself or herself in the play or story. Well, this book is about "everykid" and it's written as if everykid were writing in a journal or diary.

Everykid isn't a boy or a girl. Everykid doesn't belong to any particular race or ethnic group. Everykid isn't smart or dumb. Everykid doesn't live in the city or the country. And yet, everykid is and does all these things.

If you are totally confused by now, you're probably not alone. Just forget this preface and go on with the book.

And may God's power and love flow through what I have written and what you will read.

New Year's Day

HAPPY NEW YEAR, GOD!

You know how people are always telling kids, "Just be yourself and everything will be 'super'?" Just be yourself! Well, what I want to know is how you can be yourself when you don't know who you are?

I don't know who I am. Sometimes it seems as if I'm three people—the school me, the everyplace-else me, and the secret me who lives deep inside and is really sort of religious. I even live by three different calendars. There's the regular one that begins in January. There's the school one that begins in September. And ever since I was a little kid I've heard about the church calendar. It begins in Advent which is always late November or early December.

I've decided that the only way to figure out who I am is to think a lot about it. I've also decided that the secret me, the one who lives deep inside, the one who believes in God, is the most important one, the one I should pay the most attention to.

So, happy New Year, God! Here I am with a whole lot of questions and not many answers. Will You help me? I'm pretty sure You will.

2

SHALL I MAKE A RESOLUTION?

This is one of those times when my three calendars all collide. The church calendar is still celebrating Christmas. The school calendar tells me I've got a very long way to go before the year's over. And the rest-of-the-world calendar is shouting, "Happy New Year!"

Happy New Year. The time when everybody thinks they can start over again and makes resolutions to do a better job of it this year.

Shall I make a resolution? I can think of at least four bad habits I could try to break. Or five good ones I could try to begin.

But I guess I know myself too well. Any resolution I make today I'd just break in a week or two. Nobody else seems to take them all that seriously, and so I don't either.

No, if I'm going to break bad habits or start good ones I'll have to do it some other way. I'll have to make a resolution every single morning. And I'll have to ask God to help me keep it. I just can't do it alone.

Now let's see, where shall we start . . .

3

A NEW PERSON

I read someplace that every seven years all the cells in your body are replaced and you are a whole new person. I think that's great! In fact, every so often I look at my thumb or something to see if I can tell any difference. (Dumb!)

Seriously, though, this is just another one of those facts that points out to me what a fantastic thing God did when He created us. Every seven years a new person!

But wait. Didn't God do something even more fantastic than that? A new person. Isn't that what we become at Baptism? And every time He forgives our sins? A new person. Cleansed of our sins through Jesus' death on the cross.

That means you could become a new person every day. Every hour. Every **minute.** And that kind of change you couldn't help but notice. You'd **feel** new, as if your life were just beginning and the past didn't matter anymore.

I've heard people talk about all this in church and Sunday school for years and years. But it didn't make sense to me till right now. I guess I didn't really hear it.

A new person—me. Wow!

4

THE OLD PEOPLE

Today my Sunday school class went to a nursing home. We took little boxes of candy to the old people and we sang Christmas carols. I was scared to death.

There were so many of them and they were so old. They sat there in their chairs, and some of them looked at us like bright-eyed little birds and others just looked down. When we asked them to sing "Silent Night" with us, though, almost all of them tried. One old man even sang it in a foreign language. The nurse said it was Czech.

I can't think about this too much, God. It hurts too much. It hurts because there they are, and that's all that's left in their lives. And it hurts because I can picture me there someday, and I don't know if I could stand it.

Be with them, God. Love them and let them **know** You love them. Keep them warm and happy with Your love. They're **Yours,** God.

And, yes, I guess they're mine too. While we were getting ready to leave one old lady stroked my arm as if young skin was a miracle she could hardly believe.

"Come back," she whispered.

And I will. It's scary and it hurts. But I'll go back, God.

5

PUTTING AWAY

Today we got out the boxes, wrapped the ornaments in tissue, hung bread and peanut butter crackers on the tree, and put it out in the yard for the birds. For us Christmas is over for another year. For the birds maybe it's just beginning!

Earlier I thought I wanted Christmas to go on forever. But today I was sort of ready for it to be over. Maybe you can't go on celebrating every day. Maybe you need time in between to think about other things.

I guess that's what the people who planned the church calendar thought too. Otherwise they could have put in a lot more festivals—like one for every time Jesus worked a miracle.

They didn't, though. They left those in-between times open for other things to happen. I'm not sure just what those things are, but this year I'm going to try to find out, because I want them to happen to me. I want to **grow.**

So, good-bye, Christmas. See you next year!

Epiphany

A STAR SHONE BRIGHT

Epiphany. A hard word to spell and a strange one to pronounce. Ee-PIH-fah-nee. For a long time I've thought it was a little festival in memory of the day the Wise Men came to see Jesus. Today I learned. It's more, much more.

Epiphany comes from the Greek word that means "to show." When the Wise Men visited Jesus it was the first time Gentiles (people who aren't Jews) were shown the Savior. A star led them to Him. They saw Him. And that made all the difference. God was saying to the world, "I did not send My Son to just one group of people. I sent Him for all of you. See? I show Him to you."

So Epiphany isn't just one little festival. It's a whole season during which we Christians pay special attention to showing Jesus to the world.

And that's what I learned today. I've still got a lot of questions. Some fears too, I guess. But I wanted to grow this year, and if Epiphany is next on the agenda, well, then I'll try it.

Please help me, God. **Show** me Your Son when I get confused or discouraged.

7

ME? CHOSEN?

I learned something else yesterday—that each of us is chosen by God to do special work for Him. That's hard to understand. I'm not even one of the first kids chosen to be on a team at school. Why in the world would God choose me? Besides, I'm not sure I **want** to be chosen. It's too much responsibility.

Just think about the kind of people God chose to do His work in the Old Testament. People like Jacob and Moses. Now **there** were real heroes.

Or were they? I seem to remember Jacob doing some pretty shady things. And Moses made his share of mistakes too. In fact, didn't Moses even **argue** with God about being chosen? He didn't want to be anymore than I do. Hmmmm.

Okay then. Look at the people Jesus chose to help Him. I'll bet they were better qualified for the job.

Yeah, sure. Like Matthew the tax collector. Or Peter, who even denied Jesus.

Okay, God. You win. You must have Your own reasons for choosing people, reasons I can't understand. So if You want me, I'm Yours.

Chosen. Me!

8

THE WILDERNESS

When people like Paul and Silas and Barnabas went out to show Jesus to the world, they had to travel in the wilderness. There were robbers and storms and fierce beasts and everything out there. It must have been scary.

I'm glad I don't have to do that. Our world is a little more civilized. Well, we do have robbers. And storms. But there aren't too many fierce beasts left.

Unless—is poverty a fierce beast? Or greed? Or hate? Or . . . oh, rats! I guess we have fierce beasts too.

And that's where You want me to show Jesus, is it, God? Out there in the world? It's a wilderness, You know. Yeah, I guess You do know. After all, You care about those people who live in the wilderness too, don't You? The ones who suffer from poverty, greed, hate, and all the rest.

I don't want to go out there, God. It's scary. But if that's what You want, I'll try. Just please go with me.

9

I'M JUST A KID

There's one thing, God, that maybe You sort of forgot. You see, I'm just a kid. And most of the problems in this world are too big even for grown-ups to handle. A kid wouldn't stand a chance.

What can I do about poverty, for example? There are **millions** of people starving. I can't feed all of them. Why, the most I could do is save enough out of my allowance each week to buy one kid one meal. Big deal!

Big deal. Yes. It would be a big deal to me if I were a kid who was starving. One meal would be a very big deal indeed. It might be such a big deal that I'd start wondering about the person who got me that meal. And if I knew that person was a Christian, I might start wondering about that too. I might ask questions. One meal a week might be just what it takes to show me Jesus.

Furthermore, if about 20 kids saved enough out of their allowances to buy one meal a week, that starving kid wouldn't be starving anymore. Twenty kids. That's just about how many there are in my Sunday school class. I wonder . . .

O God! With You **anything** is possible—isn't it?

10

SIGN TONIGHT!

I heard a song once and part of the chorus went: "Sign tonight! Sign tonight! A million souls are waiting." I think you were supposed to sign up for Jesus. To be perfectly honest, the whole thing made me sick.

I can't do that. I can't stand on street corners and preach sermons or hand out tracts. I can't knock on doors and tell people they're going to fry in hell if they don't come to church with me next Sunday. First of all my mom wouldn't let me. But I couldn't do it even if she would.

The thing about all that street-corner and door-knocking stuff is that you don't even **know** the people you're talking to. You don't know their problems, their hurts. You don't even know if they already follow Jesus!

I wouldn't listen to somebody who didn't even care enough to know me, who just wanted my signature on the dotted line or my body in church.

I don't have to do it that way, do I, God? No, of course I don't. Jesus didn't. He didn't collect signatures or bodies. He **cared** about the people He talked to. He listened to them and helped them solve their problems.

I want to do it His way, God.

11

WHAT'S A PROPHET?

One time at school a girl asked me how I liked her new haircut. I said it made her face look fat. She didn't speak to me for six weeks.

Another time a teacher asked me how a particular poem made me feel. I said sort of sick to my stomach. That didn't go over too well either.

But the other day our pastor said that a prophet is someone who speaks the truth. Like a prophet might take a good hard look at our society and say that something is wrong if some people are starving and others have millions of dollars.

I **like** that. I think it would be great to be a prophet. Of course I don't know enough to be one yet. But maybe someday . . .

The only problem is that whenever I tell the truth, I seem to get in trouble. Like with that girl and my teacher. But come to think of it, the prophets in the Bible got in trouble sometimes too. Poor old Daniel even ended up in a pit full of hungry lions.

Maybe it wouldn't be so great to be a prophet after all. Maybe it's just one of those things you end up doing because God says it's your job. Maybe it won't even be my job.

Or maybe it will.

12

SOMEONE TO FOLLOW

I knew a kid once who didn't want to be a scout because he was afraid they'd make him go out in the woods by himself and he'd get lost and die. That was pretty dumb of him. He should have known that scouts have leaders to follow.

But in a way I know how he felt because it's sort of how I feel about this whole Epiphany thing. I don't want to go out there in the wilderness alone. I might get lost and die. I guess what I really mean is that I might get hurt pretty bad inside. I want someone to follow.

I can't picture following my pastor around all the time, though. Or my Sunday school teacher. It just wouldn't be practical. In fact, I can't think of one person I could follow.

Unless . . . **would** it be possible to follow Jesus in a different sort of way? I mean, I know He's always with me, but would it be possible to sort of talk to Him by praying and listen to Him by reading the Bible?

That's a **wild** idea. I'll have to think about it some more. But there sure isn't anyone else I'd rather follow!

13

HUNGER IS FOR REAL

I got excited about that stuff I wrote the other day about a starving kid. So I went to our church library and checked out some stuff about hunger. And I made a very big discovery. Hunger is for real.

It's not just a bunch of sob stories people send you in the mail or show on TV. It's true!

There are millions and millions of people in the world that don't have enough to eat. There are people in my **own** country who are dying of starvation.

And I guess what's worst of all is that this isn't happening because there's not enough food to go around. There is! It just doesn't get to the people who need it.

That's where the whole thing gets pretty complicated. The stuff I started reading talked about economic factors and trade agreements and stuff like that. I didn't understand too well. But what it **sounded** like to me was that all this food is tied up in miles of red tape while the people who need it are dying.

If that's the case, God, please help us cut that tape. Please help us feel those people. How can we show them Your Son if they're dead?

14

GOD, IT HURTS!

I can't get that stuff I wrote yesterday out of my mind, and the more I think about it, the more it hurts. Why should people be dying of hunger in a world that has enough food for them? It's so unfair!

I guess what really hurts is that I start picturing individual people. Not real people, but people who could be real. A kid like me. An old lady. A baby. Then a little bit of their pain becomes my pain and, God, it hurts! In fact, last night I hardly slept at all.

Feeding the hungry was just one thing Jesus talked about. I thought I'd try to look at some of the others too. But I'm not sure I can do it if it's going to be like this.

It's later now. I talked to mom. I was afraid she'd tell me to forget the whole thing, that I was too young to handle it. But she didn't.

She said to go ahead and think about all those other things Jesus mentioned, but while I was at it to write down some positive things a kid like me could do to help. Then, later, I could go back, look at what I've written, and decide on an area where I'd like to put most of my energy.

"Don't forget that there are other people in the world who care too," she said. "Maybe not enough, but you aren't totally alone."

And God cares. I mustn't forget that.

15

BOXES IN THE BASEMENT

Last winter mom and I used to take the bus sometimes to shop downtown. We had to pass through a pretty bad part of the city to get there, and I'd see these little kids playing outside without hats or gloves or anything. I thought then that their mothers ought to be taking better care of them.

Now I understand. Their mothers were doing the best they could. They simply didn't have any hats or gloves or warm coats to give their kids. And they didn't have any money to buy them with. Those kids were some of the naked that Jesus wants us to clothe.

I can think of one way a kid like me could help right away. Down in the basement are a couple boxes of clothes that are perfectly good but too small for me now. I'm sure if I told mom I wanted to give them to some charity she'd let me. And my pastor probably knows a good charity to give them to.

I can think of another thing too. What if I got up very early some Saturday morning, took a few dollars with me, and rode my bike to a garage sale? You can get **gobs** of kids' clothes for almost nothing at a garage sale. Then I could give them to charity too.

Yeah, I feel better now that I'm thinking of things I can **do.**

16

SICK IS BORING

I've only been in a hospital once, and that was just the emergency room. I skidded on some gravel with my bike and had to have four stitches in my chin. It wasn't much fun!

But a boy in my class had to have an operation, and he was in the hospital for a long time. He said the worst part wasn't the pain or the shots or any of that medical stuff. The worst part was being lonely and bored.

I had bronchitis last year, and I can remember how bored I got. And I was in my own home with all my own stuff around me. I can see why Jesus wants us to visit the sick.

It's kind of hard, though, for a kid to visit someone sick in person. Lots of hospitals won't even let you in. And if the person is at home your mother gets all nervous about the germs.

But you can visit sick people in other ways. You can call them on the phone or send them funny cards and presents you make yourself.

Our church newsletter always prints a list of people who are sick. I wonder if anyone on that list would like to hear from **me.**

17

DIFFERENT KINDS OF PRISONS

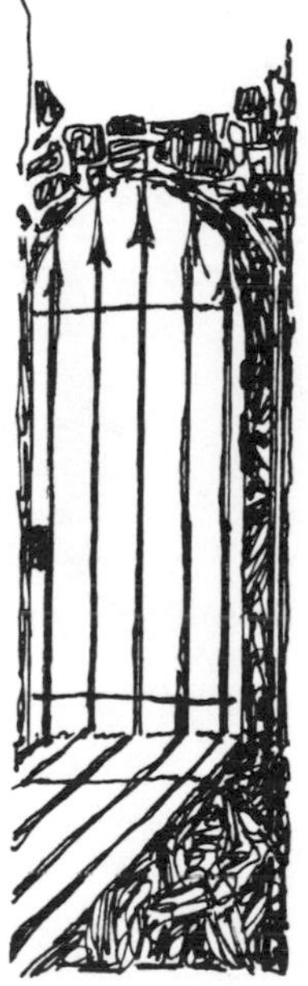

Another thing Jesus talked about was prisoners. I don't think I know any. And I don't think the guards would let me into the jail to visit them if I did. Visiting prisoners might be a neat thing to do when I grow up, but I don't see how I could manage it now.

Unless there are different **kinds** of prisons. I think I'm talking now about what my teacher calls metaphors. A metaphor is when you say one thing is something else. Poets do it a lot.

Sickness is a prison. Loneliness is a prison. Old age is a prison.

Old age! Maybe **those** are the prisoners I could visit. The people in the nursing home where we sang Christmas carols—they're prisoners just because their bodies won't let them get out and go many places. And I **know** they'd like to see me. That one old lady even asked me to come back.

I'm going to have mom call right now and find out if I can stop by there after school some day.

Hey, this is exciting. I'm going to **do** something!

18

THE FIRST TRY

I did it! The superintendent at the nursing home said they'd be glad to have me, and so this afternoon I stopped by. I went straight to **my** old lady, and she remembered me right away. Her name is Mrs. Fitzpatrick, and she came to the home about a year ago when her legs got so bad she couldn't live in her own house anymore.

Mrs. Fitzpatrick has four grownup children but they all live out of town. She hasn't had a visitor of her own for over three months! I asked her if her minister didn't come to see her sometimes, and she said, well, her old minister had died a few years ago, and she hadn't gone to church much after that because she didn't like the new one.

And then I took a deep breath and asked her if she'd like **my** minister to come to see her. I promised that I'd come with him to introduce them and everything.

She thought for a minute and then she said, "Why, yes. Yes. I would like that."

Wow! I don't know if that's showing Jesus to the world exactly, but it sure feels right. And it didn't hurt a bit. I'm even looking forward to visiting Mrs. Fitzpatrick again. She's going to tell me stories about when she was a girl. It feels so **good** to have taken the plunge!

19

AN AWFUL PERSON

There's this old man at the nursing home with Mrs. Fitzpatrick. I think he's the most awful person I ever met. First of all he kept interrupting us all the while we were talking.

"Why you want to bother with that old woman, kid?" he kept asking. "Go outside and play like other kids."

That's all he'd say, but he said it over and over like a broken record. Mrs. Fitzpatrick didn't even get mad. She just kept answering, "You be quiet now, Horace. It's all right."

Finally the old man looked her in the eye and spit right on the floor. That's when the nurse came in. She scolded him and took him off to his room.

I'm sure glad I'm visiting Mrs. Fitzpatrick and not him. **That** sort of person doesn't deserve any visitors. Even Jesus would be turned off by him.

I'm glad I wrote that last sentence, dumb as it is. It's **so** dumb that it turned my thinking around. Of course Jesus wouldn't be turned off by Mr. Horace. He's exactly the kind of person who needs Jesus most. And I suppose **that** means I should try to be nice to Mr. Horace too.

Well, I'll try. But I don't think it's going to do any good.

20

A SPECIAL POWER

I'm reading this really great book called **Sounder.** The kid that the book is about is a whole lot different from me, but that doesn't seem to matter. I can still feel every single feeling he feels. I think it takes a good writer to make you able to do that.

My teacher calls that feeling "identification." She says you start to see yourself as the character in a pretend sort of way.

My mom says it's more than that. She says it's "compassion," being able to feel with the other person. I think they're both right. And I think that reading books is a neat way of learning how to feel identification and compassion. You get to practice on so many different kinds of people.

But I think Jesus wants you to take it farther than that. I think He wants you to feel identification and compassion for people you meet out in the world. That's what He seemed to do.

And I guess it's what I did with Mrs. Fitzpatrick. I could sort of imagine what it would be like to be her, shut up in a nursing home with no one to come visit you. I could feel loneliness along with her. And because of that I didn't have much trouble thinking of things to say to her.

Whatever power it is that makes able to feel identification and compassion, I think it's a gift from God that He gives us to help us do His work. Thanks, God!

21

TOUGH BUBBLES

Every time somebody says "Martin Luther King" I think of the words "I have a dream." Dr. King said those words again and again in a speech he made. I saw part of it on a TV documentary.

Each time he said "I have a dream" you could just **see** that dream, like a bright shining bubble floating out in front of him. It wasn't a fragile bubble though. It wouldn't pop the first time someone touched it. No, it was a tough bubble.

I want a dream like that. I want something I can spend my whole life working for, something big and important that will change the world and make it better.

I don't know what it will be yet. Maybe when you're a kid you have to dream lots of different dreams before you find the one that's really yours. But I know I want it to be big. And I want it to be tough.

God, please help me dream.

22

A DROP IN THE BUCKET

I went to see Mrs. Fitzpatrick at the nursing home today, and while I was there I tried to be nice to Mr. Horace too. (The nurse says his name is really Mr. Benton, but I like to call him Mr. Horace. I **think** he likes it too. At least he sort of cackles whenever I say it.) Mom gave me two little houseplants to take with me this time—one for each of them.

Mrs. Fitzpatrick got all excited about hers. She said she's going to talk to it, and then it will grow twice as fast. Mr. Horace just looked at his and snorted.

But he **did** cackle when I called him Mr. Horace, and I think that cackle was supposed to be a laugh. At least it's probably as close as Mr. Horace can get to a laugh.

Maybe that's only a drop in the bucket, but I feel pretty good about it. After all, I'm not the only one trying to fill that particular bucket. The nurses are working at it too and so is Mrs. Fitzpatrick, I think. And even more important, God is. He's not going to let that bucket be thrown away. He **loves** it.

23

WHAT IF I FAIL?

I wonder if people in heaven know what's going on back on earth. I wonder if Martin Luther King knows that his dream didn't die when he did. Did God let him watch other people pick up that dream and march on with it?

I don't suppose anyone really knows the answer to that question. But I think it's important that **I** know dreams don't have to die. Because sometimes I get really scared that I'll try to do some important thing and I'll fail. And what will happen then?

I **am** going to fail sometimes. Everybody does. But I think I'll be able to take it if I can just remember to trust God. If I'm dreaming His kind of dream, He's not going to let it die just because I messed up. Maybe He'll give me another chance. Or maybe He'll just pass that dream on to somebody else who can take over where I left off.

It's kind of a relief to know that.

24

DIFFERENT

My school is on the edge of the city, so lots of different kinds of kids go to it. There are kids from the suburbs, kids from the country, and kids from the city itself. There are black kids, brown kids, white kids, and a few Oriental kids. And, of course, there are boy kids and girl kids.

Some of us like each other and some of us don't. I don't think anyone knows everybody. The people I like are mostly ones who are interested in some of the same things I'm interested in. The people I don't like are mostly ones who have been mean to me or to someone I like.

I don't think there's anything very surprising in all of this. What **is** surprising, though, is how people let themselves get hung up on prejudice. Okay, here's this kid who's interested in some of the same things I like and who's never done anything mean. Why shouldn't he be my friend? Just because his skin is a different color than mine? It doesn't make sense.

I don't like pizza. Maybe this kid does. **That** doesn't mean we can't be friends. Why should skin?

Personally, I think God had a perfectly good reason for making everybody different. We'd be bored stiff if He didn't. Imagine if everyone was just like me. Bo-ring!

It was a good idea, God. Help us understand that.

25

I'M NOT THE FIRST

We've been studying Joseph in Sunday school, and I just made this incredible discovery. Joseph was a human being! He did wrong things—like showing off. His brothers picked on him. He got scared and depressed. He wanted to get even. And through all of this he held on to God.

I guess what this really says to me is that I'm not the first person to face some of the problems I have or feel some of the feelings I feel. I'm not the first person who's sometimes felt there was nothing or no one to hold on to **except** God. Joseph went through the same thing. And there were probably a lot of other Bible people like that too.

Of course all of this wouldn't be any big deal if the Bible stories didn't tell you something else. But they do. Joseph not only held on to God. God held on to Joseph! He never let him go, no matter what happened.

And what **that** says to me is that God won't let go of me either—no matter what happens.

26

THE NEWS

We're supposed to watch the news every night this week for current events. I hate it. **Everything** is bad news. Murder. Robberies. Countries fighting each other.

Maybe it wouldn't be so bad if I could come up with a good reason for **why** all these things are happening. But I can't. The closest I can get is that somebody has something that somebody else wants. And **that's** no reason to kill.

I'm so confused, God. It seems to me that if we just tried a little harder the world would be a much nicer place. But we don't even seem able to **try.**

Is this what the Bible means when it talks about sin? Is sin the selfishness in people that won't let them even try to make the world nicer?

I can see why You sent Jesus, God. We **need** forgiving. But I don't think we're taking much advantage of it. Is that because too many of us don't know or don't really understand what Jesus is all about?

Is that why You want some of us to get busy and show Him to the world?

27

HOW MUCH WILL IT COST?

How much is all of this going to cost, God—this showing Your Son to the world? Oh, I know it's not going to cost me much money. I don't have much money to spend. But I have a feeling it's going to cost me a lot of other things.

It's already costing me time. A couple days a week I'm not watching TV after school anymore. I'm going to the nursing home instead.

It's costing me pain too, because everytime I see or hear about one of Your people hurting, God, I hurt too.

And it's costing me energy. It takes energy to care, God.

But it's going to cost even more, isn't it? I have a funny feeling about that.

The strangest thing of all, though, is that I don't mind. I feel almost like a lump of clay. I've handed myself over to You, God, and You can do whatever You want with me. **Use** me, no matter how much it costs. (The bit about the clay is from Isaiah.)

None of this makes much sense according to the rest of the world. But then You aren't the rest of the world, are You, God? And the way **You** think, it makes a lot of sense!

28

PEACE ON EARTH

I found a Christmas card behind my bed last weekend. (Actually I find a lot of interesting things behind my bed on the rare occasions when I move it.) This Christmas card showed three penguins, all wearing little Santa Claus hats and singing "peace on earth!"

Well, that got me to thinking. Not about penguins in Santa Claus hats but about peace. Then my mom came into the room. After she finished fainting over the fact that I was cleaning behind my bed, I asked her what she thought had happened to that peace the angels sang about on the first Christmas.

"Let me quote you a line from a hymn," said my mom. (She loves to quote things.) "'The peace of God, it is no peace, But strife closed in the sod.' That means that living with God's peace is like doing battle all your life. It's a very active sort of peace."

"But that's not what the rest of the world means by peace," I said.

"Nope," said my mom.

Things sure are different with God. **Active** peace. I'll have to think about that.

29

PEACE AT SCHOOL

Since I thought I'd figured out what "active peace" was, I decided to try spreading a little of it at school this week. There's this kid who's fairly new, and nobody likes her very much. She's one of those kids that it really is sort of fun to tease because she gets made right away and then starts to cry. And there's a particular group of kids that teases her all the time.

Well, I began thinking how she must feel, and I decided it must be lousy. I mean, if anyone needed to feel a little peace, that girl did. So I started out the week by being nice to her. When some kids from the group knocked her books off her desk I picked them up. And I ate lunch with her.

It really wasn't all that bad either. I finally found out that she's interested in the stars—astronomy and stuff—and once she started talking about that she was sort of interesting. I'm also probably the only kid in school who's ever seen her smile.

This afternoon I asked my mom if that's what she meant by God's active kind of peace.

She grinned and hugged me.

"That's what I mean by a nice kid," she said.

30

SOME KIDS ARE AGAINST ME

I ate lunch most of this week with that girl, and boy, did I get in trouble. Not with the girl. Not with the teachers. With some of the other kids.

One guy walked by and purposely dropped some trash in the middle of my plate. Later another girl knocked **my** books off **my** desk. And someone else stuck a note on my bike that said, "Pick your friends a little more carefully." They'd stuck it on with bubblegum.

I've never been a particularly popular kid at school. But I've never been picked on either. For about 30 seconds after I found the note I wanted to cry.

Then I got mad. There is no reason for the other kids to mistreat that girl. She hasn't done anything wrong. She's just a little shy and sensitive. I'll be friends with that girl if I want. I **will** be friends with her because I know I should be.

This is going to be rough, God. Please help.

31

BATTLEFIELD LEARNING

They caught the guy who put the note on my bike. A friend called me this morning and told me. A monitor saw him trying to do it again just before school let out and turned him in to the principal. I don't think he'll try that trick again. But it's still going to be rough. I've also had my milk spilled and found a dead roach in my desk.

The girl? Her name's Maggie. And she's going to lend me a book about the stars. She also said maybe I can come over some evening and look through her telescope. I **don't** want Maggie to know what's happening to me. It'd just make her feel bad.

In a way, though, this isn't such a terrible thing because I've learned some stuff. First of all I've learned that I can take it. I'm not scared of those kids, and I wouldn't have known that if this hadn't happened.

Second, I've learned that not everyone **has** to like me. If you really do the stuff you say you believe in, you probably will make some enemies.

And third, I've learned that God **is** with me at times like this. I can practically **feel** Him.

That makes the whole battle worthwhile.

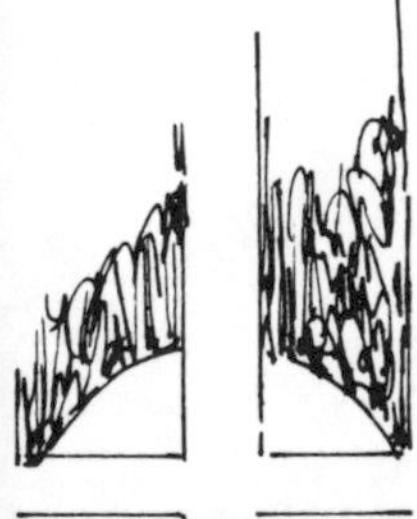

32

THE KINGDOM

The fact that I want to do this work for God, no matter how much it costs me, doesn't make sense according to the rest of the world. In the rest of the world you get paid a salary for the work you do. You don't **pay** to do work.

God's kind of peace doesn't make sense according to the rest of the world either. Most people think of peace as a quiet, safe feeling. God's peace gets you moving and sometimes puts you in tricky situations.

Ever since I started thinking about me and religion I've had the strangest feeling that I'm living in two different worlds. And what makes sense in one world doesn't make sense in the other.

Now our pastor preached a sermon that said the same thing! He said that Christians are called to live in the kingdom of God and in the rest of the world at the same time. I used to think the kingdom of God meant heaven, but our pastor says it's a little different. He says the kingdom of God is right **now.** He says Jesus said so. And the kingdom of God is **in** the world, but it's not **like** the world.

So I'm living in the kingdom of God—and the rest of the world too. Just thinking about it is enough to make me feel special.

33

UNCOMFORTABLE TIMES

Today a friend of mine asked me to come over and listen to records. I said I couldn't because it was one of the days I visit the nursing home.

"Do you have a relative there?" asked my friend.

"Well, not exactly," I said. "But there's this little old lady called Mrs. Fitzpatrick who I visit."

"Why?" asked my friend. "I'd never go to a place like that if I didn't have to. It's depressing."

Well, I didn't know what to say, because in one way my friend was right. I don't **have** to go to the home. And it **is** depressing sometimes.

I just didn't have the nerve to say, "Well, I'm doing some work for God, and He goes along and helps. And it doesn't matter if it's depressing sometimes because in another way it isn't."

My friend would not have understood.

So I said, "Well, it's just something I do," and left. I think my friend thought I was crazy.

Living in Your kingdom can be a little uncomfortable at times, can't it, God? Please, show me the best way to handle those uncomfortable moments.

34

WHY IS THERE PAIN?

So much of what I've learned about God is absolutely wonderful. But there's one thing I just can't understand. Why, if God loves us so much, does He let there be pain and suffering in the world?

I asked my mom and she hemmed and hawed and got a strange, scared look in her eyes and finally said why didn't I call our pastor and ask **him.** So I did. He gave me the greatest explanation, and I just hope I can remember it long enough to write it down.

He said that God did not want pain and suffering to come into the world; they are the result of sin. Okay, I can buy that. He said that, for Christians, pain and suffering leads us to repent and find comfort in Jesus.

"Ohhh," I said.

"Pain and suffering will always be with us," he continued. "But God has also given us the opportunity to comfort people and show our Christian love. Jesus said we should feed those who are hungry, clothe those who have nothing to wear, and care for those who are sick. We can show Jesus' love to the world."

I can't stop pain and suffering, God, but maybe You could help me start showing Your love to just a small part of the world, like the people I know.

35

SOMEONE TO TALK TO

It really helped yesterday talking to my pastor about that problem. I wish I had someone I could talk to like that all the time. But I can't always be bugging my pastor. He's got to make hospital calls and write sermons and stuff like that.

I can't always talk to my parents either. Sometimes the problem I want to talk about **includes** my parents and sometimes—well—I guess I feel too much like a baby running to them.

Wouldn't it be neat if the church gave each kid a religious counselor, like we have guidance counselors at school? Maybe that's what godparents are supposed to be, but mine live about 80 miles away. I think that's true for a lot of other kids too.

What the church would have to do is find some people who really like kids, who understand their problems, and who know something about religion. There wouldn't even have to be a lot of these people. Maybe all the kids in the same grade could have the same one.

Hey! Maybe our Sunday school teachers could do that job too. Mine would be great at it. I wonder what would happen if I just called her up the next time I have a problem that has to do with religion. I wonder . . .

36

ALONE SOMETIMES

Today was one of those days when I wasn't alone for even one minute. Well, I **was** alone while I did my homework, but that doesn't count because the time was all filled up with homework. I wouldn't even be writing this now if I hadn't **stolen** the time by deciding to take a shower in the morning. I hate days like this.

It's not that I don't like people. Most of the time I want to be with them. I'd feel awful if I were alone all the time. But sometimes I just need time to think and maybe even pray a little. I usually put off saying my prayers till I'm in bed, and then sometimes I fall asleep in the middle of them. I hope God understands!

It seems to me that Jesus used to go off to be by Himself every so often. And if **He** needed to do that, I sure do. Maybe I'll just have to take a long hard look at all the stuff that's filling up my days and cut some of it out. After all, it's for the sake of my health—my **spiritual** health!

37

I CAN'T SAY GOD WORDS

Today I was at the nursing home, visiting Mrs. Fitzpatrick, when this lady came into the sunroom (that's where we usually sit along with a bunch of the other old people). This lady went right up to an old woman who's had so many strokes she can hardly talk and said, "Do you accept Jesus Christ as your personal Lord and Savior?"

I think the old lady got scared by the suddenness because she started to cry and make these awful, grunting noises, and one of the nurses had to come and take her to her room.

"Crazy religious fanatic," mumbled Mrs. Fitzpatrick as the lady who'd asked the question left. Lots of the other old people looked mad too. And to be perfectly honest, I was right with them.

Part of it was the whole impersonal, street-corner preacher thing that always turns me off. But part of it was the words she used. Not in my wildest dreams could I picture myself saying, "Do you accept Jesus Christ as your personal Lord and Savior."

Now if someone I felt close to happened to ask me how I'd managed to get through a difficult situation, I could say, "Well, I sort of think God helped me."

Or if someone asked me how I could possibly forgive so-and-so for the horrible thing they'd done to me, I might say, "I guess it has something to do with Jesus and the way He died for forgiveness. I really believe that."

Maybe what it all comes down to is that we each have to talk about God in our own language. Mine just doesn't happen to include what I call "God words"—the phony-sounding stuff. Is that all right, God?

38

A SONG IN A STRANGE LAND

There's a story that goes along with one of the psalms in the Bible. The people of Israel have been captured and taken as slaves to the land of their enemies. While they're there, their enemies start taunting them and asking them to sing one of their religious songs. The people of Israel sing this psalm, and one of the lines is "How can we sing the Lord's song in a strange land?"

Except they did, of course, because they sang the psalm—or at least part of it.

I think that lots of times God is asking us to sing His song in a strange land. Most of our world is a strange land to me—even my own neighborhood and my own school sometimes. It can be scary there, and I could get hurt inside if not physically too. But if I sing God's song, part of the scariness goes away.

Oh, I don't mean sing out loud. I'd probably just get laughed at or locked up. But there's a way you can walk and act, a smile you can have just behind your eyes, that somehow says to the world, "There's a song inside that person and it's a good one."

I'd like to do that more often. God, could You let me hear Your song a little louder?

39

THE LITTLE MINISTER

The Little Minister is the title of a book we have downstairs in our living-room bookcase. I think it's a classic, but I don't know anything else about it because I've never read it.

The title, though, got me thinking. In a way aren't all the people in the church who do work for God ministers? Someplace I once heard the phrase "priesthood of believers." I think that may mean the same thing.

It sure is a neat idea. I mean, here we have this person wearing black clothes and a funny white collar and most of the world says, "There goes a minister." If they don't want to have anything to do with religion, they just keep away from people dressed like that.

But what most of the world doesn't know is that there's a whole army of ministers who don't wear special clothes. They're plainclothes ministers and some of them care just as much about doing God's work as the ministers in uniform.

How about that? Me a little plainclothes minister. I like it!

40

I FELL

What a day! Anything that possibly could go wrong did go wrong. Right off the bat I discovered that my best friend isn't speaking to me—and I don't know why. My teacher gave a pop test and I know I failed it. Later she chewed me out in front of the whole class about a paper I'd written. She said it was sloppy, careless, and generally poor work. And that's just the beginning.

This afternoon I got called to the principal's office. He wanted to know if I knew anything about some bike stealing that's been going on. He said someone had seen me hanging around the bike racks. Well, that someone must have seen someone else who looks like me, and I told the principal that. But he didn't act like he believed me.

I took a long time getting home from school because I was

walking slowly and thinking about all that had happened. And when I got home, mom was furious because I'd missed an appointment at the dentist's. I honestly just forgot! Dad will be furious about that too when he hears, because our dentist makes you pay for missed appointments unless you call 24 hours ahead of time.

When I was a little kid and fell down, it seemed like there was always someone right there to pick me up again and make me feel better. Well, I've sure fallen down now and there's no one. Is there? God?

41

A REAL SACRIFICE

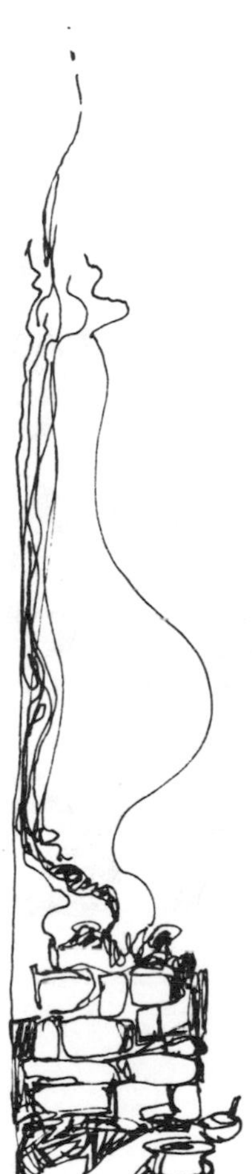

Today I came up with another religious question. We don't do burned offerings and that sort of thing in our churches anymore (and I'm glad we don't), but we still talk about sacrifices. What are they and why do we have them? Didn't Jesus take care of all that?

Well, I decided that this was the perfect problem to try calling my Sunday school teacher about. I did and I honestly think she was glad! She asked me if she could have a little time to think about my question and maybe look at a couple of books, and then she'd call me back. She did too.

"A sacrifice," she said, "is something set apart or made holy. That's what the word literally means. When we sacrifice something today, we set it apart and ask God to use it or help us use it in some special way in His work. That's why it's usually something that's pretty important to us. We want to give God the best thing we can."

"Could you give me some examples?" I asked.

"Well, money's the one most people think of first," she said. "But I think there are better things. Like maybe a whole day of your time. Or a big chunk of caring—or even love."

Well, that really made sense to me. I mean, those things don't get in the way of what Jesus did at all. In fact, we make sacrifices like that just **because** of what Jesus did. We want to show our love for God.

I guess in a way I'm sacrificing some of my time by going to the nursing home. But it doesn't really feel like it because I like it. Must be another one of those strange things about living in Your kingdom, God.

42

A RELIGIOUS FANATIC?

Good grief, I wonder if I'm becoming a religious fanatic? I'm paying attention to the church calendar. I think about religion almost every day. I pray almost every day. I **know** a lot of my friends don't do that. Is there something the matter with me?

Well, if there is, that's just tough because I like being this way. Before I felt sort of like a plant walking around everywhere on its skinny little white roots. Now I feel like those roots are in dirt—good clean dirt—where they ought to be. Maybe that's not a very religious picture, but it says the way I feel.

Actually, when you stop to think about all God has done for us—making us and our world, saving us, taking care of us—I don't see how anyone could feel any other way. I don't see how I went around ignoring God for days on end.

So, here I am, a religious fanatic. And it's great!

43

OPPRESSED

I saw this horrible movie the other night on TV. It was all about this lady who was caught being a witch back in the 17th century. Actually the movie never came out and said she was a witch, but all her neighbors thought so. And the way they punished witches back then was to make them lie on the ground. Then they put boards on top of them and rocks on top of the boards. They just kept piling up rocks until the person was crushed to death. It gives me goosebumps just to think about it.

I've read the term "oppressed people" lots of times in newsmagazines. Our pastor uses it sometimes in his sermons too. It means people who are poor or terribly ill in some way or who live under a dictator. I wonder if those oppressed people feel sort of like the lady in that movie, as if all the awful things in their lives are just pressing down on them, and there's no way they can get loose. God, I couldn't stand it. I know I'd die right away.

Please, be with the oppressed people. Lift off some of those things that are crushing them. And help us not add new things.

44

THE AMBULANCE

Today I was with some friends from school, walking along the street and having a good time, when an ambulance went by. Its siren was screaming and the lights were flashing. I couldn't help myself. I stopped right in the middle of a sentence and turned cold all over. It only lasted a minute, and then I was okay again. But that always happens to me when an ambulance goes by.

I think that during that moment I'm picturing me on the inside, horribly hurt and in pain. Or else I'm picturing someone I love. It's an awful, helpless feeling.

Today, though, I finally figured out what to do about it. I'll pray, just a simple little prayer like: "Be with them, God. Let them know You

are with them so they won't be afraid." That's what I'd pray for me if I were in the ambulance because I think being afraid would be the worst part of it. And so that's what I'll pray for all those people I don't know.

Then I won't have to feel helpless anymore. I'll have helped in the best way I can. I'll have handed those people over to God.

45

HOW ABOUT THE CHURCH?

Yesterday afternoon my mom helped me take those boxes of clothes to a charity that will give them to people who need them. Today I was telling my friend about it and about going to the nursing home to see Mrs. Fitzpatrick.

"Why are **you** doing all that?" asked my friend. "Isn't that what your church is supposed to do?"

Well, the answer just bounced right off my tongue.

"I **am** my church," I said. "We all are."

"Oh," said my friend. "I never thought about it like that before."

To be perfectly honest, neither had I. But I guess I've been watching it happen all along. I do my thing and my mom does hers. My dad does his and the people across the aisle do theirs. And when you put all those things together, they are God's work and we are the church doing it.

We're more than just a group of people, though, each one doing something different. The secret is that we all follow the same leader. Jesus. He's the One who brought us together in the first place, and He's the One who holds us together, even when some of us mess up. That makes us different from every other organization. And it means we have tremendous power.

Thank You, God, for our different, wonderful church.

46

THE ANIMALS

I read a prayer today that I just love. It goes like this:

"Dear Father, hear and bless
Thy beasts and singing birds,
and guard with tenderness
small things that have no words."

A lady called Margaret Wise Brown wrote it. (She wrote lots of children's books too.) I especially like the last line. That's the thing about animals that really gets to me—they can't talk to you. Sometimes I'll look at a bird with bright black eyes and wonder, "What are you thinking, you smart-aleck little rascal?" Or I'll look at a dog's big sad eyes and wonder if its thoughts are really sad too.

I know it's our job to look after the animals, God, but sometimes we don't do it very well. We're cruel to them or else we just forget them, like I sometimes forget to feed the cat.

But You've promised, God, that You know every time a sparrow falls. Jesus said that when He was talking about how great Your love is. Take care of them, God—the sparrows and all of them. And help us to a better job too.

47

THE FRONT LINE

A while back I wrote about the ministers in uniform and all the rest of us who are plainclothes ministers. I said that this reminded me of an army. But I forgot to mention some people who have one of the toughest jobs of all, the ones who work on the front line. Missionaries.

For a long time I thought that missionaries didn't have it so hard anymore, that all the killing and stuff was in the past. But my dad says that isn't so. He says missionaries are still killed sometimes, either by natives who don't understand why they're there or by hostile governments.

Maybe being afraid of death isn't the worst part of it though. I think I'd be bothered more by all the pain and suffering I had to see. Of course I'd try to do something about it, but if I were in one of those countries where people die like flies every day I might begin to give up hope. It's hard enough for me just **reading** about those things.

Be with the missionaries, God. They're our front line. Give them extra strength when they need it. And if they start to give up hope, show them for sure that You are God and Your will **will** be done.

48

A MAN AT CHURCH

There's a man at my church who works at a medical school. He does some complicated kind of research. I always thought that sounded sort of neat, but I never really thought too much about it. And now he's made a discovery that might mean the end of some terrible disease children get.

A man at **my** church! That just about knocks me over! Here I've been writing all this stuff about us being the church together, and he's been quietly working away in his lab and coming up with his great discovery. And he's one of **us.** He's doing God's work too. His discovery is **part** of God's work.

It makes me so proud that I almost want to cry. Thank You, God, for this man. Thank You for helping him do his work. All those children he may someday help will probably never know him. So I'll say their "thank You" too. Thanks!

49

HIS TOO

Today mom and I went shopping downtown. That means we rode the bus through that bad part of the city again. The kids were outside playing again, and some of them didn't have any gloves or hats. There were men outside too, several bunches of them just standing around on street corners and talking. I guess they didn't have any jobs to go to and were in their wives' way at home.

That's what I saw. And then all of a sudden I saw something more. For just a tiny second I saw those people—the kids and the men and the women inside—as You must see them, God. I saw them as Your children. You love every one of those people just as much as You love me. Every one of them is absolutely precious to You. Oh, it's hard to put this into words, but I saw it and I felt what You must feel. It was tremendous, God.

If everyone could have a tiny second like that and if those tiny seconds could go on forever, hate would just dry up and die. Prejudice would sneak away and never be seen again. All people really would be brothers and sisters because they'd all know and love the same Father. You, God.

Will we ever get to that point? Will You help us?

50

WHAT'S CONSTRUCTIVE ABOUT CRITICISM?

If there's one thing I can't stand it's when someone tears you into tiny pieces and then, when you **dare** to speak up for yourself, says, "What's the matter? Can't you take a little constructive criticism?" At that point I could just about fly up to the ceiling and stick there with a big SPLAT! And yet grown-ups are always doing that to kids.

It's not so much that I mind people telling me about something that's wrong with me. I suppose I'd really rather know, so I could try to change that thing. But I'd much rather they told me about just one thing at a time instead of listing all my faults at once. And I could handle the situation much better if they told me privately, in a quiet, friendly sort of way instead of yelling at me in a voice that would shatter glass or smugly looking down at me as if they didn't have any faults at all.

Well, maybe this is just one of those things you have to live with. If it is, God, please help me live with it without getting so mad every time it happens. And even if the person isn't speaking very constructively, maybe You could help me **find** something constructive in what he or she says. At least that way some good might come out of the situation.

51

LOVE MEANS YOU GOTTA SAY, 'I'M SORRY'

I never did understand that song, "Love Means You Never Have to Say I'm Sorry." It's when I hurt the people I love that I most want to say I'm sorry. And for some reason I seem to hurt the people I love more than anybody else.

I guess there's a good reason for that. When I'm around strangers or people I don't know very well I usually act sort of stiff and formal. I try to remember my manners and make a good impression. But when I'm around the people I love—my family and my good friends—I'm more relaxed. I let more of the real me show. And sometimes that real me hurts people.

Of course I always feel awful the minute I've done it. That's why I have to say I'm sorry. I have to know that the person hasn't stopped loving me because of the thing I've done. I have to let them know that I love them even though I did that thing. I don't see how you could **not** say I'm sorry if you really love the person.

God, I probably hurt You more than anyone else. I do the things You don't want me to do. I don't do the things You do want me to do. Sometimes I even forget You. Maybe that hurts You most of all. But, God, I do love You. And even though I **know** You won't stop loving me, I want to say I'm sorry. I want **my** side of our relationship to be all right too.

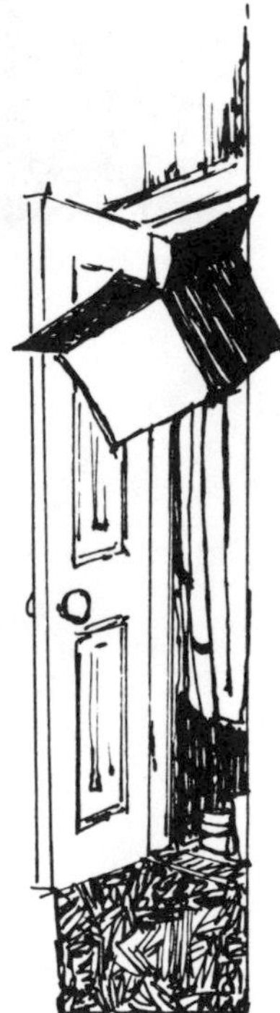

52

I GET SO MAD!

Sometimes I get so mad that I honestly don't know what to do. Maybe everything has been going wrong all day, and then I open my closet and this box falls off the shelf and hits me on the head. I could just **kill** that box. Or maybe I'm having a discussion with my friend, and she absolutely refuses to understand what I'm saying, no matter how many ways I say it. Then I usually start yelling and calling names—like "Dumbie!" and "Pighead!"

When I'm that mad it's almost like something else has taken over my mind, some superstrong power. I hardly know what I'm doing or saying. I guess the phrase "lose control of yourself" really describes what happens to me. And it's scary.

Oh, I don't think I'd ever kill anybody or even hurt them very much physically. But I could sure say some awful things and hurt them in that way. And I might even punch a little.

The worst part is that getting so mad doesn't do the least bit of good. It doesn't make the box hop back on the shelf, and it doesn't help my friend understand me any better. All it does is help me get rid of some of my feelings, and there must be better ways to do that.

God, please help me with this temper of mine. Show me how to get rid of my angry feelings in ways that won't hurt anyone. Help me learn how to control myself. Thank You, God.

53

LAZY? I'M RELAXING!

If there's one thing I love it's one of those days when you don't **have** to do anything. You don't have any homework, your room is reasonably clean, and there's no place you have to go. Some people might get bored with days like that, but not me. I can just lounge around for hours and **be.**

Unfortunately, I'm usually right in the middle of one of those great nothing days when some grown-up decides to point out to me that I'm not doing anything. Now this is no news to me. I know I'm not doing anything. I'm not doing it on purpose. But, more often than not, the grown-up seems to think there is something wrong with this. He or she seems to think I'm being lazy.

Why can't grown-ups understand that sometimes kids really need time just to be? After all, we spend most of our lives going to school and doing stuff around the house. We also spend a lot of energy growing and trying to keep on top of all the weird emotional things that seem to be happening to us. We **need** a little rest sometimes. It's not the same thing at all as being lazy. And when we do have work, we do it.

God, could You possibly help grown-ups understand that a little better? Maybe you could help me explain it to some of the grown-ups I know. What I'd **really** like to do is convert them. I'll bet most grown-ups haven't had a good nothing day in years. They've forgotten how great it feels. What do You think, God?

54

I REALLY AM ROTTEN!

Today some of the kids at school picked on my friend Maggie again. And I didn't do a thing about it. I was tired. I was sort of depressed. I just didn't want to get involved. So I pretended I didn't see what was going on. God, I hate myself!

Maybe if it were just that one thing I could get over it. But I'm always doing rotten things. Even when I do **good** things I don't always do them for the right reasons. Like when I help somebody. I'm not always thinking about making that person feel good. I'm thinking about the good feeling **I** get from helping. I'm really just being selfish. And when I sing to God in church. I'm not always thinking about Him. Sometimes I'm just enjoying the neat feeling I get from singing aloud. Selfish again.

God, how can You stand me? You know all these rotten things about me. You probably even know lots more that I'm not aware of. Can You really forgive all that rottenness? Can You really wash it all away and give me another chance time after time after time?

Yes, You can. I know that. And furthermore, You do it because You love me. I don't see how You do it, God. You are too big for my understanding.

55

ME AND MY BIG MOUTH

I was with a bunch of kids today, and all of a sudden it was like part of me stepped to one side and started watching what was going on. And do you know what that part of me saw? It saw a mouth. Mine. Going and going and going.

Now you might think I was saying something terribly important. Explaining a math problem or talking about the world situation or something. Wrong. I wasn't saying **anything.** Just blabbing. And blabbing and blabbing.

Why do I do it? I'm going to think about that question for about four minutes.

It didn't take that long. I know why I do it. I do it so people will pay attention to me. It makes me feel good when people pay attention to me. It makes me feel important. And I like to feel important.

God, I don't think someone who wants to follow Jesus should be so hung up on feeling important. After all, **He's** the important one. That's why we follow Him.

Please help me with this problem. Help me notice when my big mouth starts shifting into high gear. Help me turn it off and save it for when I have something really worthwhile to say. Help me remember that I **am** important to You, so I don't have to go around proving I'm important to everyone else.

56

LITTLE THINGS

If someone came up to me and said, "Hey, how'd you like to rob a bank?" I wouldn't have any trouble saying no. I don't want to kill anyone or hijack a plane or bomb a building. It's not the big sins that bug me. It's the little things.

The other day my teacher made a really sarcastic crack to me. Boy, did I want to say something back. Fortunately I didn't. But I did yell at my friend on the way home from school—and just because I was still mad at the teacher.

Homework is another little thing that gets to me. Sometimes I'd like to tear some of my books into little tiny pieces and flush them down the john. I guess you might say I want to kill them.

Another friend of mine just got a new bike. My bike is old and I'd love to have a new one. But I'm not going to get it. And so I just look at my friend's bike and think, "Why him and not me?"

Little things. But, boy, can they make you miserable!

I say the Lord's Prayer almost every day. Almost every day I pray, "Deliver us from evil." Please deliver me from evil, God—including the evil little things.

57

WHAT'S PROUD?

For weeks now I've been working on this science project. I mean, it is a science project to end all science projects. Finally I turned it in. And I got an A+ on it! Boy, did I feel proud of myself.

Then I felt guilty. It's wrong to feel proud. Christian people don't feel proud. I blew it again. Didn't I?

This isn't the first time I've felt guilty for feeling good about myself. But this time I'm going to work it through. I hate feeling guilty. And I don't see why I can't feel good about myself sometimes.

First of all, God made me. And God does good work. Oh, I know I fell into sin along with everyone else. But God took care of that too. He sent Jesus. Through Jesus God forgives me. I'm all clean and ready to go again. Can't I feel good about that?

Secondly, God helps me. I'm sure He was with me while I worked on that science project. He helped me find some neat ideas, and He helped me carry them out. I'd be the first person to admit I didn't do it alone. But can't I feel good about this thing God and I did together?

Maybe that's the secret. Maybe it **is** okay to feel good about yourself and some of the things you do as long as you remember that God helped you do them. I don't think you even have to say it out loud all the time. I didn't have to say to my teacher, "Oh, God helped me do that project. He should get part of the A+." I think it's enough just to remember myself that He helped.

Hey, I feel better about this. I feel proud of the way I worked it out. And thank You, God, for helping!

58

WHAT'S HUMBLE?

Thinking about proud yesterday made me think about humble. That's another thing that's always given me trouble. What's it mean to be humble?

Somehow I always picture this creepy little person, skulking around and saying, "Oh, don't take any notice of me. I'm nobody."

Or I picture saying to someone, "Hey, you really have nice hair." And that person says back, "Oh, no. It's really rather stringy, you know."

There's something very phony about that kind of humble. But I'm not sure what the right kind is. I think I'll ask my Sunday school teacher.

I called her and she said I picked the perfect time to ask her about humility because she's just been thinking about it herself. She even read some stuff about it. She said that as far as she can tell real humility is simply forgetting about yourself. You don't do that when you go around telling everyone what a nothing you are. You're thinking about yourself very hard, even if it is in a putting-down sort of way.

If you're really humble, though, said my Sunday school teacher, you are so wrapped up in God and other people that you honestly just don't think about you. She said that Jesus is the perfect example of a humble person. And nobody ever heard Him putting Himself down!

Maybe part of following Jesus is paying closer attention to how **He** did things. Maybe I'll have to start doing that.

59

SHOWING OFF

There's this guy in my class at school who is the most incredible show-off I've ever met. Today we had some free time in class to catch up on assignments or read a library book or anything else as long as it was quiet work. Well, this guy couldn't stand it. He **had** to show off and let people know he was there. So he started making pretend burping noises; and when the teacher told him to stop it, he just got louder and louder. Finally she sent him to the principal's office.

He's done this sort of thing before, and I've always just labeled him a silly show-off and forgotten it. But today I couldn't get him out of my mind. Maybe it was all the thinking I've been doing about proud and humble. I don't know.

Nobody shows off like that unless they really have a problem. And what's the problem? Well, I guess it's sort of the same problem I have with my big mouth. It's a real need to feel important. And that's hard to handle.

In a way I'd like to help this guy. But I can't see myself just walking up to him and saying, "Listen, you're important to God so stop trying to prove it to everyone else." He'd probably belt me. I'd have to know him a lot better before I could say anything like that to him. And I don't especially want to know him any better. I don't like him.

Does that matter, God? Did it matter to Jesus? Nobody much liked old crooked Zacchaeus, did they? And yet Jesus went home with him. It made all the difference in Zacchaeus' life too. Shall I try, God?

60

RIGHT AND WRONG

Someone once said to me that it's not hard to know the difference between right and wrong. What's hard is making yourself do the right thing. I don't agree. I think it's very hard to know sometimes what's right and what's wrong.

Oh, I don't mean that it's always hard. Most of the time it **is** wrong to steal and it's right not to steal. Although if you're stealing an important secret for your government—like a spy would—then maybe it isn't wrong. I'm not sure about that. I'll probably never have to make that choice anyway.

But almost every day I have to make some decision that involves right and wrong, and frankly, I don't always know if I've done the right thing. Should I tell this person something that might hurt his feelings but might help him too? Should I be nice to that person, even though she isn't the kind of girl my parents would want me to be friends with? Should I let my parents know about something very wrong that's going on at school, or shouldn't I worry them?

Those are the hard decisions, and I'm sure I've messed some of them up. But I guess all I can do is ask God to help me make the decisions in the first place, do what I **think** is right, and then trust Him to forgive me for the times I mess up. Maybe He'll even use some of my wrong decisions to make things work out in the right way after all. He can!

61

GUILT IS A SQUIRMY FEELING

Today this kid asked me to come over to his house. I didn't want to go. I don't like this kid. He's boring. So I lied. I said that I couldn't come because my mother had a bunch of stuff for me to do at home. And now I feel guilty. I **hate** feeling guilty. It's the squirmiest feeling I know.

I don't feel guilty because I didn't go to this kid's house. I feel guilty because I lied about it. There's no reason why I couldn't have said, "Aw, no thanks. I think I'd rather stay home today." That would have been the truth, and I don't think it would have hurt his feelings either. But, no. I panicked and came out with a lie instead. Result: The squirms.

Well I guess you live and learn. Maybe next time I'll take a minute or two to think instead of letting just anything pop out of my mouth. Meanwhile, I'll ask God to forgive me. At least I can be sure He'll do that. And then maybe I'll go see if there **is** a bunch of stuff I can do for mom. That ought to help to get rid of some of the squirms too.

62

AND WHERE IS GOD?

Epiphany is over, but I don't think I'll ever be the same again. I don't think I'll ever stop wanting to do God's work. It's in my bones and my feelings now and it's there pretty strong.

Recently I wrote about the tiny second when I seemed to see more people the way God sees them—as His children. Today I saw something else. It was like one of those overhead transparencies where you can flip one sheet over another and keep adding things to the total picture. Today I saw Jesus.

He was there in that bad part of the city I wrote about, walking along the street. He didn't have warm clothes to wear either. But He didn't look sad. No, He looked strong and full of life. As He walked along He had something to say to each person He met. Sometimes it looked as if He was comforting them, and other times it looked as if He was telling a joke. But after He passed, each person He'd talked to seemed changed. It was as if some of Jesus' life had gone into them and given them new hope.

No, I didn't really see any of that. It was just a picture, sort of like a movie playing in my mind. But I wish I could see it. And I suppose that's the part of Epiphany that's going to stick with me from now on. I want to show Jesus to the people who need him. I want to show Him so clearly that He can change them, that some of His life will find them.

After all, He is God. And He is with us.

63

GIVING UP?

Some of my friends are giving up things for Lent. One girl is giving up chocolate. Actually she's giving it up because it's bad for her complexion, but she thought Lent would be a good time to start. One guy is giving up football. He's a smart aleck. Football season's over anyway. Another girl is giving up movies. I think she's pretty serious about it.

Frankly I can't get turned on by the whole idea. It reminds me too much of New Year's resolutions. Everybody makes one, and everybody knows it's going to get broken right away. In fact, Lent seems to be nothing more than a second chance for those people who didn't quite make it the first time round with their resolutions.

Well, so much for how the rest of the world looks at Lent. But what about the church? That sort of bothers me too. It seems to me that it's a time of year set aside to be gloomy. I'm going to have to talk to someone about this.

I talked to dad. He said Lent is a period of time before Easter when we think about Jesus' suffering and death. We remember that he paid for our sins and won eternal life. That isn't gloomy.

I don't think I'll give anything up for Lent this year. At this point in my life it would be just a phony gesture. But I **will** think about following Jesus. There's nothing phony about that!

64

LOOKING INSIDE

I've already made one discovery. You can't think about following Jesus without looking inside and thinking about yourself too. Maybe that's because we're people with **feelings;** and those feelings can either help us follow Him, or they can mess us up.

Here's how it started with me. The first question I asked myself was "follow Him where?" I think that's a pretty logical question. The answer's logical too. We all know where Jesus ended up. On a cross. Oh, I know God made Him alive again. But the cross came first. And Jesus even said someplace in the Bible, "Pick up your cross and follow Me."

Well, that's where my feelings jump in loud and strong. And they're mostly one kind of feeling. Fear. I don't want to be hurt. I don't want to die. I know that following Jesus doesn't literally mean that you'll die on a cross. But I suspect you'll go through some awfully rough times. And that scares me.

God, all I really understand right now about following Your Son is that it's scary. Help me with that, please. Give me the courage to follow Him anyway—wherever it leads me.

65

LOOKING OUTSIDE

Yesterday I thought about following Jesus, looked inside myself, and found one very scared kid. Today I think I'll try looking outside. By "outside" I mean several things. The Bible. History. Other people.

And what do I see there? I see more fear. I see the people of Israel, scared to death to cross the Red Sea. I see Peter, so scared that he tells everyone that he doesn't know Jesus. I see people hiding in the catacombs or being thrown to the lions for their faith. I see my pastor actually admitting to all of us in one of his sermons, "Sure I'm scared!"

But I see something else too. I see God drying up the Red Sea. I see Jesus forgiving Peter. I see those early Christians dying with glory written all over their faces. I see my pastor helping more people than he probably even knows.

I see sacred people, sure. But I see God with them, helping them. I see Jesus leading the way, picking them up when they fall down, dusting them off, and giving them a little shove to get them going again.

I see a whole wonderful parade outside. And I want to be part of it.

66

TWO LITTLE LETTERS

The other day this kid asked me to be on a committee to decorate for a party that's coming up at school. "Sure!" I said. Another kid suggested that we start taking swimming lessons together at the Y. "Great!" I said. My teacher asked if anyone would like to spend extra time taking care of our animal collection after school. "Me!" I said.

How am I going to do it all? I say yes to all these things because they all sound so neat at the time. I never stop to think that every yes means a whole bunch of hours. And I **need** to spend more time on my schoolwork.

I was complaining to my mom about all this. She listened and listened and then she sighed.

"I thought we'd taught you how to talk before you were two," she said. "But I see that we left out a very important word. It's a simple one. Just two letters. N and O."

"Ha, ha," I said. But of course she was right. I **don't** know how to say no. And I think I'd better learn—fast.

Maybe it's all part of learning to think before I say anything. You know I need help with that, God. Next time could You help me remember that I really can say those two little letters? And that sometimes I really should?

67

FEAR WITHOUT A NAME

I never know when it's going to happen. Sometimes it comes at night, just when I'm ready to go to sleep. Sometimes it comes in the middle of the afternoon, when I'm sitting in school and nothing much is going on. Sometimes it comes in the early evening when I look out the window. Once it even came in the middle of a church service. I call it my monster, but what it really is is fear, a strange fear that has no name.

I could understand it if I was afraid of something in particular—like a storm or a test the next day or even a person. But this fear doesn't seem to be **of** anything. It's just fear. And that makes it a hundred times as frightening.

Do You know what it is I'm afraid of at those times, God? Is it maybe something deep in my subconscious—like death? I don't think about death very often, and I never think about dying myself. But just writing the words "death" and "dying" doesn't make me feel afraid. I think I trust You to take care of all that.

So here I am, still left with this nameless fear that creeps up on me sometimes. Surely, whatever it is, it isn't too big for You to handle. Help me remember that the next time it comes.

68

I WANT PATIENCE—NOW!

Somebody needlepointed a sign for my mom, and that's what it says: "I want patience—now!" Maybe I should get out my needle and do up a sign just like it for me. Because that's sure the story of my life. I can't stand to wait for **anything.**

When I was a little kid I used to get all upset the day after my birthday because I'd have to wait a whole year for the next one. I felt the same way about Christmas, Easter, and Halloween. I've gotten a little better about holidays now, but I'm still awfully short on patience.

Now the kind of things I can't stand to wait for are personal things—like changes. I decide one day that I'm going to concentrate a lot more on my schoolwork. The next day I'm ready to scream if I don't get perfect grades. Or I decide that from now on I'm going to be more cheerful, and the first time I feel crabby I'm ready to hit myself over the head.

I guess what's bothering me most right now is this whole business about following Jesus. I want to be good at it right away. Of course I know how dumb that is. I'll probably never be **good** at it. It's not the sort of thing you get good at. You just do it, because you love Him and you want to. And whenever you make a mistake you ask Him to forgive you and set you back on the right track. He's not going to run out of patience, so there's no point in your doing that either.

Help me be more patient, God, and especially with me.

69

TO OBEY OR NOT TO OBEY

Ever since I was a little kid in Sunday school, people have been telling me that I should be obedient. I should obey my parents, all my other grown-up relatives, my teachers, my pastor, my Sunday school teacher, and policemen. I accepted that when I was a little kid and expected to get punished when I didn't obey. Now it's getting more complicated, though.

There's a girl at school whose parents are divorced. She spends every other weekend with her father and the rest of the time with her mother. When she's with her mother she's allowed only two sweet things a day. When she's with her father she can have all she wants. But then her mother asks her how much she's had, and she gets in trouble if it's more than two. This poor girl says she's really confused because her parents are always contradicting each other like that.

I'm glad I'm not in her situation. I don't know what I'd do. It's hard enough for me when my Sunday school teacher says we shouldn't fight, and my dad says I should learn to defend myself, and my guidance counselor urges me to sign up for karate.

God, when those situations come up, help me know what to do. I guess I'd better stick with my parents for the most part, since they're responsible for me. But if they ever ask me to do something that really confuses me or that seems to go against my conscience, help me be able to talk with them about it. They're pretty great people. I know they'd help me work something out.

70

THAT SNEAKY SNAKE

I sometimes wonder why Satan decided to disguise himself as a snake when he tempted Eve. You'd think when she saw that sneaky old thing hanging around the tree she would have been suspicious right off. Maybe not, though. I sure get fooled sometimes by temptation.

"Do this," it whispers, "and everybody will think you're great. Oh, maybe it's a little bit wrong. But what's one little sin when everybody will like you?"

Or maybe there's something I ought to do, like study for a test or be nice to a person. "Why don't you just put that off till tomorrow," whispers that sneaky snake temptation. "By tomorrow maybe your teacher will have canceled the test. Or maybe someone else will start being nice to that person and you won't have to bother."

That snake seems to know all my weakest points. He says just the things I want to hear, things that make something wrong seem almost right or something right seem sort of silly. And sometimes I listen.

Forgive me for those times, God. Help me put my snake detector in better working condition so I'll **know** what's going on. And, once I know what's going on, help me tell that miserable snake to get lost!

71

COMING HOME

I almost didn't pray today. I was so busy I figured, "Oh, God will understand. He knows how much I have to do. Besides, He knows what I'd say in my prayers anyway. There's no need for me to bother saying it."

But I couldn't stand it. Whether **God** needed to hear me say my prayers or not didn't matter. **I** needed to hear me say them. I needed to talk to my Father in heaven about some stuff that was bothering me. I needed to know that He was listening and that He cared. I also needed to thank Him for some neat stuff that happened today. I wanted to list all the stuff and say "thanks" instead of expecting Him to read my mind.

That's when I figured it out. Prayer is like coming home. You've been out in the world and lots of things have happened—some good and some bad. Maybe you feel great and maybe you feel a little bruised inside. Either way you feel a lot better if you can just talk to someone about it, someone you can tell **anything** and know He'll understand.

Talking is just part of it, though. Part of praying is listening too. Not exactly with your ears. I've never heard God speak to me in words. But I have felt Him with me. I've felt myself wrapped up in love and forgiveness. It's a feeling I can't begin to describe. But I never want to be without it.

So I guess I'll go on praying. I think I'm hooked on it. Thank You, God, for welcoming me home whenever I come.

72

DISCIPLE SOUNDS LIKE DISCIPLINE

Disciple is a funny word when you stop to think about it. Funny-strange, not funny-ha-ha. It's a word we don't use much except in connection with Jesus' disciples. And then we usually just think of the Twelve, although my Sunday school teacher says Jesus had many, many more disciples than that.

I suppose that everybody who tries to follow Jesus is really His disciple. That includes me. But it's hard to think of myself that way. "Disciple" sounds so heavy and serious. In fact, it sounds a lot like "discipline" and that's not one of my favorite words because it reminds me too much of punishment.

Maybe it shouldn't, though. After all, when you talk about disciplining your body, you really mean you're training it to be able to do certain physical things. Maybe a disciple is just someone who's in religious training so he or she can follow Jesus.

If my body gives out in the middle of a race, there's not much I can do. I've lost the race, and no one can help me win it. But my religious self has a much better chance. Jesus has already won that race for me. He's defeated sin and death, and He's passed the victory on to me. I don't follow Him in order to win something. I follow Him because He's Jesus. And He even helps me do that.

This is awfully complicated, but I think I do understand one thing. Following Jesus is where I want to be.

73

WHY DOESN'T HE LIKE ME?

There's this person I know—a grown-up—and I think he's really great. In a lot of ways he's the sort of person I'd like to be when I grow up. He's funny and smart. He cares about people, and he's good at helping them. He's a Christian. But he doesn't like me.

Oh, he never said so. But sometimes you can just tell those things. It's as if everything I do seems to rub him the wrong way, and he's always trying not to look irritated when I'm around.

If it were just one thing I did wrong, I'd really work to change that thing. I so much want him to like me. But it's not just one thing. I think it's everything that goes together to make me me, and I sure can't change all that.

I feel so hurt about this, God. And I feel helpless too. I don't think there's anything I can do—except maybe have patience? Do You think that might work, God? Do You think that if I just go on being me, someday he'll realize that I'm not such an awful person? Could You maybe work on him a little bit, God?

74

HE ANSWERED!

God answered my prayer! I know He did! This is how it happened:

I prayed last night about this grown-up that I really like but who doesn't like me. And after I finished praying, I felt so much better that I sort of relaxed about the whole thing. Well, I saw this guy today and, sure enough, he snapped at me for no reason at all. If that had happened last week I would have curled up in a miserable little ball and rolled away to my corner. But I was feeling relaxed. I was feeling like the whole situation was in God's hands. So I said what I really wanted to say.

"Why are you angry with me?" I said. "You seem to be angry with me whenever I'm around, and that really makes me feel bad."

At first he looked surprised. Then he looked confused. And then he looked sad and sorry and—well, almost gentle.

"I'm sorry," he said. "I'm not really angry with you. In fact I like you very much. The thing is, you remind me so much of myself when I was your age. I see you doing the same things and making the same mistakes. I don't want you to be hurt by those mistakes, so I guess I pick on you. It's really myself I'm picking on."

Wow! I remind him of himself! That's a fantastic compliment because maybe it means I have a chance of growing up to be the kind of person he is. Anyway, I'm sure we're going to be much better friends from now on.

Maybe God didn't send me any letters. Maybe He didn't speak in a thundering voice out of heaven. But He sure answered my prayer. Thanks, God!

75

I AM ME!

I am different. I am not like any other person in my family or at my school or in my church or in the world. Some people, especially at school, probably even think I'm weird. And at one time—maybe even yesterday—that would have bothered me a lot. But not now. Because I know for sure that I am me, and that makes everything all right.

I'd better explain that a little more. Today I was all alone in the house for a while. I was listening to a record of Beethoven's Seventh Symphony. Not many kids I know listen to Beethoven. But I do because I like it. It makes me feel grand feelings.

Anyway, I was listening, and I felt a grand feeling all right. But it was different from any other grand feeling I've ever felt. It was a feeling as if someone had just said to me, "You are you. I made you that way. I love you that way. You will go on being you for the rest of your life. And I will go on loving you."

Maybe that doesn't make much sense either, because nobody really said anything to me. I just felt as if someone had. And I felt so **good** about being me! About being different!

Was that You, God? Do You sometimes reach out to people when they are listening to beautiful music? Do You sometimes talk to them in ways that are not words but that make them feel so wonderful they could burst?

Thank You, God. Thank You for reaching out to me. And thank You for making me different. Thank You for making me **me!**

76

WHY DO I DOUBT?

Why? Why can I be so sure about God on one day, and the next day start wondering if He even exists? I've heard people talk about "the seeds of doubt," and that's the perfect way to describe what happens to me. It's a if someone planted something in my mind when I wasn't looking, and before I know it that little seed has grown up into a huge ugly weed. Doubt.

Then I panic. I feel so terrible and so guilty about even feeling doubt that I just freeze. I can't think straight. I'm ashamed to tell anyone else what I'm feeling, and I don't know how to get rid of the doubt myself.

God, please help me. I can't hide the doubt I'm feeling from You anyway, so I might as well talk to You about it. Why am I doubting You? Is it because I can't see You with my eyes or hear You with my ears or touch You with my hands? But lots of times—most of the time—that doesn't bother me at all. Why is it bothering me now? God, I can't figure this one out. I'm only human. You're going to have to help me.

I'm only human, God. Is **that** why I doubt? Does that make You so mad at me that You won't want to have anything to do with me ever again? Of course not. I know better than that. You don't just wash Your hands of people. You've proved that again and again.

Okay, God, I'll relax a little. I'll let You see me through this problem like You've seen me through so many others. And do You know what, God? It's a funny thing. For someone who's doubting that

You even exist, I sure am awfully worried about how You feel about me!

77

ME AND MY ENEMY

I have an enemy. Actually I probably have more than one, but this girl has been my enemy for as long as I can remember. We've never been able to agree about much of anything. If she said the sky was blue, I'm sure it would look green to me. If I said the sun was shining, she'd be positive it was the moon.

I'm making it all sound silly and petty, though, and it's not that way at all. She's done some things that have really hurt my feelings. And I guess I try to hurt her sometimes too, if only to get back at her. There is nothing Christian in the way I feel about this girl, and sometimes that bothers me. After all, it says in the Bible that we should love our enemies.

Well, I don't think I can love this girl. I wouldn't even know where to start.

I guess You know what I'm leading up to, God. Do You suppose You could do something about this terrible relationship between me and my enemy? I'm not asking You to help me love her right off the bat. But maybe if You could just show me something to **like** about her, that would be a start. Maybe You could help her find something to like about me too. I realize all this may take a while. But it's worth it, isn't it, God?

78

THE ZODIAC AND ALL THAT

Some kids at school are really into astrology and all that occult stuff. Some of them don't even see other people as **people** anymore. They see them as astrological signs. "Here comes a Pisces." "Oh, she's a Gemini. No wonder she's a little weird." Maybe I could have gotten hooked on all that stuff too, except that I once read all the characteristics for my sign and realized that they fit my mom and dad just as well as they fit me. And the three of us were born during completely different times of the year.

It **would** be nice to be able to buy a little book at the beginning of the year and have it tell you everything to expect and to watch out for every single day. It would be nice to be able to pigeonhole people by when they were born and know exactly how to act toward them. But I don't think it works. The one day I did read my horoscope it told me to beware of visitors from afar. The only person who visited us all day was the lady next door, and she brought a chocolate cake. Now I just read the funnies.

Some kids really are taking all this astrology stuff very seriously, though, God, and I sort of worry about them. They're believing in something that isn't real, and someday they're going to be horribly let down. They're also pulling away from You when they put their faith in astrologers. I try to help them a little by making jokes about astrology whenever I can. But they need Your help too, God. Please show them that no matter when they were born they are Your children. And let them see that the only thing they really need to know about the future is that it's in Your hands.

79

MY BODY

Sometimes when I look at my body I think it is the most marvelous thing in the world. No, I'm not being vain. I'm just so absolutely knocked out by how God has made me. Take my feet. They hold up the whole thing and move it around and jump and dance and run like the wind. And they aren't even all that big!

How did God ever think them all up—all those parts of the body and all the tiny intricate things they do? It just amazes me.

I don't think my own particular body is the greatest in the world, but I do think it's a good body, and I like to feel good about it. I like to feel that I'm keeping it in the best shape I can, so it can do all those jobs. I like it to work so well and so smoothly that sometimes—like when I'm really running—I hardly know it's there at all.

I love the way my body feels when I wake up in the morning—all warm and stretchy and reaching out to meet the day. I even like the way it feels in the evening—tired and relaxed and ready to dive into sleep.

I could say a lot more about this, God. I could talk about cells and mitochondria and all the millions of other neat things that are part of my body. But I won't. I'll just say thanks!

80

WHAT'S EVIL?

Not too long ago I noticed that the word "live" spelled backwards is "evil." That fascinates me. It makes me think that maybe that's what evil is—living backwards. Look at all the good things about life. Health. Joy. Beauty. Kindness. Love. And, of course, God. Evil turns its back on all those things. It's unhealthy, sad, ugly, cruel, hateful. It has nothing to do with God.

Some people I know say that evil doesn't exist. They say it's all in our minds. Well, our minds may be one of the places evil most often works, but that doesn't mean it doesn't exist. I don't see how anyone can look at our world and not see evil.

I've got to admit that evil scares me sometimes, especially when I think about those people who worship Satan or commit mass murders. Then evil seems like such a huge powerful force that I'm afraid it will swallow all of us up.

That won't happen, though, will it, God? Because no matter how huge and powerful evil may seem, You are more powerful still. Evil will always lose as long as You're fighting on our side. You showed us that when You raised Jesus from the dead.

Help me not to be afraid of evil, God. Protect me and keep me strong so I can fight against it too.

81

DEATH

I've begun to think about death more often lately. Maybe that's because of Lent. We seem to spend a lot of time during Lent talking about how Jesus died. My teacher says that it's not unusual for kids my age to think about death. She says that for the first time we're ready to think about it. Well, here are some of my thoughts:

First of all, I think the hardest thing about death is the fact that you are separated from the person who died. You can't talk to him. You can't see him. I personally believe that we'll meet again in heaven some day. But that's a long time away, and sometimes I don't want to wait that long.

The next thing that scares me about death is that it's so unpredictable. It **could** happen to someone I love—even a young person. I have a way of handling that fear, though. I just sort of turn all the people I love over to God. If **He** wants them to die, I guess I can't argue with Him. But I'd rather know He's in charge instead of someone else.

The third thing that bothers me about death is the fact that I'm going to die someday. I don't want to do that. I like life too much. And actually, I can't really believe that I **will** die. Even though I know it, I can't believe it's true. Maybe that's because I'm so young. Anyway, I handle my fears about my own death the same way I handle the fears about people I love dying. I turn myself over to God. He was the one who gave me this life. I didn't do one thing to help. He'll give me the next life too. That's what Jesus' resurrection is all about.

Death is a big, scary, painful subject, God. If You don't mind, I'll leave the whole thing in Your hands. Okay?

82

WHAT WILL HEAVEN BE LIKE?

Whenever I think about death, the next thing I think about is heaven. I start wondering what it will be like. I don't think there will be these big pearly gates with St. Peter sitting outside, letting people in or turning them away. I think that's just a picture people have in their minds. And I don't think we'll all turn into angels, sitting around on clouds and playing harps. The Bible never says we'll turn into angels. Angels are angels and human beings are human beings. I **would** like to meet an angel or two in heaven though.

In fact, there are several things I'd like to have happen in heaven. I'd like to see a lot of people who've already died—people I know and people I've just heard about. I'd like to know everything and understand everything. I'd like to never feel hurt or sad or lonely again. And, most of all, I'd like to be with Jesus. I'd like to spend hours and hours with Him.

My Sunday school teacher says the Bible doesn't tell us very much about heaven. It paints a few pictures, but they're hard for us to understand, just as it would be hard for a person who'd always lived in a cave to understand what it's like to live on top of the earth.

Maybe we don't need to understand too much about heaven now. Maybe God wants us to focus most of our attention on the life we have. And maybe He feels we **do** know the most important thing about heaven—the fact that we'll be with Jesus. The Bible does tell us that. And I guess it's enough for me.

83

GRIEF

That's the other thing that goes with death. Grief. It's the way you feel after someone you love has died. I've never yet felt it for a person, but I've felt it when one of my pets has died and that's been bad enough. Grief tears you apart inside, and no matter what anyone says, it won't go away until it's ready to.

My mom says anger is a part of grief. You're angry at God for letting that person (or animal) die, and you're angry at the person for dying. She says part of grief is saying, "this didn't really happen," and part is saying, "yes, it did happen." And part—a big part—is just hurting.

The last time I felt grief, I didn't try to make it go away. I just faced up to it and let it wash over me like a big wave. I cried when I wanted to cry. (Crying really helps with grief. It lets some of the pain out.) I thought about my pet a lot. I talked to my parents about her. And I talked to God about her. None of this made the grief go away, but I think it made it a little easier to live with.

Then one day I was able to think about my pet without hurting so much. The memories began to make me feel better instead of worse. I knew I'd made it then through one more grief.

God, I don't know what I'd do if some person I love died. I don't know if I could handle a grief that big. Be with me whenever that time comes, God. Help me remember that You love the person even more than I do and that You will make everything all right. Help me remember that because of Jesus You will give that person life forever. Help me make it through grief.

84

WHY BOTHER?

We were talking about death in my Sunday school class (I guess I was the one who brought it up), and this one girl got very upset.

She said, "I don't see why we bother trying to live a good life and do the right things and care about people when all we're going to do is die anyway."

I knew there was something wrong with her thinking, but I didn't know what to say to her. My Sunday school teacher did a great job.

"You're right, Sarah," said my teacher. "If all we had to look forward to at the end of life was death, life would seem sort of pointless. God knows that too. And that's why He's let **us** know that death isn't the end of everything. In a way it's just the beginning of a much better life with Him."

"But how can I **know** that?" asked Sarah. "I can't talk to a dead person and make sure all that is going to happen."

"No, you can't, Sarah," agreed my teacher. "The only way you can know something like this is by faith. You know that God has promised it will happen. You know that God has always kept His promises in the past. So you have faith that He will keep this promise too."

"What if I have trouble having faith?" asked Sarah.

"Ask God to help you with that too," said my teacher.

Sarah felt much better after that. (To be perfectly honest, so did I.)

85

LITTLE DEATHS

This evening I talked to my mom and dad about death at dinner. I thought they might be upset that I was thinking about death, but it didn't seem to bother them at all, and they talked very openly with me about it. Basically we all believe the same things, and that made me feel good. But my dad said one thing I'd never thought of. I really liked it, so I'm going to write it down.

Dad said that in a way we all go through a lot of little deaths while we're still alive. Each time we fail at something that means a lot to us, each time somebody puts us down so badly that we feel wiped out, each time we think that we're really in the bottom of the pit—each of those times we sort of die inside.

And then—here's the good news—each of those times God lifts us up and makes us feel alive again. He gives us another chance, a new job to do, a person who cares about us, forgiveness.

I think it was brilliant of my dad to come up with that idea. And it's **true.** At least it's true in my life. In a way it makes me feel better about the death that comes at the end of life too. It's sort of like God keeps His promise all along so I can be sure that He'll keep it at the end.

Thank You, God, for all the little resurrections. And thank You for the promise of the big one too.

86

THE SECRET SINS

When I look inside myself and try to be perfectly honest, I see some sins that are so bad that I wouldn't dare talk about them to anyone—not even my mom and dad. I can't even bear to think about them for very long because they make me feel so horrible. I suppose other people have sins like that too, but it's hard to believe it. Somehow I feel that I must be the only person who's **that** awful.

I don't want to write very much about those sins, God, because of how they make me feel. What I'd really like to do is hand them over to You. I can do that, can't I?

Please take my secret sins, God. Forgive them. Scrub them away so they'll never be a part of me again. I ask this in the name of Jesus, who died on the cross for me. Amen.

87

TRY, TRY AGAIN

I've been reading this great book called **Caddie Woodlawn.** It's by Carol Ryrie Brink and it's based on stories about her own grandmother and how she grew up in Wisconsin during pioneer days. In one of the stories, Caddie's little brother is supposed to get up during a school program and recite, "If at first you don't succeed, try, try again." Only someone has taught him another version of the saying too. "If at first you don't fricassee, fry, fry a hen." He gets so scared during the program that he stands up and says the second version. The teacher almost falls apart.

The story made me think about how often we mess up the first time—and sometimes the second and the third times too—and have to try, try again. Take my temper, for example. I just about think I have it under control when POW! It blasts out all over the place and I have to try again.

It sure would be discouraging if I didn't know that God forgives all the mess-ups. He does, though. He wipes them clean away. So each time I try I can forget about all the times that have gone before. It's like I'm trying for the first time. And God's right there with me, helping.

88

JESUS

It seems as if I should spend at least one day this Lent thinking just about Jesus. After all, if it weren't for Him we wouldn't have any Lent. We wouldn't have any Easter. We wouldn't have any church. We wouldn't have any anything. Jesus is right there in the middle of everything we believe in.

And yet sometimes it's hard to think about Him. I wonder if that isn't because we hear about Him so often and in so many ways. I don't mean just curse words. I mean on bumper stickers and billboards, on TV commercials and radio programs, in books and in songs. And sometimes people don't paint a very good picture of Him. They show a pink and white, namby-pamby sort of person who went around smiling and saying sweet things all the time.

I don't think Jesus was much like that. I think He was pretty tough. He had to be to do the job He did. And the Bible sure doesn't show Him saying very many sweet things. The things He said were hard, true things. Things like, "Take up your cross and follow Me."

I guess the Jesus I believe in is the one the Bible shows me. He's God's Son. He came to earth to be with us, to show us God's love, to teach us about living in God's kingdom, and to win over sin and death forever. And He did it. I wish I'd known Him then. I'm glad I know Him now. And I'm glad He's given me this wonderful invitation to follow Him.

89

MY FUTURE

When I think about The Future (in capital letters), I picture a misty gray fog. You can't see anything at all, and in a way it's sort of scary.

When I think about my own future, though (no capital letters), the picture is a little different. I see school, school, and more school. I guess there's no way to get around that. And, to be perfectly honest, there are parts of school I really like. I think I'll like it even better when I get a little older.

Beyond school, though, I just don't know. I don't know what sort of job I'll get. I don't even know what sorts of jobs there will **be** by then. My dad says the job market is changing very fast these days. I don't know if I'll get married. I don't know if I'll have kids. I don't know if I'll make enough money to live comfortably. I don't know if I should even try.

I guess if you wanted to sum up my future in three words, those words would be "I don't know."

And yet I'm not at all depressed about it. Because I really do believe that whatever my future is, God will have a hand in it. He'll use me in the ways He knows are best.

I really believe that, God. Don't let me forget it if the going gets a little rough.

90

WILL I BE GREAT?

Back to my future. I wonder if I will be great. Will I be a daring missionary who leads thousands and thousands of people to Jesus? Will I be a powerful politician who is responsible for legislation that will help solve the problems of my country? Will I be an artist and express great truths in my painting or music or writing? Will I be a scientist and save countless lives with the discoveries I make?

I'd like to think that God will use me in some great, magnificent way. But I suppose there's every chance that He might not. He might want to use me in little ways instead. I might lead just one person to Jesus—maybe a little kid. My powerful political activities might be limited to voting in the wisest way I know how. My artistic life might consist of singing in the church choir. And scientifically I might just learn to bake a cake my family can bear to eat.

That doesn't sound very exciting to me now, but it might be what God has in mind for me. And if it is, I can be sure that I will have as good a life, as important a life, as the greatest great person who ever lived. Because I am God's child and He will use me in the best way for me. I have a few requests I'd like to make, but I'm perfectly happy to leave the final decisions up to Him.

91

WILL SOMEONE LOVE ME?

In a way I suppose that question is more important to me than whether I'll be great or not. I really would like to think that someone will love me—and me specially—someday. I think it might be sort of hard to go through life alone. It'd be hard socially and in other ways too, I think.

Songs, movies, stories—they all tell you that people were meant to go through life in pairs. And yet not everyone does that. Jesus didn't. I guess it would have been hard for Him to be married with the kind of life He lived. I wonder if He didn't get lonely sometimes, though. After all, He was man as well as God.

I suppose there's a chance that I'll go through life alone too, but I don't think I'll let it worry me too much right now. There's probably just as good a chance that someone will love me. And in either case, I can be sure of God's love. Maybe that's what kept Jesus going. Maybe it's what keeps lots of the people who are alone going. It **is** a powerful force.

God, if it is Your will, let someone love me someday. But if it isn't Your will, then let me be very, very sure of Your love.

92

GROWING UP IS NOT FOR WEAKLINGS

People are always talking about how wonderful it is to be young. Older people, that is. I've never heard a young person say that. It's tough to be young!

First of all, you're always too young for some things—like staying up as late as you want to or going certain places. When the relatives come to visit, you get stuck eating with the little kids. You're too young for grown-up conversation.

But at the same time you're too old for other things—like crying when something makes you mad or playing as much as you want. "Act your age," say the grown-ups. Sometimes I'd like to stamp my foot when they say that. But I'm too old.

The worst part about being young, though, is the growing up part. All this wild stuff is happening to your body, and somehow your feelings get involved too. "Growing pains," says my mom in a wise voice whenever I'm feeling especially emotional. She's right too. It hurts.

God, growing up is not for weaklings. It's a good thing You made us kids young enough to take it!

93

CLOTHES

Tonight I asked my mom and dad for a new, special kind of tennis shoes.

"They cost a fortune!" said my dad.

"You have a perfectly good pair of tennis shoes already!" said my mom.

And they were both right. What I couldn't seem to explain to them is that right now everyone is wearing this new, special kind of tennis shoe.

Later I asked myself why it is that I want to be like everyone else. Aren't I glad to be myself—unique, different? Well, yes. I am. But sometimes I still want to be like everyone else—especially where clothes are concerned. It's a way of telling everyone I'm okay. It's a way of making sure that everyone accepts me. It's safe!

O God, none of those reasons have anything to do with living as Your child, do they? **You're** the reason I'm okay. **You** accept me and that's the important thing. Safety shouldn't be so high on my list.

The thing is, God, I don't know if I can give up wanting to dress like the other kids just yet. I don't think I'm quite strong enough. Could You go on loving me even if I'm just one of the pack on the outside? Could You remember that the me on the inside is still struggling to grow? Could You help me grow—one step at a time?

94

CHANGE, CHANGE, CHANGE

Last weekend we drove to a place where we used to go for picnics when I was a little kid. It used to have lots of trees and a little brook and a field with cows nearby. Now it's a motel, complete with swimming pool and neon sign. I was so disappointed.

My mom says that she lived in two different houses when she was a kid. One of them is now under a superhighway and the other is under a parking lot. She says she's afraid that one of these days progress will get going so fast that it'll catch up with her and pour blacktop all over the house she's living in.

I used to think that only old people moaned and groaned about change, but I'm beginning to understand how they feel. It's scary!

I don't know that there's much I can do to stop it either. I guess that's why it's important for me to hang onto the one thing that will never, ever change, no matter what happens to the rest of the world. God.

Thank You, God, for always being You.

95

DO YOU BELIEVE IN GOD?

That's a question kids ask one another sometimes, especially late at night at slumber parties when everyone's feeling sort of relaxed and serious. Most kids say yes too, although there is usually one or two who like to say they're atheists. I think they think it sounds cool.

My pastor talked about believing in God last Sunday, and he said that none of us can believe in God by ourselves. He said we're just not capable of it. He said that God not only gives us all these wonderful things, like life and His love and forgiveness, but He's even the One who helps us believe in them. It's His Spirit who does that job.

I guess it's a good thing I'm not God. If I offered all that to people, and they refused to take it on their own, I'd get my feelings hurt and say, "Phooey on them! "And **then** what kind of shape would we all be in?

But not God. If we hurt Him, He sure doesn't let it show. He helps us take the things He offers. He draws us to Him and gives us faith.

96

DOES RELIGION HAVE TO BE SERIOUS?

I would have made a lousy Pilgrim. From the pictures I've seen of them, they all looked serious and gloomy. Not that I don't look that way some of the time. But I don't think those folks ever smiled!

Somewhere I read that they thought religion was strictly a serious business, and since they wanted their whole life to be religious, they were serious all the time. I guess life was a lot tougher back then, and that would help make them gloomy too.

But I don't think God wants us to be that way—not even about religion. I think He wants us to laugh at some of the funny things He made—like penguins falling into the water and kittens going crazy over their own tails. I think he wants us to smile at the sky and laugh at the puddles.

Sure, there's a time to think about our sins and feel sorry for them. But isn't there also a time to feel good about being forgiven, maybe even to laugh at the great joke God pulled on sin and death? After all, death is dead. When you stop to think about it, that's enough to make you laugh right there.

Thank You, God, for all the funny things. Thank You for laughter.

97

BROKEN AND WHOLE

I was reading a book of nursery rhymes to my little cousin today. He just loved the one about Humpty Dumpty and asked me to read it over and over again—the way little kids do. Whenever we got to the bit about "All the king's horses and all the king's men couldn't put Humpty together again," he'd shout it along with me and laugh and laugh. Little kids are kind of vicious sometimes!

Later this evening I got this really wild idea. Why couldn't Humpty Dumpty be a rhyme about Adam and Eve too? After they fell into sin, they were broken into so many pieces that no one could put them together again either. Except God.

That's how we are too when we get all caught up in the wrong things we do. We're broken and we sort of drag around, hoping to find someone who has the magic glue that will make us whole again. But no one does. Except God.

God can take any one of us, broken as we may be, and make us perfectly whole again. He does it with love and forgiveness. That's better than magic glue too, because when God's done with us, there aren't even any cracks left.

Maybe I ought to start writing religious nursery rhymes.

98

HOW CAN I PRAISE HIM?

Sometimes it just overwhelms me—all that God has done for us. Nobody else could do it. Nobody else could have that much power or patience or love. Only God. And how in the world can I even begin to praise Him for what He has done?

What could my puny little off-key voice possibly do for Him when I'm singing in church? What could my silly little words possibly say in prayer that's worth His listening to? Even if I could write a piece of music that used every single instrument in the world and had a chorus for every single person to sing, it wouldn't be enough.

And yet from the beginning of time His creatures have praised Him in the only ways they know. And He seems to like it.

Maybe that's because God isn't some great music or literary critic in the sky, just waiting to point out the wrong notes or misspelled words. What He hears is the love behind our little songs and prayers and, even though that love itself isn't perfect, He understands and likes it.

So, in spite of all my limitations, puny voice, misspelled words, and all, I praise You, God!

99

SPRING IS SPRUNG

"Spring is sprung.
The grass is riz.
I wonder where
The flowers is."

That's one of my grandma's favorite poems this time of year. You can always count on her to say it at least once. And I always laugh—just to make her feel good.

Nevertheless—I love that word "nevertheless"; it sounds so important—nevertheless, spring **is** sprung, and I feel absolutely tremendous! I could go out there and roll in the grass and shout at the sky and kiss violets. Of course my mother would kill me if someone else didn't come along and lock me up first.

And the really great thing is that I feel this way four times a year: The first day spring smells like spring; the first baking-hot day of summer; the first crisp day of fall; and the first magic snowfall of winter.

How utterly brilliant of You, God, to give us seasons! I know they aren't the same everywhere in the world, but You give everyone **some** sort of change. Even if everything else in life is dull and boring, there's always the next season to look forward to. God, I know you don't need me to tell You all this. Or do You? Anyway, I'm going to say it: You did a wonderful job!

100

BEAUTIFUL THINGS

Yesterday I got all hysterical over spring. Today I want to make another confession that might sound sort of silly. Sometimes beautiful things make me want to cry. A mountain can do it, or a deer running free, or a tiger in a cage, or a piece of music, or a poem. So much feeling wells up inside of me that it has to get out somehow, and sometimes it does it through tears.

It's not that I'm sad exactly—except maybe for the tiger. It's that I'm **touched**. Someplace inside me is a little spark of something that usually lies quiet and resting. But when I see or hear something beautiful, the little spark wakes up and glows so brightly that I almost can't handle it. It almost hurts. And yet it's a good hurt.

Maybe none of this makes much sense the way I've described it, but I think it's something that other people feel too. In fact, I think it's a gift from God. Someplace in the Bible the apostle Paul says that we should think about beautiful things. I'm sure he got that crying sort of feeling about them too sometimes and knew what a special gift it was.

So, God, I praise You again—this time for all the beautiful things and the feeling they give us.

101

A GREAT TIME FOR EARS

Today I decided it was time my ears got a little special attention, so I whipped out my calendar and decreed it National Ears Day—at least for me. And did my ears have a ball!

Normally it's my nose that gets turned on by bacon, but today my ears had their chance. "Sizzle," said the bacon, and my ears perked up like a bunny's.

Then those fortunate ears got to go outside, and would you believe that there was a breeze blowing through the trees and making soft, sighing noises—the kind that makes ears sort of melt into happy little blobs on each side of your head?

Next we listened to animals, my ears and I. To birds singing and a kitten mewing and a dog up the street giving the milkman a great deal of trouble. It was almost like a symphony of animals. We tried to listen to the worms crawling underground too, but the worms were being very quiet today, and my ears only got a little muddy.

And then! It started to rain and my ears ran inside (with me close behind) to hear what the rain sounded like on the roof and the window and dripping down the chimney. Ear ecstasy!

Next there was music, dishes in the kitchen, my dad laughing, pop fizzing into a glass, kids playing outside, a train in the distance, my mom saying, "Goodnight."

Thank You, God, for ears.

102

HE DIDN'T HAVE TO DO IT

God did not have to make this world. He did it because, for some reason of His own, He wanted to. He did a very good job of it too. And then we messed it up. At that point, God could have said, "Well, that's enough of those little monsters. I'll just wipe them out and let My world go on the way it was without them."

But He didn't. Instead God took care of the little monsters, got them out of trouble whenever they got themselves into it, listened to their tales of woe, and gave them a promise to hold onto. He didn't have to do it. But He did.

God went a little farther too. He kept His promise and sent His Son to show the little monsters how much He cared. His Son taught and healed, listened and loved. And the little monsters killed Him.

At that point you'd think God would have thrown up His hands, taken Jesus back to heaven, and let the little monsters destroy themselves.

But He didn't. He raised Jesus from the dead so that the little monsters would never have to die. He gave them forgiveness once and forever. He turned them from little monsters into His own children.

He didn't have to do it. But He did. Because He loved them. He still does.

103

I'LL NEVER DENY HIM

How could Peter do it? How could he ever deny Jesus? Just think of all the things they'd done together. There was that first great catch of fish when Peter met Jesus. There were all the miracles—the healings and the feeding of the 5,000. There was the transfiguration when Peter actually heard **God** talk about His Son. There was the time Jesus saved Peter from drowning. All those times and many, many more. And yet Peter could say to the servant, "I don't know the Man." I could **never** do that!

And then I think about that part of the Bible where Jesus says, "Whatever you do for the least of these My brothers you've done for Me." How many times have I denied "the least of these?" How many times have I turned my back on someone who could have used my help? Lots of times. And each of those times I was denying Jesus.

No wonder Peter went out and wept bitterly later that night. What else could you do? And he didn't even know what was going to happen in just a few days. He thought this was the end. He didn't know the beginning was just around the corner. He didn't know that after the Resurrection Jesus would give him an incredibly important job to do—"feed My lambs."

Forgive me, Lord, as You forgave Peter. Forgive my denials. Give me new jobs too, new chances to "feed Your lambs."

104

MY CROSS

"Take up your cross and follow Me." That's what Jesus said. It makes me wonder. What **is** my cross?

Is it all the things that are wrong with me? My sins and weaknesses? The part of me that wants to do wrong things, the part of me that doesn't want to do right things, the part of me that doubts, and the part of me that is afraid? Are these things my cross?

Or is my cross the sort of world I live in? Is it my family where we sometimes fight too much? Is it my school that sometimes seems so full of cliquishness and competition that I can hardly stand it. Is it the world with all its greed and pain and bombs and death? Are these things my cross?

I don't think I know the answer. What I do know, though, is that no matter what my cross is, it feels lighter when I'm following Jesus. Maybe that's because I know He carried that other cross and won out over all the things it stood for. Maybe that helps me know that together we'll win out over the things that make up my cross too.

Well, here I am, Lord—cross and all—trying to follow You. I can't do it alone. You know that. I'd stumble in a minute and this cross would crush me. But You won't let that happen. You'll guide me every step of the way. So let's go on. I'm ready. And thank You, Lord.

105

THE TIME BETWEEN

What did they do for all those hours after Jesus died? Jesus' disciples, I mean. It doesn't sound as if any of them really knew that He would be alive again on Easter. After all, they were awfully surprised when they found out He was. That time between when He was crucified and when He showed Himself to them must have been terrible for them.

I think it says somewhere in the Bible that they hid in a house. I guess they were afraid the Romans or the Chief Priest or that someone would come after them too. I probably would have been afraid too. But what did they talk about? Did they remember the things they'd done with Jesus? Did they cry for Him? Did they pray?

In a way, that period of time for them reminds me of how we feel after someone has died. We're told that the person will be alive again, but we don't always act as if we believe it. We get scared thinking about our own death. We remember things. We cry. And—sometimes—we pray.

If we could just remember what happened to the disciples! Their time of grief was so short, and then they had Jesus with them forever. That's how it will be for us too—**because** of Jesus.

God, please be with those who are grieving now. Help them live through their grief and, even in the middle of it, help them see a glimpse of Easter, the Easter Your Son has won for all Your children.

106

THE INCREDIBLE EMPTINESS

How brave those women were—the ones who went out to the garden where Jesus was buried to put spices on His body. They certainly didn't know He was going to be alive, or else they wouldn't have brought the spices. And they must have known there was a good chance they could run into the soldiers who were guarding the tomb. Those soldiers could have given the women a rough time. Why, they might even have arrested the women for being followers of Jesus!

But they went. And when they got there they found an empty tomb. Usually we think of emptiness as a sad, disappointing sort of thing. If someone gave me a box wrapped up as a gift and the box was empty, I'd sure be disappointed. But for this one time in history, emptiness was the most wonderful thing anyone could find, because it meant Jesus was **alive**.

The women didn't seem to understand that right away, but they sure found out fast. And what a feeling they must have known then. I think the feelings of joy I have now are just great, but my joy must just be a little drop next to the ocean of joy they felt.

God, You did such a marvelous, marvelous thing. For those women and for all of us. How can we possibly praise You enough for it?

107

GUILT

Let me start off by saying loud and clear that I feel a lot of guilt. Sometimes I think I even feel guilt about things I shouldn't feel guilt about, and then I feel guilty about **that**. I have so many thoughts and feelings that I'm not always able to control, and they're the things that make me feel most guilty of all.

Some of them are thoughts and feelings about my parents. I get terribly angry with them sometimes, even though I don't always show it. Some are thoughts and feelings about me. I want to do things or I think about doing things that I know are terribly wrong. And some of them are thoughts and feelings about God.

I get so caught up in the terribleness of these thoughts and feelings that I start to believe that God can't—or won't—forgive them. I wish there were a big junkyard someplace where I could just dump them and forget about them, but I can't really believe that forgiveness is there for the taking.

But it **is**! Even the nastiest, worst thought or feeling I've ever had isn't too nasty for God to forgive. If it were, then Easter wouldn't be for real. And Easter **is** for real.

God, help me remember that when I start to get overwhelmed by guilt. Help me see that Your love is much, much bigger than my guilt. Show me the empty tomb and let me realize what that really means. It means forgiveness—for everything!

108

GOD'S BIG 'YES!'

I went to see Mrs. Fitzpatrick at the nursing home today, and on the way I counted all the signs that began with the word "no." There was "No Parking," "No Right Turn," "No Left Turn," "No Animals Allowed," "No Shoes, No Shirt, No Service," "No Children Under 14," "No Loitering," and "No Checks Cashed." That's a lot of noes for one short bike ride!

I told Mrs. Fitzpatrick about them and she laughed. "It's a 'no-nothing' world we live in," she said. "Aren't you glad that God of yours says yes!"

Well, that just took my breath away. First of all, it's the first time Mrs. Fitzpatrick has talked about God without me bringing Him up. And then for her to say such a neat thing!

Because God **does** say yes. He says it to me, just as I am, sins and all. He says it to everyone if they'd just listen. He says, "Yes, you are Mine." "Yes, I love you." "Yes, I forgive you."

In fact, that might be one very good way of defining Easter. Easter is God's big "yes" to the world.

109

VICTORY!

Our team at school won a big victory last week and, boy, did it feel great! I screamed so much that I could hardly talk afterwards, and I think everyone else was in the same shape. I was a **little** bit sorry for the kids on the other team, but maybe they'll beat someone else next time. And meanwhile it sure feels super to be a winner.

I wonder if that's how Jesus' disciples felt after God made Him alive again. Their team had won, and the team of sin and death had lost—forever. They didn't even have to bother feeling sorry for sin and death. They could just concentrate on how great it was to be a winner.

I don't know why I'm wondering about the disciples. How do **I** feel about that victory? It's mine too, after all. Well, my feelings about that are pretty clear. I feel tremendous!

I guess I could lose every other game that I might play in my whole life, and it wouldn't really matter as long as that victory is mine.

Thank You, God, for Jesus' victory. And I just thought I'd mention too how glad I am that our team won.

110

ME AND MY PROBLEM

I have this problem that's been bothering me for quite a while. It's sort of a big problem, and it hurts to think about it. So mostly I haven't been. I've been letting it lie there, somewhere in the back of my mind, while I try to concentrate on other things.

Tonight, though, I said to myself, "Self, why are you being such a sniveling little coward? Daniel went marching into that pit of hungry lions. He trusted God to take care of Him. Those women marched right out to Jesus' tomb. They trusted God too. Can't **you** trust Him to help you with this problem of yours?"

Then I did it. I looked at my problem—straight on. There we were, me and my problem, eyeball to eyeball. And for a minute or two I was scared. It **did** hurt looking at that problem. It hurt pretty much.

But I discovered something. It didn't hurt so much that I couldn't handle it. Somehow God made me stronger than that pain. And after the first few minutes, I could see my problem pretty clearly. I could even begin to think of ways to solve it. Tomorrow I'm going to try one of them.

I couldn't have done that alone, God. But together we faced my problem. And do You know what? It's just a problem! Together we can solve it.

111

HOW ABOUT HOPE?

We studied this story in school: A lady had a trunk of some sort that she wasn't supposed to open. But her curiosity got the better of her, and she opened it. Out leaped trouble and pain and other awful things and filled the world. Finally she looked in the bottom of the trunk, and there was only one thing left—a little tiny creature called Hope.

This story seems a make-believe sort of way to explain how sin came into the world, and I like the picture it gives me of hope waiting at the bottom of the trunk.

Except I don't think hope is a little tiny creature—not the sort of hope God gives us. I think God's hope is an incredibly strong, powerful thing, just like all the other gifts He gives us.

I don't think hope is something we should ignore until we just can't think of anything else either. You know how people say, "Oh, well. If all else fails, there's always hope."

I think hope is there to keep us going all the time. It's because of hope that we dare to try great deeds, to change the world.

My pastor says that hope is what makes us able to believe in things we cannot see and to act as if we could see them. That sounds a lot like faith in God to me. It sure doesn't sound little and tiny!

112

INFINITY—WOW!

Have you ever stopped and thought seriously about infinity? I've tried, and I just can't do it. I don't suppose anyone else can either. But it's fun to try.

Picture two parallel lines, like this: ═. No matter how long you make them, they'll never meet. That's because part of the definition of parallel lines is that they're an equal distance apart at all points. And if they're apart at all points, they can never meet. And that's infinity.

Someone told me that some astronomers think there may be no end to outer space. It might just go on forever and ever. That makes other astronomers nervous. They'd like to think there's an end **somewhere**, even if its billions and trillions and quadrillions of light-years away. I guess they just can't handle the notion of infinity.

Even the symbol that stands for infinity in math fascinates me. It looks like a number 8 lying on its side, sort of like it's tried and tried to measure infinity and then just given up and laid down in defeat.

Infinity. It's a tremendous thing to think about. And then to think that God is **more** than infinity. Well, WOW!

113

AM I VAIN?

I saw this really strange picture once. It showed a lady in old-fashioned clothes, looking at herself in the mirror. At least that's what the picture showed when you just looked at it casually. But when you looked again, you saw that the patterns of light and dark in the picture were arranged to form the shape of a skull. Spooky!

I suppose the artist was trying to show that vanity is stupid because we all end up as skeletons anyway, even the most beautiful lady. The thought of that made me nervous, but I kept coming back and looking at the picture again and again. And then I began to wonder if I'm vain.

I guess I do sort of like the way I look. Not that I'm such a fantastically gorgeous person, but I suppose I'm used to myself. And some parts of me really are pretty nice. I even like to look in the mirror sometimes. Furthermore, I don't think that makes me vain.

It would be phony of me to go around talking about how ugly I am. It would be unfair to God too. After all, He made me and He doesn't do poor work. Even the parts of me that I don't like too much are probably right for me. (They might also get a little better as I grow up.)

So thank You, God, for all of me—even the skeleton deep inside. Please don't ever let me get carried away with how I look, either by thinking I'm too wonderful for words or by thinking I'm too horrible for words. Help me remember that You're the one who made me, and that You made me just the way You want me to be.

114

EXPLODING WITH ENERGY

Maybe it's the time of the year. Maybe it's the stage I'm going through. I don't know, but sometimes I am so full of energy that I don't know what to do with all of it.

I hope my parents never read this. They'd say they could think of hundreds of things I could do. They'd ask why **they** never see any signs of that energy when there are chores to be done. But that's not the sort of energy I'm talking about. The sort I'm talking about doesn't want to mess with chores and other **little** things. It wants to jump on the top of the world and ride it like a bronco. It wants to shoot off into space, circle around the moon, and set off fireworks for everyone to see. It's a very ambitious sort of energy.

Part of that energy comes, I think, from the feeling that it's good to be alive. Part comes from wanting so much to do something about all the parts of being alive that aren't good—like poverty and hunger and pain. And part of it comes from I-don't-know-what.

God, I hope You'll let me keep some of that special energy as I grow up. I hope it isn't a phase. Because someday, with Your help, I want to use it. Maybe I won't ride the whole world like a bronco. But between us, we might be able to patch up a little part of it!

115

MISERABLE

I feel awful. I feel tired and depressed and hopeless and sad and AWFUL. There isn't even any good reason for me to feel this way. Nothing in particular has gone wrong at school or at home or with my friends. I just feel awful because I feel awful. And I hate it.

At times like this I don't want to be around anybody. I'm sure they must be thinking that I **am** as awful as I **feel**. To be perfectly truthful, I don't even like to be around myself when I'm feeling like this. I'm horrible company. I'd just like to shut myself off like a radio until I start playing a better tune. Except I can't imagine when that time would be.

The most awful part about feeling so awful is that I can't picture ever again feeling any other way.

Well, God, I guess You're the only One who can bear to put up with me when I'm feeling like this. That's the only good news I can think of. It's funny, though. Just thinking that You won't go away does make me feel the tiniest bit better. Maybe I'll make it, God. Do You think so?

116

TOP OF THE WORLD

I don't believe it. Yesterday I felt like the monster of the pits and today I think I could play a whole symphony single-handed. And there's no reason for this feeling either. Nothing in particular happened at school or at home or with my friends. I just feel terrific because I feel terrific. And I love it.

At times like this I want to be around other people. I want them to catch whatever it is I'm feeling. I want to infect everybody I meet with happy germs. But I don't mind being alone either. There are a million things I'd like to do by myself, and even if I didn't do any of them I could just listen to my own thoughts and be entertained. I'm very good company when I'm feeling like this. I can't imagine how I could have ever felt any other way.

How do You feel about me when I'm like this, God? Are You glad? Are You thinking, "Now **that's** the way I like that kid to feel"? It sure is the way **I** like to feel. Thank You, God, for helping me out of the pits and up here to the top of the world.

117

MOODY ME

Today I'm not in the pits or on top of the world. I'm someplace blah in the middle. It's better than the pits, but it still leaves a lot to be desired.

All these moods really wear me out. I **never** seem to feel the same way two days in a row. It's like being on a Ferris wheel every minute except when I'm asleep.

I asked my mom if maybe there was something the matter with me. She smiled that wise smile again, but this time she didn't just say, "Growing pains."

She said, "There's a lot going on with you right now. There's a lot going on in your body and that affects your feelings. But there's a lot going on with your feelings besides what your body is doing to them. You're in an in-between place, and that's hard on anybody."

She reminded me of how my dad felt when he was getting ready to change jobs. Talk about moody! She told me that she'd felt that way too once before I was born, when they were going to move from a place she really loved.

"And both your dad and I felt that way when we were your age. Everyone does to some degree. You'll live through it, honey. People do."

It's not much comfort right now to think that I'll live through this. Sometimes I'm not sure I **want** to. But it does help a lot to know that my parents understand what's going on, that they don't think I'm some sort of freak. I don't know if everybody's parents would let them know that.

Thank You, God, for parents who bother to talk to me about important stuff like this.

118

TODAY, PLEASE!

When I read Bible stories, I see how God was always breaking into people's lives. He broke into the lives of the people of Israel and got them out of Egypt—even when they were afraid to go. He broke into Sarah's life and sent her Isaac—even though she laughed at Him. He broke into the lives of an awful lot of people when He sent Jesus to earth.

It must have been wonderful back then, knowing God could break into your life at any moment and change everything. It must have been sort of scary too. But I think I could take the scariness. I'd just like God to break into our lives and change a few things.

I told my Sunday school teacher that, and she said, "But He does!"

"When?" I asked. "I've never seen Him."

"When somebody brought you to church or Sunday school for the first time, God was breaking into your life," she said. "When you went to visit Mrs. Fitzpatrick at the nursing home, God was breaking into her life. When . . . "

"Wait a minute!" I said. "That wasn't God. Those were people."

"Oh, come on," she said. "Aren't you always asking God to use you? Do you think He doesn't answer those prayers of yours. Do you think He doesn't answer the same sort of prayers when other people pray them?"

I thought for a minute.

"You win," I said.

You **do** break into our lives, God. Help me notice it a little more—today, please!

119

FLOWERS TALK TO ME

Flowers talk to me. They really do. So do butterflies and raindrops and snowflakes and birds' eggs. Maybe that sounds goofy, but it's true.

Flowers say gentle things with colors and smells and little motions when the wind blows. Butterflies say happy, carefree things with the dances they dance in the air. Raindrops say serious, thoughtful things with plops and splatters and long streaks on the window pane. Snowflakes say clean, peaceful things with lacy swirls and tiny taps. Birds' eggs say cosy things with warm, smooth shells and life inside.

Yes, maybe it sounds goofy, but sometimes, when I'm listening, I can hear all those things.

I can hear one thing more, too, from flowers and butterflies and raindrops and snowflakes and birds' eggs. And this thing I hear with every ounce of me inside and out.

I hear all those things saying in clear little voices, "God made us, and He is good."

120

AMEN!

Today I suddenly began to wonder just what the word "amen" means. Good grief, I've been saying it at the end of prayers and singing it at the end of hymns for years and years, and I don't even know what it means. That's crazy!

Well, I asked my dad, and he said it means "let it be so."

"Let it be so." That's sort of like an extra little "please" on the end of the prayer, isn't it?

Or is it more? Are we asking God to let it be the way we've prayed for? Or are we asking Him to let it be the way He knows is best?

I had to go back and talk to my dad some more about that.

"A little of both, I think," he said. "God wants us to ask for the things we want. But He wants us to trust Him to do what's best too. So we say 'amen' to both."

God, I probably pray for some dumb things sometimes. Then it's a good thing You don't give me what I want. You answer my prayer, but You say no. Other times, though, You do give me what I want. And both times I've said, "Amen." Help me remember that that "amen" applies to what **You** want too, to what You know is best. Thank You, God. AMEN!

121

MY GRANDPARENTS

I wonder why grandparents are so very different from parents. Grandparents seem to have boxes and baskets of patience tucked away somewhere. They never act as if they'd like to ship you off to the

North Pole for a while. Anyway, I just love my grandparents. I wish we saw them more often.

One of the things I really like is when they start telling me stories about my parents when **they** were kids. They never tell the same stories my parents tell. My mom, for example, absolutely loves to tell me how much time she spent taking care of her little sister. My grandma, though, tells me about the time my mom chased her little sister around the kitchen table with a broom. Now **that's** the kind of story I like to hear!

My grandparents remember other neat things too. Like the games they used to play and the clothes they used to wear and the time their parents took them to the fair. I love to hear stories like that, and I don't think my grandparents ever get tired of telling them.

My grandparents never get tired of giving me surprises either. My parents say they spoil me. But it's not the **things** they give me that I like so much. It's the surprise part and the fact that I know they have as much fun giving the stuff as I do getting it.

Did You plan life that way on purpose, God? Did You know that grandparents were exactly what a kid needed sometimes? And that maybe kids are just what grandparents need sometimes too? I suspect You did. You understand us people awfully well!

122

HIS BODY

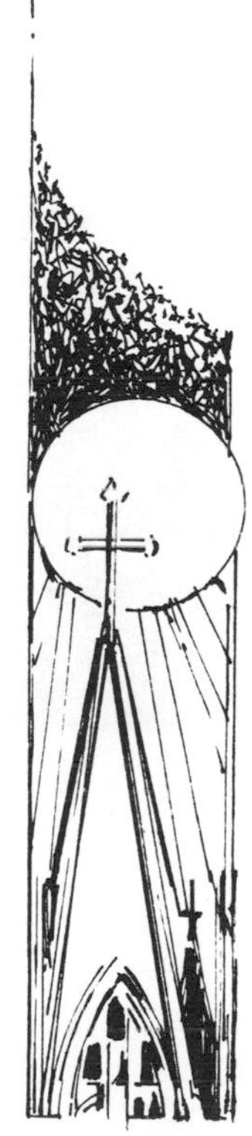

People are always talking about the church being Christ's body, with Him as the head. To be perfectly honest, that picture struck me as sort of strange. I kept wondering dumb things like whether I was a little toe or a fingernail. I guess I was being sort of childish.

Now that I stop to think about it, calling the church Christ's body is a wonderful way to think about it. You don't have to carry it to extremes and talk about fingernails and stuff. You can look at it in bigger ways, and then it says a lot.

For example, no one part of the body can do anything without the help of the others. My foot can't decide to walk someplace without the rest of me going along. And that's true for people in the church too. I couldn't be going to the nursing home and trying to help Mrs. Fitzpatrick if the people in my church weren't there to give me some ideas about what to do and the courage to do it. I wouldn't have even **thought** about going to the nursing home if it weren't for the people in my church.

But there's another way this picture of the church as Christ's body really works. The rest of my body would be absolutely useless without my head. It wouldn't know what to do or how to do it. I'd be dead. Jesus is the head of the church body. And without Him we wouldn't know what to do or how to do it. **We'd** be dead.

We're the body. He's the head. That's just perfect!

123

HOLY PEOPLE—US?

Whenever I think of the word "holy," I see it printed in gold letters, like on the front of a Bible. I always figured it was a very special word that sure didn't have much to do with old everyday me.

Then our pastor started talking about "holy." And, boy, did he open my eyes!

He said that "holy" means "set apart." And he said that that is exactly what we are—God's holy people. God has set us apart to love and serve Him and to follow His Son.

The really neat thing is that God isn't exclusive about all this. There isn't an "in" group that is set apart and an out group that isn't and never can be. **Anyone** can be one of God's holy people. Part of our job is make people **want** to be.

Holy people—us. Me!

124

POWER THAT NEVER STOPS

Somebody at school did a science project about a perpetual motion machine. Supposedly once you get it started, this invention never stops moving. "It doesn't need any power at all," said the kid who made it.

But that's not true. It's using some sort of power—gravity or some other natural force I guess. And it's using the power the kid put in it to get it started in the first place. Besides, somebody could stop it just by knocking it over. The kid had to stop it when he brought it to school. He'll have to stop it when he takes it home again. That little machine is really dependent on people for its power.

And that reminds me of the church. It—**we**—can't do much on our own either. We need some sort of power to get us started and keep us going. We get that power from God's Spirit. He's a lot better power source than some kid, too. He's not going to let anybody knock us over. He won't turn us off when He has something else to do. He really is dependable.

I guess the church is the best perpetual motion machine I know. And that's because it has such a good power source!

125

I CAN'T STAND PHONIES

There are some people in my church who get all dressed up on Sunday morning and sit there in their pews looking terribly religious. Then, when the service is over, they get up and go home. They may say a tight little "hello" to one or two people, but that's all. They don't want to have anything else to do with us.

I don't understand that at all. How can they **sit** there, hearing about God's love, singing about it, praying for the strength to show it to the world, and not show the least little bit of it to the people worshiping with them? I think they're nothing but a bunch of phonies, and if there's one thing I can't stand, it's phonies.

My mom says I should be more charitable. She says that I don't really know these people. I don't know what sorts of problems they have—physical or with their families or in their minds. They may be doing the best they can, considering what they're up against.

Well, maybe she's right. It sure isn't my job to judge those people. I wouldn't want **them** judging **me**. But I do wish church could be a different sort of experience for them.

God, if there's anyway I can help, please show me what it is. Maybe all I can do is go on being happy and excited about my church myself. Maybe they'll catch some of what I—and many others—feel. Could you make them a little less immune, God?

126

PART OF OUR BODY IS HURTING

A lady in our church just had to go to the hospital. It's bad and she'll probably have to have a serious operation. Her husband has to travel a lot because of his job, and they have three little kids. I don't know this lady very well, and I found out all the stuff about her just by listening to some of the adults talking. But, God, I feel so bad for her. She's one of us, and I don't want her to have pain. I don't want her little kids to be scared and lonely either, and I don't want her husband to worry.

This is what's it's all about—being part of Christ's body. When one of the other parts hurts, you do too. And in a way it's harder than hurting for someone you don't know, like a starving person in another country.

But in a way it's easier too, because at least you can do something. In fact, I got all fired up about doing something for this lady and her family. But I couldn't think of what to do. So I asked mom.

She grinned. "Well, honey, some of the other parts of the body have been busy too. One family is going to keep the kids. A whole group of people are ready to bring food once the lady comes home. And either the pastor or someone else will visit her every day in the hospital."

"But what can **I** do?" I asked. "We don't have room for three kids, I'm a lousy cook, and I don't think they'd let me in at the hospital."

"You could pray," said my mom.

Pray. Sure. That's part of being the body too, isn't it. God, be with that woman. Keep her safe and don't let her hurt too much. Be with the rest of her family too. Take care of them—all of them. They're ours.

127

TRY TO REMEMBER

Our church is more than a hundred years old. And nobody **in** our church is that old. That means that there's nobody left who was part of our church a hundred years ago.

And yet those people were as much a part of this church then as I am now. They cared about it in the ways I care about it. They brought their dreams and their gifts and their prayers and their praise to it, just as I do now. They cared for the sick, taught the little kids, baptized and married and buried. They **were** the church. And then they died and handed the church on to us. In many ways, we owe our church to them. If they hadn't cared, it wouldn't be here.

Thank You, God, for all those people who went before me. I know they're with You now. But thank You for lending them to us for a while. They helped bring us to You.

128

MR. OSWALD'S TONE-DEAF CAT

Whenever my grandmother hears someone singing badly, she says, "Good grief! That's worse than Mr. Oswald's tone-deaf cat!"

Well, there's this man who usually sits behind my family in church, and if I didn't know his name, I'd think he was Mr. Oswald in person. Or maybe he has that cat tucked under his jacket. You cannot **believe** the noise that man makes when he sings. If he gets one right note out of a whole hymn, it's purely by accident. And he's loud enough to drown out Niagara Falls.

For a long time I got mad every time I heard him sing. What right did he have, I wondered, to inflict that terrible noise on all the rest of us? One day it bothered me so much that I turned around to look at him. And I saw the most incredible thing.

He was smiling. Not a tiny, polite smile, but a huge, grinny smile. He was smiling while he was singing. And somehow I got the feeling that his whole heart was in that smile. That man was praising God with every ounce of his being, and if some of the ounces were off-key, well, what did it matter?

For a minute I felt about one inch tall because of all the ugly thoughts I'd had about him. But somehow his smile was catching, and I couldn't feel too bad. Instead I turned back around and went on singing myself—about four times as loud and six times as happily.

129

I LISTENED

I used to think that church was a great time for figuring things out. I mean, there was the sermon, a whole block of time when you couldn't do anything else anyway. I used to work out what I was going to do with the rest of the day or maybe even the whole week. Sometimes I'd decide what I was going to give mom or dad for their birthdays or Mother's Day or something. And sometimes I'd just tell myself stories—the kind where I was the hero and everybody cheered.

Not anymore. Last Sunday I listened to the sermon. And do you know what? Our pastor had something to say! He was talking about how we are the church, and a lot of what he said filled in some blanks in the stuff I've been thinking myself.

Oh, there were a couple of parts I didn't quite understand. Our pastor uses some pretty big words sometimes. But I asked him about those confusing parts while we were leaving church, and he didn't mind explaining at all.

I wonder how many neat sermons I've missed while I was off being a hero in one of my stories. I guess from now on I'll stay in church—and listen.

130

THOSE OLD PRAYERS

Another thing I sometimes don't pay attention to in church are those old prayers, the ones the pastor usually reads while everyone else just listens. I've heard them so often that I'd almost forgotten the words really had meanings attached.

But today I looked at some of them for myself. Some of them actually go back hundreds of years, even though the language might have been made a little more modern in the versions we use. And what surprised me most of all was that those people way back then were praying for exactly the same kind of things we pray for now. Things like peace among people, enough food for everyone, safety for those we love.

I don't suppose that should surprise me. We wouldn't be using the prayers in the first place if they didn't apply to us. But I'd never realized how well they apply because I've never really listened.

Well, I guess I'm going to start listening to them too, maybe even praying along. There is something sort of special about a whole group of people praying the same prayer that other whole groups of people have been praying for hundreds of years.

Don't You think so, God?

131

AT HIS TABLE

I've got to be perfectly honest and confess that I don't completely understand what Holy Communion is all about. I mean, I don't understand how it works. Not with my mind. I know I like taking it though. And I like the feeling I have after I've taken it. A clean, warm, strong sort of feeling.

My mom says that no one really understands it. She's says it's a mystery that only God understands. Baptism is sort of like that too.

In a way I'm glad I don't completely understand. Understanding would make it just a thing for my mind. But Communion is more than that. It involves every part of me. And it makes me feel a part of something much bigger than me.

Thank You, Jesus, for giving us this Sacrament. Thank You for being with us whenever we celebrate it. Thank You for what it does for us—this wonderful, wonderful mystery.

132

JUST SUNDAY MORNING?

One of my friends at school asked me a strange question today.

"Don't you get tired of spending every Sunday morning with all that religious stuff?" she asked. "There are so many other neat things you could be doing."

"No, I don't mind," I said. "I like it."

But then I got to thinking. I don't just spend every Sunday morning with religious stuff. I spend **lots** of time with it. I guess I'm to the point now that if I don't pray or a least think about God on a particular day, that day feels hollow and wasted.

It's not a guilt thing either. I don't do it because I think God expects me to and will zap me if I don't. I want to do it. I get sort of hungry for it. It keeps me going.

That's a hard thing to explain to someone who's never felt it. I don't know if my friend at school could understand. I don't know what church she goes to—or if she goes at all.

God, I'll bet there are a lot of people like my friend. Help them get to know You better. They're missing so much!

133

ALL THEY WANT IS MY MONEY

That's what I heard this man say as he was coming out of church. His chin jutted out and he was obviously mad. And the funny thing is that all our pastor said was that stewardship is part of our responsibility as Christians. He didn't even mention money!

In fact, I don't think he meant money at all. Or if he did, it was just a little part of what he meant. He was talking about us being stewards of everything God puts under our care—the earth and its resources, our own bodies, our gifts and talents, our time and energy.

But somehow that man heard him say "money," and that's kind of scary. It means that man is worried about his money and is ready to stop anyone from taking it away—even the church. I wonder if he has a lot of it. He doesn't look poor and he drives a neat car.

I guess it really isn't any of my business. I just feel sort of sorry for that man. It must be awful to be so suspicious that you can't even listen to a sermon without getting mad. It must be awful to care that much about money.

God, I've got to admit that I care some about money. I'd just as soon have enough to get along. But please don't let me ever care as much as that man. Let me put first things first in my life—You.

134

THE PEOPLE UP FRONT

I wonder how it feels to be one of the people up front in a church service—the pastor or the organist or one of the assistants. I wonder if they feel more religious than I do, closer to God.

I think it would be neat to be up there, wear special robes, and read from the Bible or preach a sermon or play an inspiring piece of music. I think it would be scary too. What if you messed up right in the middle of a worship service? Well, I guess God forgives the people up front just as much as He forgives the rest of us.

Sometimes we call the people up front ministers. But then we also talk about all of us being ministers. I guess the ministers up front take care of the ministers in the pews so that the ministers in the pews can go out and take care of the rest of the world. That's neat!

I know that our ministers up front do a lot more than preach sermons and read from the Bible. They spend an awful lot of time with people, helping them solve problems, comforting them when someone dies, and stuff like that. It's a lot of responsibility.

I wonder if I could do a job like that someday. I wonder if God wants me to. I guess He'll let me know if He does.

135

THE OTHER KIDS

Not all the kids I go to church with go to the same school I do. And since I make most of my friends at school, there are some kids at church that I hardly know at all. All of a sudden that seems wrong.

After all, those kids at church and I are linked together in a way that's more special than any other way. We're really members of the same family. How can you not know members of your family?

I guess I just haven't bothered. It takes time to get to know people, and it's risky too. Maybe some of those kids won't like me. Maybe I won't like some of them, and then I'll be stuck with them.

But isn't that how it is in a family? You're pretty well stuck with the people you have, and they're stuck with you. And that's not such a bad thing. Not when you love the people.

I can see where this is heading. I'm going to have to join one of the groups at church. I'm going to have to make a special effort to get to know those kids. Not because God will get mad at me if I don't, but because suddenly I can't stand **not** to. They're my brothers and sisters!

136

THE LITTLE OLD LADIES

Have you ever noticed how many little old ladies seem to hang around churches? I guess I see more little old ladies there than anyplace else I go. And I started to wonder why.

First of all, I suppose there are more little old ladies than little old men because men die sooner. A lot of the little old ladies at church are widows, I know.

What's it feel like to be a widow? To have lived with someone for years and years and then to suddenly be alone. I get depressed just thinking about that. It must be awful. Our society's a hard place for people who are alone. It must be even worse when you're not used to it.

Maybe that's one reason little old ladies like to hang around the church. Maybe they don't feel so alone there. They feel close to God, and they feel close to other people. They're part of a family again.

One thing is for sure. Little old ladies do a lot of work around the church. They cook dinners, fold bulletins, arrange flowers, hold bazaars, and probably a lot of other things I don't know about. It seems that they're the ones who take on the jobs that no one thinks to say "thank you" for.

I praise You God for the little old ladies. Be with them and fill them with Your love so they won't feel lonely. Help the rest of us to show them how much we love them and appreciate them too. Amen.

137

HOW GOD SEES

We've been studying the story of David, and in it is this great Bible verse that says God does not see the way people do. People look at appearances; God looks at the heart. God said that to Samuel when He wanted Samuel to anoint David king.

I think that I will remember that verse for the rest of my life. It's so **comforting**. There are a lot of times when I must look like a real dunce to the rest of the world. It's good to know that someone can look past all that and see me as I really am.

Oh, not that what I really am is so great. I guess when God looks at my heart He sees some pretty bad things sometimes. But He's ready to forgive them. You can't always say that for the rest of the world.

That verse does more than comfort me too. It makes me want to look at people a little differently than I usually do. It makes me want to try to see them the way God does. That's not easy for me. I really do get hung up on appearances. But I'd like to change.

God, would you help me start seeing differently?

138

A GREAT TIME FOR EYES

This is it—National Eye Day for me. Mostly I've used them to look at people, because of what I wrote yesterday. But a few other things slipped through too.

The first person I saw after I woke up was my mom. Now my mom tells me she isn't in the least beautiful. But ever since I was a little kid I've thought she was one of the most beautiful people in the world. I'm still not changing my mind.

Next I saw a very large brown dog taking a very small old man for a walk. Close behind him came a large white handkerchief, and close behind the handkerchief was our mailman. He sweats a lot. He told me once that it helps the mail slide through the slots a little more easily.

"Enough of people for a minute," said my eyes at this point. "We want to check out a few other things."

They did. A row of birds sitting on a wire like a bunch of oversized clothespins on a high clothesline. A butterfly quietly going crazy all over the lawn. A cloud that looked like an elephant on a skateboard.

I took my eyes inside so the rest of me could have a drink of water. They accidentally looked in a mirror.

"Blahhh!" said my eyes. "Let's try again tomorrow."

Smart alecks.

I praise You, God, for eyes.

139

OUT IN THE WOODS

My friend talked to me about church again today.

"Why do you have to get all dressed up and go to that special building to worship God?" she asked. "Isn't it a lot easier to feel His presence out in the woods or someplace like that?"

Well, I've got to admit that I **have** felt God's presence out in the woods. It's hard not to when you're surrounded by so many beautiful things He's created. I like the quiet too and being alone with Him and my thoughts.

But church is a whole different thing. It's more than a place where **I** worship God. It's a place where **we** worship Him—me and my church. Some of the great stuff that happens wouldn't happen if those other people weren't around.

For example, I need other people to teach me about His Word. I need other people to sing with me. It sounds—and feels—different when there are a lot of us. I need other people to pray with me—and for me. I need other people to gather around His table with me.

I think God sort of shows Himself to us through other people. I think He uses people as channels for His love. And I sure need that love too.

I still intend to go out in the woods sometimes and feel His presence there. But on Sunday mornings I want to meet Him with—and through—His other children.

140

DON'T I EVER GET A VACATION?

"Okay," said my friend. "So you're hung up on going to church. You say you really like it. But don't you ever get a vacation?"

A vacation. Well, I've got to admit that I've thought about it sometimes. Especially on those Sunday mornings when I simply cannot get my body out of bed. I even told my mom one morning when I felt like that, that I wanted a day off. She said okay. I couldn't believe it.

So, long after everyone else had left for church I lay there. I didn't sleep; I just lay there—and tried to feel luxurious. It didn't work.

One little part of me felt guilty, but that didn't bother me as much as the overwhelming feeling that I was missing something! My family—my church family—was all together doing the things we love to do, and I was left out.

The whole week went wrong after that. I had the empty, missing feeling every single day. The next Sunday morning you'd better believe I was up and dressed at the crack of dawn.

"You're going to think I'm a religious fanatic," I said to my friend. "But I don't **want** a vacation from church. I tried it once and it felt as awful as taking a vacation from breathing. No more!"

"Oh," said my friend.

141

MY FRIEND THE ATHEIST

Well, my friend at school has finally confessed to me that she thinks she's an atheist. It's funny too. She says it as if she's proud of it. She says you've got to be a really tough person to make it on your own. Church is for sissies who have to believe in a lot of superstitions to keep them going.

I said something really bright back to her, like, "Well, that's how you feel."

I didn't want to get in an argument with her right then. First of all I was too mad at being called a sissy. And second I wasn't sure what to say. I'm sure now though.

I'll tell her that at our age I'm not smart enough and she's not smart enough to figure out intellectually whether there is a God.

Besides, believing in God isn't something that you do only with your mind. You do it with some other part of you too—your heart, I guess. That's a different way of knowing, and in that way I do know there's a God.

My argument probably won't convince her. I think she's made up her mind that it's cool to be an atheist. But it's sure done a good job of convincing me!

God, please be with my friend the atheist. Give her the faith to know You. Help her understand that You're not a superstition. You're very, very real.

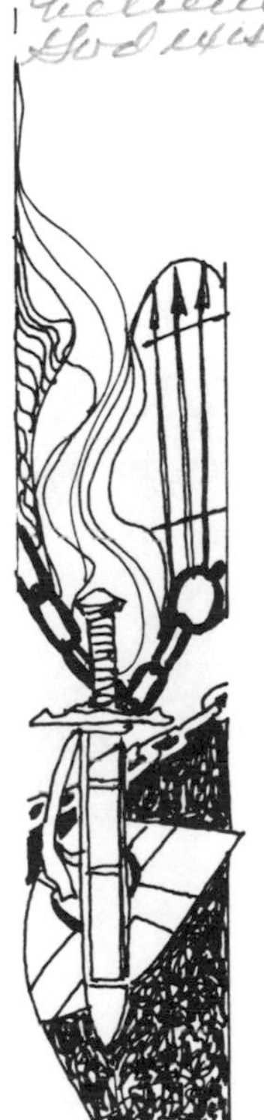

142

THE INQUISITION AND ALL THAT

Today my friend the atheist began telling me about all the awful things the church has done in the past. She talked about how we tortured people in the Inquisition. She talked about how we went on the Crusades just so we could loot and plunder. She talked about how corrupt we were in the Middle Ages. She painted an absolutely dreadful picture.

"Okay," I said finally. "Maybe people in the church did do all those things. But people outside the church did the same sorts of things. Oh, they fought their wars for different reasons, and they tortured people for different reasons. But they did it too."

"Yeah, but I thought the church was supposed to make better people of you," said my friend.

That stumped me for a while. But then I began to get a glimmer of an idea.

"I don't think that's really what the church is about," I said. "At least it's not the most important thing about the church. It's not the thing that comes first. What comes first is a bunch of people who admit that they are pretty rotten. They come to the church just because they **do** need God's forgiveness. Once they start feeling themselves full of His love, they start acting better. But the forgiveness part comes first. And it takes some people a long time just to get to the point that they know they need it."

"That's a dumb argument," said my friend.

"No, it isn't," I said.

"Yes, it is," she said.

God, please get to work on my atheist friend. Otherwise we aren't going to be friends much longer.

143

SUNDAY SCHOOL

A lot of kids I know think Sunday school is stupid. They make fun of it, and they try to get out of going whenever they can. I've felt that way too sometimes, especially when I have a teacher who treats us like a bunch of little kids. But I don't think Sunday school **should** be that way. After all, what it really is, is a bunch of grown-ups sharing something that means a lot to them with a bunch of kids who still have a lot to learn about it. If only so many teachers wouldn't treat us like babies!

I said that to my mother, and she reminded me of what she always says when I accuse **her** of treating me like a baby.

"Well, prove to me that you're grown up."

It makes me mad when she says that to me, and this time it made me mad too. But deep inside a sniggly little something tells me she might be right.

I started thinking about how things go in those bad Sunday school classes. What usually happens is that the teacher says something like, "Now Jesus says we mustn't steal. Let's all write that on a little card and carry it in our pockets all week."

We **know** that. What we want to know is what do you do when one of the neatest kids in your class asks you to cheat. That's the kind of problems we have. And I think most of us would like to talk about them.

Maybe we should just tell our teacher that. Maybe **that's** the grown-up thing to do. It sure beats looking bored and throwing paper airplanes around the room.

144

I **SMILED** AT COMMUNION

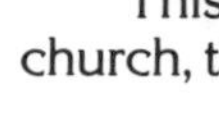

This week I shocked myself right out of my shoes. We were at church, taking Communion. Everyone was very serious, the way they always are, and the organ was playing some very serious music.

But I started thinking about all the love and forgivness God was giving us with Communion, and when the pastor got to me I just couldn't help myself. I **smiled**.

And, boy, was I scared. I thought maybe I'd committed some terrible sin. I was afraid the pastor might even refuse to serve me.

But then the second shocking thing happened. He smiled back at me! It was wonderful. All at once I didn't feel as if I were taking Communion by myself—just me and God. I felt **connected** to my pastor and to all the other people who were taking it too.

There's nothing wrong with feeling like that, is there, God? Isn't that how Jesus **wants** us to feel? I'm sure it is. Thank You, God, for the smile You had me smile at Communion. And thank You for letting there be someone to smile back.

145

I WANT THE CHURCH TO DO MORE

Tonight on TV there was a special program on world hunger. It really upset me, because nowhere in the whole program did I see the church doing anything. I realize that the people who put together the program probably just left us out. But if we were doing more—**lots** more—about problems like hunger, they wouldn't be able to leave us out. We'd be so obvious they'd **have** to show us.

I guess that in a way I'm afraid my atheist friend watched the program too and that tomorrow she'll make some smart-aleck crack about us having no part in it. I guess I should remember what I said to her the other day about our being people who need forgiveness too.

But I **still** wish the church would do more. Surely there are enough of us who feel God's love and want to share it with others.

God, this really bothers me. Please help me think straight about it. Help me see what the church **is** doing. But don't let me be content with that. Don't let any of us be content. Help us also see all the people who don't know You and Your love. And then help us get busy!

146

IF THE BUILDING BURNED DOWN . . .

I read a story in the newspaper tonight about a church whose building burned to the ground. No one was hurt, but the building was a total loss.

It gave me chills to read that story. I **love** our church building. It may not be the most beautiful one in the world, but it's ours. Everything in it is so dear and familiar. To see it burn down would be as bad as—or maybe even worse than—seeing our own home burn down. I couldn't **stand** to lose my church.

But wait a minute. The story in the paper didn't stop there. It said that the people whose church burned were now meeting in a school gymnasium. It said they hadn't made any plans for rebuilding their church right away. Apparently they were involved in too many other projects at the moment.

If they're still meeting and if they're still involved in projects, aren't they still a church? Isn't it really the people who are the church? They can get together to worship God and serve Him anywhere, even in a tent or on a vacant lot. God isn't locked into a particular building and neither is the church.

I sure hope our church never does burn down, God. But if it did, I guess we could take it. Because it wouldn't really be the church burning down. That's something You'll never let happen.

147

IT'S TOO EASY

I keep thinking about what my friend the atheist said—about the church just being for sissies. She wouldn't have been able to say that centuries ago when people were hunted down and killed for being Christians. Christians had to be tough people back then. Now I guess we don't have to be so tough. At least not in this country. Maybe it's too easy to be a Christian here these days. Maybe that's why we look like a bunch of sissies.

But I don't really think all of us are. You can't be a sissy and follow Jesus. You can't look at all the pain He makes you look at. You can't hurt for people the way He does. You can't stand up and tell the truth the way He did. Maybe you can call yourself a Christian and still be a sissy. But I don't think you can really live like one.

Or maybe there's still another way of looking at it. Maybe we **are** sissies—by ourselves. Maybe it's God who makes tough people out of us. After all, He's the One who gave those long-ago Christians the strength to go on following Jesus. He's the One who gives us strength to follow Jesus too.

I guess I don't mind so much being a sissy, God. Not if You'll go on making me tough!

148

WHY AREN'T THEY MORE FRIENDLY?

Last Sunday I watched a new family who came to our church. The ushers said hello to them very politely and showed them where to sit. Then the ushers said good-bye to them when it was time to leave. And that was it. Nobody else spoke to them at all.

Now I **know** a lot of the people in my church. I know how loving and friendly they can be. But those new people don't. All they know is what they saw at that one service. And I'm afraid we must have looked very cold to them.

Sure, it's hard to talk to new people. You don't really know what to say after you've said, "Wasn't that a nice sermon?" and "Isn't the weather fine?"

But it's even harder **being** a new person. I've been in that position too.

Maybe I should ask my pastor if there are ways we could act more friendly toward new people. Couldn't some people in the congregation be responsible for talking to them too—the sort of people who are just naturally friendly? All they'd have to do is invite the newcomers to coffee hour or Bible class or something like that.

Maybe I **will** talk to my pastor. And maybe I'll do something else. After all, I'm part of my church too. If that family comes back next week, maybe **I'll** talk to them.

149

I NEED THEM

I **did** talk to my pastor about newcomers. And he thought my idea of having certain friendly people in the congregation responsible for talking to them was fantastic! He's even going to call a meeting of some of those people this week.

"Of course I'd really like the whole congregation to feel responsible for newcomers," he said. "That's part of what a church should do. Welcome the stranger. But I'm afraid it'll take time for us to reach that point. And meanwhile, your idea is a very good one. Boy, I wish we had more kids like you around. We need you."

I could have fainted. My pastor said the church needed **me**. All because of one simple little idea that just came from keeping my eyes open. Wow!

You know, this tells me something very important about myself that I hadn't realized before. I **need** to be needed. It's one of the greatest feelings in the whole world. And to be needed by my church, well, that's even more special.

Thank You, God. Thank You for letting me know that they need me. Because it's a sure thing that I need them.

150

WHAT'S MY JOB?

I'm still pretty excited about my pastor's response to my idea about newcomers. What he said about the church needing me makes me want to do more and more and more. But I'm not sure what to do. I look around at the other folks in the church and it seems to me that the adults have a much easier time of it. They can serve on committees or do repairs on the building or help take care of the money. Kids don't get to do stuff like that. And it may be a long, long time before I get another bright idea like the newcomer thing.

I asked my dad what he thought I could do and he said, "Just what you are doing. Being you."

Well, it took me a while to figure that one out. I guess what he meant, though, is that most of what I do is sort of like guerrilla warfare. I strike wherever I see a chance to strike—like visiting Mrs. Fitzpatrick at the nursing home and getting my pastor to visit her too, or talking to my Sunday school teacher about the things that are really important to kids my age. And when I do strike, I ask God to help me do the very best job of it I can.

Well, God, if this is the way you want me to go on serving Your church, it's okay with me. Just please keep on helping me do a good job. I can't do it alone.

151

A BIG OLD SHIP

Today I saw another one of those movies in my mind, the kind I can sometimes make happen when I'm all alone and thinking hard about something. It was the church I was thinking about today. And all of a sudden the movie started.

I saw this big old ship afloat on the ocean. It was full of people, all kinds of people—young and old, rich and poor, scared and brave, silly and smart. The captain of the ship, of course, was Jesus.

We sailed all over, from country to country and island to island. And everywhere we stopped, we all got off and tried to bring people back to the ship to meet our captain. We knew that if they really got to know Him, they'd want to get on the ship too. And we always had plenty of room for more.

Sometimes one of the scared people would start to cry. Then the rest of us would try to comfort him or her. Jesus always helped. Sometimes one of the silly people would fall overboard. Then the rest of us would try to rescue him or her. Jesus always helped then too.

But the neatest thing was that we didn't really think much about where we were going, about where the end of our trip would be. That didn't seem to matter. What was important was that we were on the ship—with our Captain.

152

TREES

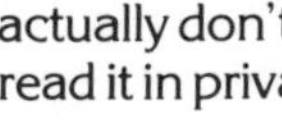

No, I am not going to write a corny poem about trees (although I actually don't think that one by Joyce Kilmer is so bad if you could just read it in private and not have to talk about it in class). I've got to admit that I'm terribly impressed by trees, and whenever I start getting unimpressed, I close my eyes and try to picture the earth without them. Then I get impressed all over again.

Today I was noticing especially the color of trees. For a long time, when you're a little kid, you think that trees are green things with brown trunks. Period. Then one day you really look at a tree and it's like having a new set of eyes.

Right now the sun is shining on the tree outside my window. The leaves are dark green, light green, about a million shades of medium green, yellow, and white. The trunk and branches are dark brown, medium brown, tan, and almost black. Tonight all that will change and the tree will look really black, purple, blue, and maybe silver.

I know that trees serve all sorts of useful scientific functions in our ecology. But right now I'm happy just to look at this one.

Thanks for trees, God. They were a wonderful idea.

153

EXCUSES, EXCUSES!

Every time I tell my parents the reason I can't do something, they say I'm making excuses. Well, maybe I am sometimes—like when I really don't want to do something but am afraid to say that. But sometimes my reasons are perfectly good, and I wish my parents would understand.

This afternoon, for example, mom wanted me to run an errand. I was in the living room, sort of draped over the couch, reading a book. Maybe she thought I was just loafing. But I wasn't. It was a book-report book; and I was not only reading it, I was at an especially tricky part, thinking up what I was going to say about it. But mom didn't hear my reason for not wanting to run the errand. She heard "excuses." So I ran it. And when I got back, I had to think through that tricky part all over again.

Maybe my excuses and I are a little like the boy who cried "Wolf!" Maybe I give them so often that when a real reason comes along, no one takes me seriously. I hate to think that's the case. I'd rather blame my parents. But I think maybe it **is** true.

God, please help me not to make so many excuses. And when I give reasons, please help me make them sound very reason-able.

154

THE DOWN-PUTTER

There is this girl at school who I simply cannot stand. She's always putting everyone—and everything—down. If you say to her,

"Wasn't that a great book?", she'll say, "Oh, I didn't like the ending." Or, if they're super books (like the **Chronicles of Narnia** by C. S. Lewis) and she couldn't possibly think of anything bad to say about the story, she'll complain that the print's too small or the cover is ugly.

She's even worse about people. A doesn't wash her hair often enough. B bites his fingernails. C is dumb in math. She can't find anything good to say about anybody. I think she must be a miserable person. She certainly does her best to make everyone around her miserable. And so, naturally, people avoid her.

I guess that makes it even worse. Then she's more miserable, and everything and everyone look more miserable to her and . . . I'm making myself dizzy.

I know what will happen if I try to be this girl's friend. She'll go on down-putting and I'll go on trying to be patient and then one day I'll have had it and I'll blow up at her.

Maybe that wouldn't be such a bad thing, though. Maybe she **needs** someone to tell her what she's doing. Maybe I ought to tell her calmly before I get to the blowing-up point.

Would You help me handle this problem too, God?

155 WHAT THAT GIRL DID!

Everybody is talking about a girl we know—a high school girl—and what she did. The other people get together and whisper about it. The kids just talk aloud. I guess you can guess what the girl did. She's going to have a baby, and she isn't married. (I wonder why everyone keeps saying **she** did it—as if some boy didn't do it too.)

I can just imagine how the girl must feel. Scared, embarrassed, ashamed, alone. Her first day at school after everyone knew must have been rough. Not as rough, though, as the first time she went to the grocery store. For some reason grown-ups are much worse about this sort of thing than kids. Kids just ask stuff like, "How do you feel?" and "Are you going to get married?" Grown-ups point their fingers and say "Tsk tsk!"

Then, last Sunday, that girl did the bravest thing I've ever seen. She wore her maternity clothes for the first time—and she went to church. (I forgot to mention that she goes to our church.) When she walked in, you could hear people catch their breath. I tensed up all over like an Olympic athlete. I was ready to kill the first person who whispered. But no one did. And the girl had made her point.

Without saying a word, she said, "All right, I have made a bad mistake. But God's forgiveness is big enough to cover that mistake. Would everybody else try to forgive just as much?"

Help them do that, God—especially the grown-ups. That girl is going to have some hard times ahead. She'll need grown-ups to help her. When she does, God, please let them be there.

156

BABY-SITTING

Tonight I had another baby-sitting job. It still seems funny to think of me baby-sitting. I can still remember when I had to **have** baby-sitters. And now I know how some of them must have felt!

Baby-sitting can have its bad moments. Like when the people expect you to clean their house along with taking care of their kids. (I go to those places just once—then never again.) Or when they don't leave you anything to eat. (I get horribly hungry when I'm baby-sitting.) Or when the kids won't do a thing you tell them. (I'm getting better at figuring out ways to handle them.) Or when the kids are all in bed, and the house starts making noises at you. (Sometimes I call my mom and just talk for a while.)

But there are great moments too. Like when a little kid gets out of the bathtub all damp and squeaky clean. Or when you go into their rooms after they're asleep, and they're flopped all over the bed like little rag dolls. Or when they want to say their prayers with you. That **really** makes me misty eyes.

Baby-sitting is a big responsibility. I know that, God. Be with me while I'm doing it. And help me do the best job I can.

157

ANOTHER BIRTHDAY

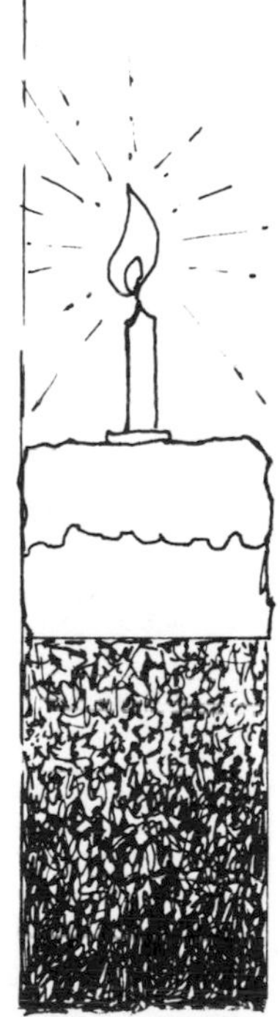

For a long time I didn't understand what Pentecost was all about. Oh, I knew that a long time ago God sent His Spirit to Jesus' friends in Jerusalem. There were tongues of flames over everyone's head and a rushing wind and people could understand what other people said even if they didn't speak the same language. Actually it all sounded sort of spooky to me, and I tried not to think about it too much.

But this year I sat down and read the Bible story (it's in the first part of Acts), and I made the neatest discovery. Pentecost is the day the church was born!

Before Jesus went back to heaven, He promised His friends that God would send them the Holy Spirit. On Pentecost that's what God did. And right away Jesus' friends began doing the sorts of things **we** do in church. Peter preached a tremendous sermon, and a bunch of people who heard him decided that they wanted to follow Jesus too. So they got baptized.

It was God's Spirit who made all that happen back then. He made the church to be born. He gave it the power to do the things God wanted it to do. And it seems to me that He hasn't stopped working through the church ever since.

So, happy birthday, church. And many happy returns of the day!

158

PETS

I think pets are one of the greatest things since sliced bread (that's one of my grandma's expressions). I mean, just stop and think about it. What do pets ask from people? A place to sleep and some food that sure doesn't cost much compared to people food. Maybe a walk now and then or some playtime.

And look at what they give. Company. Protection sometimes. Mouse-free houses sometimes. Above all, love. Love without questions. A pet doesn't stop to figure out whether or not a person deserves love. It just loves. The ugliest person in the world doesn't have to feel ugly around a pet. The pet simply doesn't care what he or she looks like. It just loves. I wonder how many people who have been so lonely that they could die have hung on to life because one little animal loved them. I'll bet there have been a lot.

The world would certainly seem an empty place, God, without animals. Worse even than without trees. Thank You for pets. They are part of Your creation. And please help all pet owners take care of them as they should.

159

STROKES

Today somebody said something very nice about me. And what did I do? I puffed up like a pigeon in a puddle. I felt great! I don't think I said anything very profound in return. I probably just mumbled, "Thanks," and turned beet red. But that's okay. It's hard to talk when you're perched on a cloud two miles above the earth.

I used to think that there was something wrong with needing to hear compliments. I used to think that you should be so self-confident that you could make it entirely on your own. Well, I don't think that anymore. Because the fact is that I need strokes. And I think most everyone else does too.

And that reminds me of something. I wonder if I've handed out any strokes lately. Sometimes I forget. I can be thinking of some neat thought about a person, but I somehow never get around to saying it. Maybe I'm just a tiny bit embarrassed. But if that person who said the nice thing about me today had felt that way, I wouldn't be feeling so good.

Thanks for the strokes I get, God. Help me remember to give my share too—not phony stuff, but real, honest compliments.

160

AIR

If there's one thing I don't usually think about it's air. Oh, I can get excited about pollution control and all that. But the air that's right here all around me—well, I just sort of forget it.

Not today, though. Today there seemed to be something special about the air. Or maybe it's my nose that's feeling special. Or maybe the fact that it's really and truly summer makes everything seem a little special.

Anyway, this morning I stepped outside and I didn't just breathe the air. I drank it. It had a softness about it and yet a tang that made it suddenly seem real to me. It wasn't a bunch of invisible stuff. It was part of God's creation, one of those miracles of nature.

During the day I got busy and forgot about air. (Of course, I didn't stop breathing!) Once again it was only a bunch of invisible stuff.

But this evening I went outside again. The air was still soft, but the tang was gone. Instead there was a faint, gentle sweetness, as if a long way away honeysuckle was blooming, or jasmine. Once again I drank instead of breathed.

God, this may be the only time in my life I do it, but I really want to thank You for air. I not only need it, I like it!

161

ME THE KLUTZ

Who else do you know that can trip over shoestrings when they're going barefoot? Who else meets the world elbows first? Who else is purple as a prune most of the time? Who else's friends call them Scrubbyknees? Well, here I am—the World's Champion Klutz.

Most of the time I can laugh about it—through my tears. But occasionally it really gets to me. Like when I bumped into my math teacher and knocked her into the principal, who was getting a drink at the water fountain. **That** was a little messy. Or when my dad gives me the platter of barbecued hamburgers to take inside and I trip over a piece of gravel one millimeter in diameter and we have to send out for a pizza instead.

After all, my feet are part of me. So are my elbows and knees and all those other parts of my body that seem to think they belong to someone else. You'd think they would pay a little attention to what I want them to do.

Oh, well. Mom says I'll get better with age. Personally I sort of doubt it. By the time I'm 21, I'll probably be the world's largest living bruise. At least then I'll be able to make some money out of my klutziness. Charge admission and all.

God, please keep me from doing any serious damage to myself or anyone else till I outgrow this—if I ever do.

162

SMOKING

A lot of kids at school are already smoking. I don't understand that. They know how terrible it is for them, but they do it anyway. And I mean **really** smoking. Inhaling. I'm sure they do it to make themselves look cool. But, first of all, they don't really look cool; they look sort of dumb, like little kids in grown-up clothes. And secondly, even if they **did** look cool, they're paying too high a price for it.

I can understand why some grown-ups smoke. They started back before everybody knew how bad it is, and for some of them it's almost impossible to stop. I remember when my dad stopped. We weren't sure who'd end up in a padded cell first—him or the rest of us. What I can't understand is how someone could **start** now.

Of course the ads are really sneaky about smoking. They make it look like the minute you light up a cigarette you're suddenly the most beautiful woman or the most handsome cowboy in the world. They tie a bunch of good things—like horses and gorgeous sunsets and babbling brooks—onto smoking and think that people will feel they all belong together. But even a kid like me can see through that.

God, please help the people who are trying to stop smoking. Please help kids understand what a dumb thing it is to do to their bodies. And please don't let me ever even **think** about starting.

163

MY FAVORITE WORDS

Other people have favorite colors, favorite foods, favorite songs. So do I. But I also have favorite words. They aren't necessarily words I use a lot—at least not out loud. But they're the words I like to **feel** in my mouth, hear in my ears. They're words I would use in poems if I were a poet.

One of my favorite words is mouse. Mouse. It's such a cute word, a little word. Somehow it sounds like a mouse.

Another of my favorite words is loam. It means earth, the kind of earth you plant things in. And the word itself—loam—is somehow dark and rich and wet just like the thing it means.

The meaning of the word doesn't always matter to me, though. I like the word grey (spelled with an e, the way the English do it), but grey isn't one of my favorite colors. In fact I think it's sort of a sad color.

I once read about an Italian man who said he just loved the words cellar door. He didn't even **know** what they meant. He just liked the way they sounded. Cellar door. They do sound a little like singing.

My most favorite words, though, combine both sound and meaning. They're Christ Child. They are strong and yet gentle. They sing too—a bright, joyful song. And they touch me somewhere deep inside.

Thank You, God, for words. They're useful—and they can be so beautiful too.

Help us to each day use words that are encouraging, positive, & meaningful. Let our words glorify you, Lord.

164

DAYDREAMS

I wonder if everyone else spends as much time daydreaming as I do. Oh, I don't sit around for **hours** doing it. But I bet I daydream at least once every day and sometimes more than that.

In a lot of the books I've read, kids who daydream are always seeing themselves as the hero of some big adventure. I like to daydream like that sometimes too, but it's not my usual kind of daydream. In my usual daydream I'm in some neat place—the woods maybe or on the beach by the ocean. I may be playing with animals or looking for shells. And if there's another person in my daydream it's usually someone I don't know (not in real life, I mean), and that person is a very good friend, someone I love and who loves me.

I suppose daydreams could be bad for you if you spent all your time in them and didn't pay any attention to real life. But I'm not that way. I like real life too. In fact, someday I'd like to make some of my daydreams come true. I'd like to go to the places I dream about, do the things, meet the person.

Would You help me do that, God? Someday?

165

POLITICS

Every so often I feel that I should get very serious and think about politics. These spells usually last less than an hour, just long enough for me to try to read a newspaper or watch a news program and figure out what's going on. I never do.

I hear Joe Smith make all these wild and wonderful promises about what he's going to do if he gets elected. He also manages to hint that his opponents couldn't begin to do the same things. Then Fred Jones comes on with a set of wild and wonderful promises all his own. After Fred comes Mary McGee. By then I've stopped listening. I don't think any of them could keep those promises. They're just carrots to get us—a bunch of donkeys—to follow them.

I finally told my dad how I felt. I thought he'd be shocked and think I was unpatriotic. But he just laughed. He said he's felt the same way many times himself. "The thing is," he said, "is that intelligent voters have to pay attention to a lot more than campaign speeches." Then he started talking about voting records and stuff like that. In a way it made sense, but it sure sounded complicated too. Maybe that's why kids my age aren't allowed to vote.

God, please guide the people who can vote to make good

choices for the rest of us. And please be with the people who get elected and keep them honest and strong and caring.

166

MY TALENT—MAYBE

I've been thinking a lot about this, and I suspect I know what my talent is. That's an exciting feeling—and scary too. After all, a talent is like a special gift from God. He doesn't just give it to you for no reason at all. He expects you to use it and use it well. A talent brings with it a lot of responsibility.

Of course, it will take me a long time to find out if this talent is real. I'll have to learn as much as I can about how to use it. I'll have to practice using it over and over again. I'll have to figure out whether I want to make a career out of it or just do it in my spare time. Most of all, I'll have to decide how I can use it to serve God.

But it's there now and I feel like it's some precious secret inside of me. That talent could make a lot of difference in who I am and who I grow up to be.

Thank You for this gift, God. Help me use it wisely and well.

167

DO I RESPECT MY PARENTS?

I was over at a friend's house today when he had a fight with his parents. It was over some dumb thing, the way lots of fights often are. But at one point his parents (actually it was his mother) said something that really shook me. She said, "We're your parents. You should respect us."

I didn't really think the argument had anything to do with respect. My friend felt one way about something and his parents felt another way. They were simply disagreeing. But it bothered me that his mother said, "You **should** respect us." I think that when respect becomes a "should" kind of thing it stops being respect.

Take me and my parents. I think I respect them. I feel that they're good people with good ideas and good beliefs. I trust them to give me wise answers to questions that are important to me. I ask their advice and I usually take it. I'm proud of them. Surely all those things add up to respect. But respecting them doesn't mean I have to agree with them all the time.

I like yellow. My dad likes blue. My mom likes red. Does that mean we don't respect one another?

I don't think you **can** force someone to respect you. Fear you, maybe. But not respect. I **do** respect my parents. That's something I give them because of the kind of people they are. The neat thing is that

I think they respect me too, and that says something about the kind of person I am.

God, I'm glad You put me into my family. We have our faults, but we have enough respect to go around too!

168

THE STORM

We had the most incredible storm today. The sky became dark as night, all the leaves turned inside out, the wind began to blow in great huge gusts, and then the rain came down—**waves** of it. The thunder boomed so loud that you could feel it in the floor, and the air was practically alive with lightning. For a while there I was scared pea green.

Afterwards I thought for a while about what made the whole thing so scary, and I think I've figured it out. For that period of time, I felt totally out of control. I wasn't even sure if anyone else I knew was in control. It was as if nature had taken over and was showing all of us what puny little things we really are. We couldn't stop the wind or the lightning or the rain. All we could do was sit it out.

I cheated though. When the storm got to its scariest, I called in someone I knew could handle it, someone who never lost control. You, God,

169

AN OLD-FASHIONED WORD

Today I was reading a story in an old book that my dad's had for years. The story was about soldiers fighting some long-ago battle, and they kept using a word that I almost never hear people use today. Honor.

I asked my dad what it meant, and he grinned and said what he always says, "Look it up in the dictionary." So I did. There were a bunch of definitions, but the one that came closest to what the soldiers were talking about said: "A sense of what is right, just, and true."

That's pretty heavy. But I guess it had to be if those soldiers were willing to die for it. I seem to remember a lot of other people in history who died for honor too—people like philosophers, martyrs, even scientists.

I wonder if I have a sense of what is right, just, and true. I think I do—in a way. But my sense of honor is somehow all tied up with what the Bible teaches and the church. It has a lot to do with following Jesus too.

God, if I'm ever in a situation where I have to die for that honor, please give me the courage to do it. But I guess I'm more likely to have to **live** for it. Give me the courage to do that too.

170

ENERGY

One of the things you learn about in science class at school is energy. There are two kinds: kinetic, which is energy at work, and potential, which is energy stored up and waiting to go to work. Sometimes, especially in the summer, I feel like I have a lot more potential energy that I do kinetic energy. It's there all right, but it just doesn't happen to be working at this particular time.

I wonder how much energy each of us really has inside. If there's enough energy in one little atom to blow up an entire city, and if each of us is made up of more atoms than you can count—well, that's a powerful lot of energy. But I don't think I'd much enjoy turning myself into a bomb.

Then there's the fact that energy is never wasted. It just goes on being energy—unless it happens to be matter for a while. I don't think I've explained that very well (it's sort of complicated), but maybe my summer problem is that too much of me is matter and not enough is energy.

I like thinking about scientific stuff. And whenever I do, I always end up right back at God. **Nobody** could have come up with a world like this except Him. Nobody.

171

THE DIFFERENT CHILD

Today while I was at the store, I saw a woman with a child who was different. I think brain-damaged is the term to use. This little boy must have been about six years old, but he acted like he wasn't yet two. And somehow he looked different too.

I didn't want to stare at him, because I know how I'd hate someone staring at me. But I didn't want to ignore him either, because that would be cruel. So I looked for a moment or two, smiled, and then went on down the aisle. The little boy didn't notice. But his mother did and she smiled back at me. It made me feel great, like I'd done the right thing.

God, I know You have some reason for letting children be born like that, even though I don't understand what it is. Sometimes I could almost get mad at You thinking about it. But I try not to. I try to trust You instead.

But, God, please take especially good care of those children and the other people in their families too. Let them know in as many ways as possible that You really do love them.

172

AND EVERYONE WILL KNOW MY NAME

I don't know what I want to be when I grow up. Not for sure. But somehow whenever I start thinking about what I'll be, it's something that will make me terribly famous.

Everyone will say, "Look at those paintings!" or "Listen to that sermon!" or "what a fantastic discovery!" And I'll be very modest and say with a little smile, "Oh, it was nothing."

HAH!

I guess everyone has crazy thoughts like that sometimes. But I'll bet not everyone has a mother like mine. I was telling her about how famous I'd like to be and this is the question she asked me:

"How would you feel if you painted the great paintings or preached the sermon or made the discovery and no one knew who you were. For some reason you were anonymous and only God knew what you had done. How would you feel then? Hmmm?"

"You are a rat," I told her. "At first I think I'd hate it. I'd want everyone to know **I'd** done those things. Then maybe I'd get used to it. And after a while I might even like it. After all, people don't bug you when they don't know who you are. And the really important thing is that the picture gets painted or the discovery made—not who paints it or discovers it."

"Very good," said my mom, making a rat face.

Help me do whatever I do as well as I can do it, God. And if no one but You knows I've done it, well, I guess that's plenty!

173

THE ALCOHOLIC

A friend of mine just told me about a really rough problem she has. Her dad's an alcoholic. She says it's not like the movies where the guy comes home drunk all the time and beats his wife and kids. At least it's not that way with **her** dad. But he and her mom do have terrible arguments sometimes. And lots of times her dad just doesn't come home at all, or else he staggers in and flops on the bed.

"It must be horrible for you," I said. "Isn't there anything anybody can do to help?"

"Well, my mom's going to Al-Anon now," she said. That's a place where relatives or friends of alcoholics can go to meet with a lot of other people in the same situation. Mom says it really helps. But what we want most of all is for dad to join Alcoholics Anonymous. That's the group where alcoholics help each other."

"Won't he join?" I asked.

"No. The thing is, he doesn't really **want** to stop drinking yet. And you have to **want** to stop before you can even begin to try."

God, please make him want to stop. Make him see what he's doing to himself and the people who love him. And help them too. Make them strong enough to stick with him until You get to him.

174

BETRAYED

My friend betrayed me. I told him a secret, something I'd told nobody else, and today two other people told me he'd told them.

I'm furious, absolutely furious. But more than that, I feel hurt. **Why** did he do it? Did he just not care? Did he think my secret was so unimportant that he'd use it to make himself more interesting to other people? Did he think I was so unimportant? I guess that's partly what hurts so much. This person that I cared about doesn't really care about me.

I don't know what to do now. Should I call him and tell him I know what he did? Should I wait till the next time I see him and then be terribly cold? Or should I try to forget the whole thing, pretend it never happened? One thing is for sure. I'll never tell him a secret again.

God, help me know what to do. Help me get over this terrible hurt—and the anger too—so I can think more clearly. Help me forgive my friend (because deep down I know that's the best thing to do). And please God, keep me from ever doing something like this to someone else.

175

WHY DO WE FIGHT?

Boy, did we have a humdinger of a fight in my family tonight! Everyone was yelling at everyone else and finally everyone stamped out of the room. We're just managing to speak to one another again now, but we do it very very cautiously. And the funny thing is that I can't even be sure what the fight was all about.

It was as if all at once there were these three entirely different animals locked in a cage together. Each one of us wanted to do something different, but there wasn't enough room for that. So we turned on each other.

I suppose it is like that in a family sometimes. Everyone can't do what he or she wants all the time. Sometimes you have to give in and let the other person have a turn.

It sounds easy written out like that. But it sure isn't easy when real people get in the act.

God, please help us understand one another a little better. We love one another, but I think we need Your help to show that love more often. We especially need to show it when the things we want all conflict. Help us then, God.

176

THE QUILT

If there's one thing I love, it's big old quilts. The kind made up of patches from all different colors and patterns of material. Over there in one corner is Cousin Mabel's favorite polka-dot dress. Here's Baby Joe's first sunsuit. And here's what's left of mom's apron after she spilled gravy all over it last Thanksgiving. Quilts are like a collection of stories stitched together with a piece of thread.

And (here is my own brilliant idea for today), the Bible is like a quilt. It's a collection of stories too. Over there Daniel is facing the lions. Here Miriam is singing a song of praise. Here Jesus is healing a blind person.

The thread that holds all those stories together, though, is the most important thing about the Bible quilt. It's God's love. It goes around and over and under and through every story. Without it they'd all fall apart.

Thanks for that idea, God. (I'm pretty sure it came from You.) But even more, thanks for the Bible—and all the love that's in it.

177

BAD WORDS

No, I'm not writing this about the kind of words we usually think of as bad, the kind that look like this—@+?//*!—in comic books. I'm writing about words that do bad things to people. I thought I knew most of those words, the kind people use to describe people who are different from them in some way—maybe in race or in the country of their ancestors. I never use those words.

But today I found out that a word I've been using for years is bad in the sense that it hurts some people. That word is handicapped. I don't suppose I'd ever thought much about where the word came from. I just assumed it meant someone who had something physically (or maybe mentally) wrong with them, like a blind person or a crippled person.

But words have histories just like people and countries do, and the history of handicapped isn't very nice. It goes back to a time when people with physical problems were looked down on by almost everyone else. The only way they could make a living was to beg, with a cap in their hand. Cap. Hand. Handicapped. That's where the word came from, and even though it doesn't have the same meaning anymore, some people are hurt when you call them handicapped. As far as I'm concerned that's a good enough reason to ban the word from my vocabulary.

God, please help us to be sensitive toward one another. Keep us from doing the things that hurt and help us do the things that lift up. Help us be more like Your Son.

178

ONE OF THESE DAYS I'M GOING TO GET ORGANIZED

There are lots of different signs that say that. Usually people put them on their desks. They show blobby little people looking horribly frazzled. And you get the feeling that the people who own the signs half mean what it says and half realize that they probably never will get organized.

Well, I mean it! And by "one of these days," I mean maybe even tomorrow or the next day. I'm tired of wasting hours looking for something that's probably under my bed. I'm tired of having to look up my friend's phone number in the phone book every time I call (her last name is Jones), instead of being able to flip to the right page in my address book and find it there. I'm tired of always having the very thing I want to wear dirty. I'm going to get organized. I am!

The thing is, there are so many important ways I could be using my time—learning, growing, even just having fun—and it seems awfully dumb to have to miss some of them because I'm crawling under a bed or digging through a phone book.

God, if I say it once more—I'm going to get organized—and really mean it, will You help me?

179

EVIL THOUGHTS

Have you ever had an evil thought, I mean **evil**, get inside your head and refuse to go away? Well, that's what happened to me today. I'm not even going to write the thought down. It's too awful. But it almost drove me crazy.

And the more I tried not to think it, the more it kept popping into my mind. It was sort of like that joke you play on little kids when you tell them that you bet they can't go for a whole minute without thinking about a blue mouse. They squinch up their face and try as hard as they can and of course the only thing they can possibly think of **is** a blue mouse.

Well, I decided to try to figure out where that thought had come from. I didn't think **I'd** made it up. It really was too evil. So I decided the devil must have put it in my mind. And **that** scared me more than ever because I began to wonder if I was being possessed.

Finally I talked to mom.

"Everybody has thoughts like that sometimes," she said. (That made me feel better right off the bat.) "And the best thing to do when you have them is to laugh at them. It's one of the things the devil can't stand—to be laughed at."

So I did it. I pictured the devil snorting and snuffing and gasping and grunting to get that thought into my mind, and I laughed right in his stupid face. The thought didn't go away just like that, but it sure doesn't bother me as much anymore. And I have a feeling that by tomorrow, I'll hardly think of it at all.

So there, devil!

180

THE JOKE

Some friends of mine and I had a party today and we decided to play a joke on one of the girls that was there. It wasn't the kind of joke that could hurt anyone physically. In fact, it wasn't any big deal at all—just sort of silly and maybe a little embarrassing. But, boy, did it backfire.

The girl got horribly upset, started to cry, and ran out of the house. We found out later that she walked all the way home.

Needless to say, the party was ruined. And it's going to be hard on all of us to be around that girl for a while. Hard for her too, I guess.

But what really gets me is that it didn't have to happen. We didn't have to play that joke. Sure, we didn't know ahead of time that the girl was going to take it the way she did, but maybe we should have known. Maybe we should have thought about the kind of person she is—sort of sensitive—and figured out how she'd react to being embarrassed in front of everyone. But we didn't think.

I'm going to have to call her and tell her how sorry I am. I don't know if that will do any good, but it's all I can think of at the moment.

But, please, God, don't let us do anything like that again. Teach us to think before we act.

181

GRASS (THE REAL KIND)

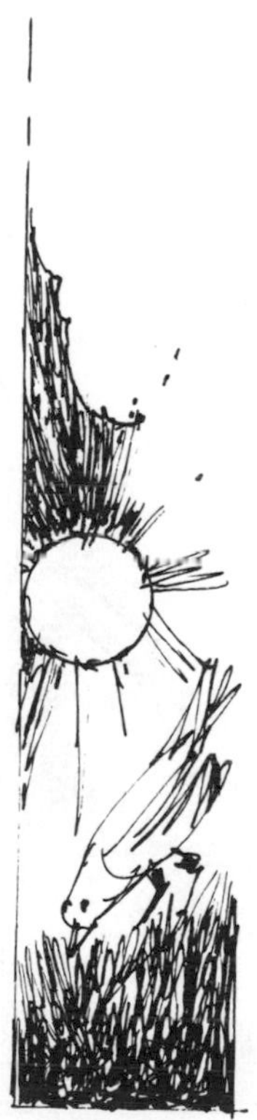

I know some kids who get excited about grass. By grass, they mean marijuana. Personally I don't intend to touch that stuff with a 10-foot pole. But I can get excited about grass too—the green stuff that grows all over our front lawn. I think it's great!

First of all it's great on the eyes. Have you ever been reading for hours and hours till your eyes feel like two fried eggs? Just try looking at some grass for a while. It's the most restful thing imaginable.

Grass is great on the ears too, especially if it's tall grass and the wind is blowing through it. It sounds like a tiny world then, where all sorts of magic is going on. I tried to explain that to my mom once. She said to cut it anyway.

Noses have been known to go stark raving mad over grass, especially right after it's been cut or just after it rains. At times like those I can even understand why cows like to eat the stuff. (I've got to admit I've nibbled a blade or two myself once or twice.)

Best of all, though, is a nice big stretch of grass applied to two bare feet. The coolness! The tickle! The . . . I'm going outside this very minute.

Thank You, God, for grass.

182

CAN I FORGIVE THAT PERSON?

It's been a while now since my friend betrayed me, and I still haven't been able to forgive him. Everytime I think about what he did I get mad, and I hurt all over again. He probably doesn't even know because I haven't seen him or talked to him since it happened. So my not forgiving him isn't hurting him. It's hurting **me**.

What does it mean to forgive someone anyway? I don't think it means that you should pretend what he did never happened. That wouldn't be real. It **did** happen. I don't think it means forgetting what happened either. If it does, I've had it, because I can't forget.

I think forgiveness means that you go on caring about the person in **spite** of what happened. You don't let what happened break your relationship. Then, after a lot of time has passed and your relationship is full of other kinds of things, maybe you **do** forget what happened.

Well, I'm ready to try that anyway. But I guess I'll have to get together with my friend first. And we'll have to talk about what happened. I'm pretty sure I won't say, "I forgive you," in those words. I'd feel horribly self-righteous if I did. So I'll try to show him in other ways that I forgive him.

God, this isn't going to be easy. Please help me.

183

SO **THAT'S** WHAT IT MEANS!

I did it! I called my friend and we got together and talked about what happened. He felt really bad, I could tell. He explained that he was just trying to impress the people that he told my secret to, and he said it was a rotten thing to do.

Well, that was about all I could take.

"Let's just go on being friends like we were before," I said.

"I don't think we can," he said, "because this thing happened. But if we can go on being friends in spite of it, I think we'll probably end up being **better** friends."

And of course he's right.

Now, here's the incredible thing. I came home feeling very, very good about all that had happened, that my friend and I were friends again. I didn't think too much about the fact that I'd **forgiven** him, but I guess that's really what I'd done. And then it hit me.

This is exactly what happens when God forgives me! We both

decide to go on with our relationship in spite of what I've done, and our relationship gets even better.

God, now that I've worked at forgiving someone, I know how hard it is to do. It just takes my breath away to think about how often You do it—and how completely. O God, I do praise You for that!

184

SARCASM IS CHEAP

There's this teacher at school that no one likes very much, and today, for some reason, I started thinking about her. The reason no one likes her is that she's so sarcastic. She'll look at a paper that someone's turned in and say, "Oh, this is just brilliant. A real work of art." But she'll say it in a flat, biting tone that lets you know she doesn't mean a word she's said.

A few kids may giggle a little when she says something like that, but no one really thinks it's funny. It's just a cheap, easy way to make someone else feel bad.

Sarcasm **is** cheap. **Anyone** can be sarcastic with almost no effort at all. All you have to do is say the opposite of what you mean and say it in a tone of voice that let's everyone know it's not what you mean. Whammo! Instant sarcasm.

That teacher could have said, "Well, this isn't a very good paper, but let's take a look at it and see what the problems are and how we can correct them." The person she was talking to might not have felt **great** about her saying that, but at least he or she wouldn't have felt laughed at.

God, sometimes I'm tempted to use sarcasm too. I want a laugh, even if it's a cheap one. Help me resist that temptation.

Independence Day

I'M FREE (I THINK)!

Everyone's talking a lot these days about being free. People want to be free to do their own thing, find out who they are, live their own kind of life-style. I guess I'm caught up in all that too. I don't want to feel boxed in by other people's rules and ideas. I want to work out my own rules and ideas. In fact, one of the things I like about religion is the freedom I get from knowing that God will forgive my mistakes. And yet . . .

And yet I can't help feeling there's something wrong with all this emphasis on freedom. I don't mean that I want to live under a dictator or go back to the Victorian days when there was a rule for everything and heaven help you if you broke one. But I don't think any Christian who really cares about what religion is all about **can** be totally free.

I can't be free of the hungry people. I can't do my own thing, worry about who I am, live my own life-style, and forget those people. Not if I honestly want to follow Jesus and show God's love the way He did. Those people will be with me and so will all the other people who are hurting. They're God's children just as I am, and I can't separate myself from them and their pain.

I guess in a way they're like chains and sometimes those chains will feel heavy. But I don't mind that because I love them. I **love** the chains that keep me from being entirely free, and I'll go on loving them until the hungry people are fed and the hurt ones healed and everybody else can be free with me. It's the only way I can feel and I'm glad.

God, is this what Jesus meant when He said, "My burden is light"?

186

DIVORCE

Well, now it's happened to someone who is close to me—this thing I've read and heard about for years. My friend's folks are getting a divorce. And my friend is tied up in little knots about it.

She says her parents have been having awful fights for years, but she never really thought they'd split up. She says they've been to marriage counselors and psychologists and everything, but none of it helped, and they just don't feel their marriage can work.

My friend says that when they first told her their decision, she immediately felt guilty. She thought that somehow **she'd** caused them to want the divorce. They talked to her a lot, and they had a psychologist talk to her too, and now she knows (at least in her head) that the whole thing **isn't** her fault. They also told her—both her parents and the psychologist—that there's nothing she can do to bring them back together again.

But I think she still secretly hopes that she can. Or that maybe a miracle will happen and they'll come back together on their own accord.

God, please be with my friend during this painful time. Let her know that she's still very much loved by her parents and by You. And be with her parents too. Keep them from being bitter and help them make wise and loving choices.

187

I WAS LEFT OUT

I just found out today. A bunch of kids I know from school had a party last week. And I wasn't invited. Those kids are some of my closest friends. I went to their parties all last year. I invited them to a party I gave. Now all of a sudden I'm left out. Why?

Maybe one of them decided to start a clique and had the party to get the people who would be in it all together. Sometimes cliques do start that way. But I know the girl at whose house the party was held, and I thought she was my friend too. I don't know why she'd want to leave me out of her clique.

Well, I guess there are several ways I can handle this. I can mope around all summer and feel sorry for myself. That sounds like a **lot** of fun. I can get busy and form a clique of my own. But I don't want to do that. I don't like cliques. And I'm not even sure if that's why this party was held in the first place.

No, I don't think I'll do either of those things. Instead I think I'll just go on being friendly to that group of kids—as a group and as individuals. I'll try to be the kind of person it's fun to be around. Maybe I'll even have another party of my own and invite them. Then I'll just wait and see what happens.

Social stuff is really very complicated, God. I'm awfully glad to know that no matter what goes on in the rest of my life, **You'll** never leave me out.

188

AM I NORMAL?

I was reading an article today in one of my mom's magazines. It was about how to raise a normal, healthy kid. And naturally I just had to ask the question: Am I normal?

First of all, I don't think I know what "normal" means. I walk, I talk, I eat, I sleep. I go to school and I do all right. I suppose all of that is normal.

But are my thoughts normal? My feelings? The things I like to do? If normal means that they're exactly the same as what everyone else thinks and feels and likes to do, then I'm not normal. Sometimes I have thoughts that I doubt if anyone has ever had before. (Or if they have, I never heard about it.) Sometimes I have very deep, very personal feelings. Those are mine, all mine. And there are a couple things I like to do that not a single other person I know likes to do.

So, am I a freak? I don't think so. I think that I'm an individual person and that God made me that way. I don't **want** to be normal if normal means being just like everyone else. I'd get bored of myself that way. With everyone else too.

Thanks, God for not making me normal!

189

POTTYMOUTH

That's what they call this guy I know. Pottymouth. He's always saying the most awful, disgusting things. It seems as if he can't even open his mouth without something ugly coming out.

The strange thing is that he thinks it makes him neat. He thinks other kids admire him for knowing all those words and being brave enough to say them. Well, somebody might laugh or be impressed for a minute or two. But after that it's just disgusting.

I wish someone would talk to this guy and tell him that he's turning people off instead of attracting them. I don't think I'm the person to do it, though. I'd have to be someone he really looks up to and admires. Like one of the older guys. Maybe that'll happen this summer. I hope so.

God, don't ever let stuff like that come out of my mouth. Don't even let it be in my head. There are so many good words to say all the things I want to say. Help me be intelligent enough to use them.

190

MY NAME

Have you ever stopped and thought about your name? I did that today and it was neat. First of all I looked it up in one of those books on what to name your baby. I never knew that's what my name meant. Pretty impressive!

Then I said my name over and over, till it didn't sound like a name anymore—just a word. I decided I liked the way it sounded too.

Next I tried to picture myself with a different name. Boy, was that a weird feeling. Obviously I am very used to my name.

I asked mom how she and dad decided on that name for me. It seems they thought a lot about it and came up with a lot of other names first. She told me some of those names. I'm sure glad they went on thinking!

I guess everyone has a special sort of feeling for his or her name. After all, in many ways that name is who we are. It's usually the first thing somene else knows about us.

The best thought I had all day, though, is that God knows my name. He knows it and He knows that it's me. He doesn't confuse me with anyone else, even if that person happens to have the same name. Of all the names in the world, **my** name means something special and important to God. Because **I** mean something special and important to Him. I'm His child.

191

A GREAT TIME FOR HANDS

Summer is a great time for hands. There's so much they can do, so much they can get into. And so today I decreed National Hand Day.

The first thing my hands did was stretch themselves, clear out to the tips.

"Yep, we're alive," they decided. "Let's get on with it."

The next major thing they did was feed my face. This made both my face and my hands very happy—not to mention my stomach.

After breakfast my hands said they wanted to touch things, all different kinds of things with different textures. So I let them touch a cat's fur and the needles on a pine tree. Some dewy grass and a warm, rough rock that had been sitting in the sun. A tender little green leaf and a feather dropped by a bird.

"Ahh," sighed my hands. "That's nice."

"Yes, but now it's time for you two to stop thinking about yourselves," I told them. "It's time you did something for someone else."

"Okay," said my hands. "How's about we pick some flowers? Then you can get that crazy couple downstairs—your feet—to help us deliver them to Mrs. Fitzpatrick at the nursing home."

"Great idea, hands," I said.

All in all, my hands had a busy day. I think they'll sleep well tonight. But they made me promise them one thing in honor of National Hand Day. That I wouldn't bite my fingernails anymore. Well, what could I say?

Thank You, God, for hands.

192

CRUEL

I saw some kids today tormenting a dog. They were gathered all around it so it couldn't get away, and they were talking and laughing about what they were going to do. I don't know what they had in mind because I wasn't quite close enough to hear them. But fortunately they never got a chance to do it, because a man came out of his house and chased them all away. He said he'd call the police if he ever saw them try anything like that again.

The poor little dog took off like a rocket in the opposite direction. It was wearing a collar, so I hope it made it home all right and is now having a good nap.

I cannot understand why people want to hurt animals. In fact, I can't understand why people want to hurt other people. It would be different—not right, but different—if someone had done something bad to them and they wanted to get even. But that certainly isn't the case with animals, and it often isn't the case with other people either. It seems that some people are cruel just because they like being cruel.

That makes me believe that there really is evil in our world. I can't think of any other explanation for cruelty. It's evil.

God, help us in our never-ending battle against that evil. Help me fight it in every way I can. Give me the courage to get involved even when I may get hurt myself. And someday, God, banish evil forever and ever.

193

THE BEAUTIFUL PEOPLE

Usually I see them in movies or ads, these beautiful people. Their bodies are slim and tanned. Their teeth are perfect and so are their clothes. They're always in gorgeous places and look like they're having a wonderful time. And, oh, how I wish sometimes that I were one of them!

You just know that these people wouldn't know a pimple if they met one. Their hair has never frizzed or drooped. Buttons never fall off their clothes. And they never catch a cold. What a life it would be!

In a way I feel about those people the way I used to feel about magic princes and princesses in fairy tales. Maybe there's a good reason for that too. Maybe these beautiful people aren't real either. Maybe they're fairy tales for grown-ups.

I think a lot of grown-ups think they're real though. I think these grown-ups even spend much of their lives working to get the material things that they think will make them beautiful people. Well, I don't want to do that. I don't want to get lost in a grown-up fairy tale. There are some material things I'd like to have when I grow up, but I don't believe those things will make me a different person.

God, help me hold on to what's really real and what's really beautiful as I grow up. And don't let me settle for anything less!

194

AM I SELFISH?

I guess I really do spend a lot of time thinking about myself. I want to understand who I am and what I can do and how I can improve myself. Does that mean I'm selfish?

Maybe I should be spending all my time thinking about other people and what they want and need. Maybe I should try to forget me entirely. Is that what God wants me to do? I don't know.

I finally talked to dad about all this. He said—can you believe it? that he doesn't think I'm selfish at all! He said there are times when I **should** think about myself, should try to understand and improve myself. He said there are even times when I should make a special effort to be nice to myself.

"But how can you say that?" I asked. "It doesn't sound very Christian to me."

"It **is** Christian," said my dad. "Because if you want to give yourself to other people, you have to make sure you have something to give. Jesus knew that. Why do you think He went away to be by Himself every so often?"

Well, no one could ever accuse Jesus of being selfish. And if He had to spend some time on Himself, I guess it's okay for me to do that too.

195

THEY BEAT HER

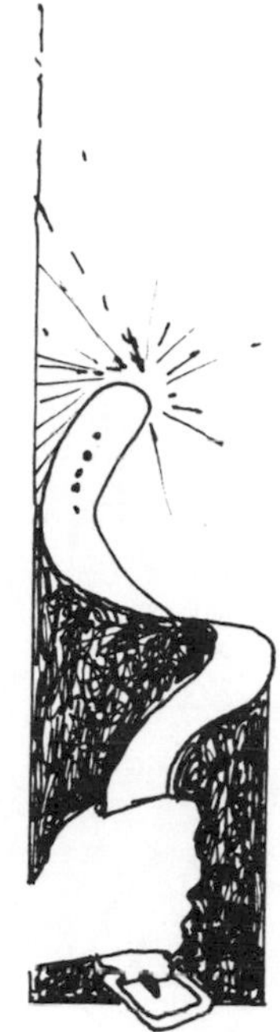

I found out an awful thing today. A girl in my class at school is what they call an abused child. Last night some neighbors heard her screaming and called the police. When the police got there she was still screaming. Finally the police got in and took her to a hospital for treatment. From there she'll go to the Salvation Army home.

I just can't believe it! I know this girl. She's very quiet and I can't imagine why anyone would want to beat her. But apparently her parents have been doing it for a long time. They even broke her arm once. I remember when her arm was broken. She said she fell down some steps.

O God, what kind of world is this when things like that can happen to a kid? It's a sick world—that's what it is. It's so sick that I can't even bear to think about it. God, please, **do** something!

And, God, be with that girl—and all the other abused children. Let them know that they have at least one Parent who will never hurt them.

196

FAMILY STORIES

My aunt and uncle came over for dinner this evening, and afterwards we all sat outside and told stories—family stories.

Like the time Great Uncle Henry swam clear across a river with his good clothes tied on top of his head. He wanted to go see his girlfriend, and the bridge was out. His girlfriend, incidentally, ended up being Great Aunt Florence.

Or the time my aunt couldn't find my cousin Freddy, who was four. She finally found him, right in the middle of one of the busiest streets in town. He was directing traffic.

"I want to be a traffic cop," he explained when she finally got him home.

I love stories like that. They tell me something about the kind of people we are in my family. They tell me something about the kind of person I am.

How about the Bible, God? Isn't it sort of a collection of family stories too? Stories about people in Your family? Don't those stories tell me something about the kind of people we are, the kind of person I am? One thing those family stories tell me for sure. We're people who are loved very much. By You!

197

I TRIED TO READ THE BIBLE

I think a lot about the Bible. I listen to it in church. I've read a lot of Bible stories. But today I decided that it was time for me to start reading the whole Bible, all the way through, from beginning to end.

Well, I got off to a good start. I read all of Genesis and all of Exodus. That's a lot of reading too. There are many, many chapters in those two books.

Then I got to Leviticus. Oh, boy! Page after page after page of rules. Some of them didn't make any sense to me at all. I guess they were rules that the Jews followed in worship and things. I gave up.

Actually I switched to the New Testament. I thought I'd read the epistles. There aren't too many stories in them, so I don't know them as well. I started with the first one, Romans. Talk about rough going! I didn't understand half of what Paul was talking about in the first chapter alone.

Well, tomorrow I'm going to try again. But this time I'm going to start someplace else. I'm going to start with the Gospel of Matthew. I'm pretty sure I can handle that. And maybe Sunday I'll talk to my pastor and ask him to make a list of the other books he thinks I can read on my own.

I **am** going to read Your book, God. But it may take me a while.

198

LET ME FLY!

Today I went out into the backyard, lay on my back in the grass, and watched the birds flying overhead. What must it be like, I wondered, to jump off into space anytime you want and soar and swoop and glide. What must it be like not to have to walk around obstacles or climb over them, but simply to fly over them as if they weren't even there.

For a while I watched one particular bird; I followed every curve and dip of her flight with my eyes and my breath. And then, for just a moment, it seemed as if I was flying with her, stretching to go higher and higher and then plunging back down with my heart in my mouth. For that moment the paths and highways of the air were mine too, and, oh, it was glorious!

The closest thing I can compare it to is being totally involved in some creative project. In writing, when the words start coming faster than you can put them down, and you completely forget where you are and what's happening around you. Or in playing a piece of music, when suddenly the music takes over, and you're only an instrument through which something much bigger than you is happening.

I know that most of my life will be spent on the ground, God. But sometimes, when I get too tied to things here or too tired by them, then, God, just for a moment let me fly!

199

THEY'RE TRAVELING

So many people I know are taking vacations right now—going to the lake or the seashore, visiting relatives out of town. One guy is even going to Europe with his parents. I wish I could go on all their vacations with them. I love being in different places and seeing new things. Just getting in the car to go to the other side of town excites me because I never know what new thing I'll find.

My mom says that I'll probably be a roving reporter when I grow up. Just me, my passport, and my pencil off to see the world, telling the folks back home about it. Sounds great!

In the meantime, though, there are all these people I know out traveling somewhere. And I have to admit that I worry about them a little. Our highways certainly aren't the safest places in the world. Even a good driver can be in an accident caused by someone else.

God, be with all the people who are traveling. Guide them safely to their journey's end. And then, God, be with them and care for them there.

200

AREN'T MANNERS PHONY?

I went to a very nice restaurant today with the family of a friend of mine. The room we ate in was beautiful and the food was super. And you'd better believe everyone took out and polished off his or her best manners.

Napkin carefully in lap. Bread broken and buttered just so. Not that fork. This one. Start from the outside. Please may I have the salt. Of course I can reach it perfectly well myself with just the tiniest bit of stretching, but that would be so utterly improper, my dear.

All of a sudden it came over me what a complete bunch of phonies we were being. In fact, most manners make me feel phony. Suppose I meet a new person. Ever so politely I must shake hands, with just the right amount of firmness, and say, "I'm so glad to know you," or some such thing. How do I know I'm glad to know that person? I've just met him. I might think he's a real creep after I've been around him a little longer. I might be thoroughly sorry that I know him.

So let's banish manners from the world, okay? Let's all just say and do exactly what we want. Down with phoniness!

I want the salt. I'm going to grab it. Whoops! Was that your milk I knocked over with my elbow? Well, order another glass. You can afford it. And so what if it spilled all over your lap? That dress looks hideous on you anyway. What do you mean you're going to punch me in the mouth? I was just being natural. You wouldn't want me to be phony, would you?

You would? You'd rather I minded my manners because they tend to make me behave a little more nicely—a little more kindly—toward others? Oh.

Could it be, God, that manners are not all bad? That they might even be one of the tools You use to make this world a better, more livable place?

201

PEOPLE ON THE WAY TO WORK

This morning I woke up early. Usually when I do that I lie in bed for a good long time and tell myself all sorts of reasons why I shouldn't get up yet. But today I got up, went out on the front steps, and watched people on their way to work. What a show!

First of all there are the people who are not really awake yet. The man next door is one of those. Fortunately he doesn't drive. Instead he kind of leans against his door waiting for his car pool to get there. When they do he staggers down the walk, clutching a half-drunk cup of coffee as if it were his dearest friend. Poor guy.

Then there are the people who obviously wish they were going to Tahiti or the Canary Islands or anywhere except to their job. They sit in their cars glumly staring straight ahead, no doubt picturing the executioner who is waiting for them with axe sharpened. Sometimes there's a whole carful of people like that, and you can't help but wonder why the car itself doesn't sink into the earth from the weight of all that gloom.

And finally there are the eager beavers. I don't know if they like their jobs all that much, but they sure seem excited about getting on with them. Even their cars look perkier than the others, and if they're riding in a car pool, they're usually jabbering a mile a minute to the people with them.

Well, God, about now they're all at work—the sleepies and the gloomies and the eager beavers. Be with all of them, please. Make it a good day for them and bless the work they do so that it will become Your work and make the world a little better.

202

WALLOWING IN SELF-PITY

It's been one of those days. Everything has gone wrong. And on days when everything goes wrong, I start remembering all the things that have gone wrong in the past. Pretty soon a whole bundle of wrong things is sitting on my back, and there I am, the helpless victim. I tried so hard—yes, I did—but the whole world was against me, and now here I am, weary and broken.

Kind of makes you want to cry, doesn't it? Well, it kind of makes me want to throw up. I just hate myself when I get on one of these self-pity jags. But I certainly do a good job of it. My best line is, "Why shouldn't I pity myself? No one else does."

Fortunately about then I begin to see how ridiculous I'm really being. Sometimes I can even start laughing at myself. Not always though. Sometimes I have to climb up out of that self-pity like an explorer who's fallen into a swamp. It's just about that sticky and messy too.

It doesn't help to think about how much worse things could be. It doesn't help to think about all the people who are worse off than I am. What helps is to **do** something—**anything**—even if I don't in the least want to do it.

Today I baked chocolate chip cookies. As soon as they were done and cooling on the racks I felt about one inch better. Then I poured myself a glass of milk and ate half of them. After that I felt a good three inches better. And so on.

God, don't let me fall in that swamp too often. I just don't like the way it feels.

203

I **HATED** HIM!

I went to the pool today with some friends, and while we were there I saw a guy I know from school. This guy's father was with him, and he was the most horrible person I've ever met. He was sitting next to another man, and all he could talk about (in the loudest voice you ever heard) was how awful kids are these days. He talked about our hair, the clothes we wear, the way we talk. He picked out specific kids at the pool (kids he didn't even know) and made fun of them.

Then he started in on his own son. "That's not the way to dive, you dumb kid. Can't you do anything right? At your age, I . . . " Of course this superathlete took great care not even to get his little toe wet!

I could feel the rage boiling inside of me. That is, at first it was rage. I was furious about the things he was saying. But then rage changed to hate. Hate for him as a person.

I don't think I've ever felt anything like that before. It was as if everything inside me was red-hot and churning. I couldn't see very well for a few seconds, and I felt like I might throw up. Then it passed, and I switched to feeling sorry for the poor kid who has to have that guy for a father.

If that's how hate feels, God, I can see why You don't want us to feel it. It's not so much what it does to the person you hate as what it

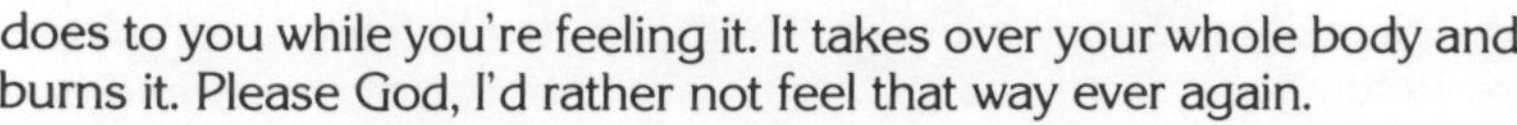

does to you while you're feeling it. It takes over your whole body and burns it. Please God, I'd rather not feel that way ever again.

204

I'M ALONE—AND SCARED

My parents had to go out this evening and I'm alone in the house. It isn't the first time they've left me. I really am old enough to stay in the house by myself. After all, I even baby-sit for other kids. But there's something different about being alone with some little kids and being alone **alone** (if you know what I mean). And there's something different about tonight. I'm scared.

I keep hearing bumps and creaks. Rustles too. And I imagine the strangest things. A face at the window. A rat watching me from the corner. (That last one would really get to my folks. We **don't** have rats.) I keep thinking about that old Scottish prayer: "From ghoulies and ghosties and long-legged beasties and things that go bump in the night, good Lord, deliver us." Long-legged beasties. Brrrrrr!

I think I'm getting my sense of humor back. After all, it is my own mind that's doing this to me. The house is no different than it is when mom and dad are here. Maybe my mind would feel better if I put a little chocolate ice cream in my stomach. I think I'll try that.

God, please be with me tonight. I'm still just a little bit scared!

205

MY FRIEND IS IN SERIOUS TROUBLE

She called me today and told me about it, this friend of mine who's in serious trouble. She doesn't know what she's going to do. She's afraid to tell her parents, but she's going to have to. They'll find out sooner or later anyway.

In a way it's her own fault that she ended up in this mess. But I can see how it happened. It could have happened to me too if I'd been in the same situation and not thinking straight. I think that makes the whole thing twice as scary. It could have happened to me.

I didn't know what to say to my friend except to encourage her to tell her folks. Sure, they'll be mad at first. Hurt too. But they're good people, and they really care about her. They'll help her figure out what to do next.

How many other kids are there who are in serious trouble and don't even have parents they can turn to? Who helps them figure out what to do next? Do You, God? Even if they don't know enough to ask You for help? Because I know some of them don't.

Well, God, I'm asking You for them. Please help all the kids who are in trouble. Show them Your love, and maybe that way they'll learn to know You. But especially, God, help my friend.

206

I COULDN'T DO A **THING!**

I keep thinking about my friend who's in trouble and wondering what's happening to her today. I guess what bothers me most is that there isn't anything I can do to help her. If only I were older or smarter, maybe I could think of a way out of her problem. But my mind just spins in the same useless circles that hers does. That's one of the worst parts of being young. You're old enough to have big problems but not old enough to know any big answers.

She just called. My friend. She was crying, but she said she wanted me to know that everything was going to be all right. She talked to her parents, and they were just great. They already have a couple of ideas about what she can do, stuff she'd never thought of.

And she thanked me.

"For what?" I asked. "I didn't do anything. I couldn't even think of anything **to** do."

"You listened to me," she said. "That was one thing. You encouraged me to talk to my parents. That was two things. And, knowing you, you probably prayed too."

Yes, I listened. I told her to talk to her folks. And, knowing me, I prayed. So I did do something. Three things. But, knowing You, God, You did the rest. You're the One who helped her actually talk to her folks and helped them listen with love. You helped them think up some answers too. Thanks, God.

207

WHY AM I ME?

Of course I know the answer to that question—all the stuff about genes and chromosomes that we learned in science. But a scientific answer doesn't stop me from wondering why I'm so lucky.

I could be a kid in some terribly poor country, waiting in line for a bowl of rice. I could be a kid in a country where war was going on all around me, and I would have to be afraid of snipers in my backyard or planes dropping bombs on my school. I could be a kid in another period of history—when dinosaurs were stalking around or thousands of people were dying of bubonic plague. Even later in history I could be one of those kids who had to work in factories 14 hours a day and most likely got crushed by machinery.

Why should I be so lucky as to be me? What have I done to deserve this life?

The answer to that is quite obvious. Nothing. For some reason of Your own, God, You've chosen to let me live in this time and this place. I don't understand that reason, God, but I'm very grateful to You. And I guess there is something I can do in return. I can remember that You care just as much about all those kids who aren't as lucky as I am. I can remember that You want me to care about them and help them too. Isn't that the best way I can use this wonderful life You've given me? Give it to others? Thanks, God, for the opportunity.

208

THE ROCK GOD COULDN'T LIFT

My friend the atheist called me today, about to burst with excitement. She'd just heard this puzzle, and she was sure it would knock me off my feet and destroy my faith in God forever.

"God is all-powerful, right?" she said.

"Right," I said.

"Well, if He's all-powerful, can He create a rock so heavy that He can't lift it? Huh? Huh?"

"Well . . . " I began.

"See, if He can't create it, then He isn't all-powerful, and if He can't lift it, then He isn't all-powerful. There's no way He can win!"

I don't know how I managed to come up with the answer I did. All those math courses and systems and stuff, I guess.

"Yes, He could win," I said. "First He'd create it, and then He'd lift it."

"But that's not fair," said my atheist friend. "It isn't logical."

"Nope," I said. "But whoever said that God had to be logical. He's God. He can be anyway He wants."

Well, my friend mumbled for a while, but she couldn't really argue with that. I mean, how can you argue with an un-argument.

How'd I do, God?

209

SLEEP

Sleep is a very strange thing to think about. First of all there's the word itself. Sleep. Say it over and over again. Sleep. Sleep. Sleep. After a while you want to giggle. It's a weird word.

Then there's sleep itself. Sometimes I want it so badly that I don't think anything could get in my way. I could probably fall asleep in a burrow full of porcupines if I were tired enough. Or drifting down in a parachute. Or just three feet away from a buried treasure worth a billion dollars.

Other times, though, I can lie awake for hours (well, maybe minutes) worrying about sleep. I mean, you close your eyes and all of a sudden you're out of control. Not only don't you know what's going on around you, but you can't even control what's going on in your mind. You could dream about almost anything, including some rather awful things.

"I may never go to sleep again," I say to myself after I've been having thoughts like that. Then the next thing I know I wake up and it's morning.

And that's probably the best part of sleep—how you feel when you've had some. Your head works, your body works, nothing hurts, and you're ready to go. I could almost see taking several naps a day just so you could have that waking-up feeling several times.

Thanks, God, for sleep. It's a marvelous invention!

210

CHOICES

It seems to me that we're always having to make choices. What to wear. What to buy for lunch. Which friend to call. Which book to read. Choices like that, though, I don't mind making. It's great to have enough clothes, enough food, enough friends, enough books to have to choose. And if I pick friend A this time, I can always pick friend B next time. Such richness!

Then there are other choices, the ones that can make a real difference in your future. What courses to take in school. What lessons to take outside of school. How much time to spend on schoolwork and how much on extracurricular stuff. That sort of choice I don't like as much. I'm always a little afraid that I might choose the wrong thing. And with choices like these you don't always get a second chance.

I guess the choices we have to make get harder and harder as we grow older. One of these days I'm going to have to decide on a college, a career, the person I want to marry. With those choices I **don't** want to make any mistakes.

Thank You, God, for fixing it so that I have choices to make. Please help me make good ones.

211

WHAT'S SELF-RESPECT?

A while back I wrote about how I respect my parents—and how they respect me. But I've heard a lot of people say that it's important to have self-respect too, and I'm not sure exactly what that means. The respect I have for my parents is all tied up with loving them, admiring them, trusting them, asking their advice—stuff like that. How can I feel those things for myself?

Well, what about loving myself? Jesus said we should love our neighbors as ourselves. I guess I can't do that unless I love myself. And I suppose I do in a way. I sure like being me. And I definitely care what happens to me.

Do I admire myself? Not if that means standing around gazing into a mirror all the time. But if it means I think my ideas are pretty good, and I like the way I act most of the time, then, yes, I guess I do. If I didn't admire my thoughts and actions, I'd try to change them. Sometimes I do.

Do I trust myself? Yes, I think I do. If I were in a tough situation, I think I'd try to do the right thing. And I think I'd have a good chance of succeeding because I'd ask God to help me.

Maybe that's the key to the whole question of self-respect for me. I **do** respect myself, but the reason I do is because God is so involved in my life. He's the one that helps me be respect-able. And I'd be pretty silly if I didn't appreciate what He does for me.

212

I REALLY PITY THAT KID

Today a friend and I were talking about a kid we know at school, a kid who has a lot of problems.

"I really pity that kid," said my friend.

"Yeah, so do I," I said.

Then for just an instant I wasn't hearing the words we were saying. I was hearing the tone of our voices. And that tone, a lofty, superior sort of tone, made me feel that pity is a very ugly thing.

When I pity somebody, I'm somehow saying that they're different from me. Their problems have put them in a different place from me, and all I can do is look at them from a distance and feel sorry for them.

I don't think Jesus ever felt that kind of pity. He wouldn't let the people with problems be separated from Him. He got there right in the middle of them, felt their pain, and tried to help them. If Jesus were talking about that kid at school . . . well, He wouldn't even **be** talking about him. He'd be talking with him.

Maybe pity is a word I should cut out of my vocabulary and a feeling I should cut out of me. Maybe sympathy is a better word and a better feeling. I'll have to think about this some more.

213

SEX

It seems as if the only thing many of my friends are interested in anymore is sex. That's all we ever seem to talk about when there aren't any grown-ups around. What is it like? How does it work? Is everything about me all right? Well, I guess I've got to admit that I'm sort of interested in it too.

After all, a lot of changes are going on inside our bodies right now. Most of them have something to do with sex. Everywhere we look we see ads or movies or songs or **something** about sex. How to be sexier. How sex messed up my life. Wow, sex is grand. You really can't get away from it. So I guess it's normal for us to be curious.

The strange thing is that most of us already know the facts about sex. Where babies come from and all that. But it's not the facts that concern us. It's how we fit into the picture. Or to be more accurate, whether we will fit in or not. Sex is such an important thing in our world that it's scary to think that we might mess it up.

And yet sex is just one more part of Your creation, isn't it, God? It's an important part since it's the way we all get here, but it's still part, and You're still in charge. Walking was an important part of my life years and years ago when I was a baby. But I didn't have the sense back then to worry about whether I'd be able to do it. When the time was right I just did it. And You helped. Won't sex be the same way? Won't You help me fit into that world the same way You helped me join the walking world? Of course You will. So I think I'll go on wondering about sex, but I'll try not to worry about it.

214

VACATION

We aren't going away for a vacation this year, which is sort of disappointing. I love being in another place where it's my **job** to relax and have a good time. I love what vacations do to my parents too. Mom and dad act about 10 years younger when they're on vacation.

I also like the way you feel when you come back from a vacation. You've been away from the normal part of your life just long enough to make everything look a little different. Somehow you can see things more clearly—like what you could do to fix up your room or why you haven't been getting along with so-and-so or what a neat person Joe X really is. Of course that clear way of seeing things only lasts a day or so, but I like it while it lasts.

This year, though, we're not going anywhere, and really I'm not too terribly disappointed. I can usually manage to have a pretty good vacation right here at home. Just being at home instead of at school is vacationish for me. It's mom and dad I'm worried about. Their life doesn't change much unless we go away.

Maybe I can do something about that. Maybe I could volunteer to make supper for two whole weeks. (After two weeks they'll be ready for a vacation from my cooking, but that's okay.) Maybe I could encourage them to go away on little trips to places around here—with or without me. There are places just a few miles from my house where tourists go, and I've never been to them.

Help us have a good vacation this year, God, even if it just means relaxing and enjoying one another a little more.

215

WHAT DO I WANT TO BE?

Grown-ups are always asking kids my age that question: "What do you want to be when you grow up?" I used to let it bother me. I used to think that I had to give them a definite answer and then try to stick to it for the rest of my life.

But that's silly. Because the fact is I have no idea what I want to be. Well, actually I have lots of ideas, but they change almost every day.

Sometimes I want to be a doctor. Sometimes a minister. Sometimes a cartoonist. Sometimes a forest ranger. And I don't think there's anyway I'm going to combine all those things into one career. I guess there are people who know what they want to be from the time they're six years old, but I'm not one of them.

And I think that's okay too. There's no reason I have to decide now. I don't even have all the facts yet.

The important thing for me is that whatever I am when I grow up, whatever I do, I want it to be something that will let me feel that I'm doing God's work along with just making money. I want to feel that He can use what I'm doing to make the world better and to show it His love. I don't usually tell people that, but it's the one thing I'm sure of. When I grow up I want to be God's servant, just as I am now.

216

I'M IN TROUBLE

Well, I really blew it this time. I did something that's definitely wrong, and now I'm in trouble The worst part is that I knew it was wrong while I was doing it, and yet I did it anyway. It wasn't an honest mistake. It was out-and-out **wrong**.

I feel awful. Here I sit around writing all these high-minded, religious thoughts, and the minute a little temptation comes my way, I give in to it.

My parents are being pretty decent about the whole thing. They know that I know I've done wrong, and they know I feel bad about it. I'm not sure if they're going to punish me or not. They don't really have to. I won't do that thing again. But if they do, it'll be okay too. I do deserve it.

God, what can I say to You? Are You disappointed in me? Or is it just what You expected from this rotten human being? No, that last question wasn't fair. You don't think of me as a rotten human being. You think of me as Your child. So I guess I did disappoint You.

I'm sorry, God, and I won't do it again. That's all I can think of to say. Please, God, forgive me and help me get rid of this awful, nasty feeling I have about myself right now.

217

ASHAMED

That awful, nasty feeling I had about myself yesterday—I think it's shame. I don't feel it anymore now, at least not about myself, although

I do feel it about the thing I did. God's forgiven me. I know that. My parents have forgiven me too. And both my parents and God want me to forgive myself, so I will. But I want to write a little more about that terrible feeling called shame while it's still fresh in my mind.

It's a hot feeling that you can almost see crawling all over you, but especially all over your face. It makes you want to look down instead of straight ahead. It throws your thoughts into a jumble because you don't really want to think clearly about the thing you've done. It makes you want to avoid people because you're sure they can tell just by looking at you how rotten you've been.

Shame is a terrible feeling to have. Even if I didn't believe in God, I think it would stop me from doing wrong things just because I don't want to feel it. But I **do** believe in God and I'm awfully glad I do because He's the way to get rid of shame. His forgiveness takes it away, along with the guilt and all the other bad feelings that go with doing something wrong.

Well, God's forgiven children don't dwell on the past. They **act** forgiven and move on to the fresh start He's given them. So that's just what I'm going to do now.

218

MUSIC

Today I put on the recording of Beethoven's Seventh Symphony and lay on my stomach on the floor and listened to the whole thing. What an incredible experience! I don't know why I don't do that more often.

Somehow music—great music like Beethoven's—seems to express all the feelings people ever feel. And it does that without using words or pictures or stories. It's like the feelings expressed in music are the pure **essence** of feelings, very strong and very pure.

I felt grandeur in Beethoven's symphony, the grandeur you might feel if you'd climbed a mountain or discovered a new continent. I felt sadness too, a sadness too deep for tears. And I felt joy, the kind of joy that makes me feel very close to God.

When the symphony was over I felt empty, but in a clean, almost holy sort of way. And at the same time I felt charged with energy, as if now it was my turn to do something grand. I don't think I could bear to listen—really listen—to two symphonies like that in a row. I couldn't handle **that** much feeling.

Thank You, God, for giving some of Your children this great gift of being able to express such monumental feelings for the rest of us. Surely they are doing Your work when they make us feel so much closer to You.

219

WATER

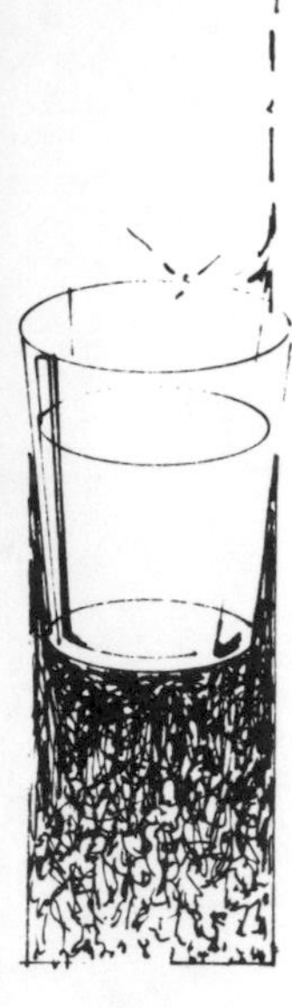

Water is a strange thing to think about. I can sit here looking at a glass of it and it has no color, no shape of its own, no smell, no taste. The minute I put some in my mouth, though, I feel better.

Of course water does have color when it's in the sea. It has the color of the sky darkened and reflected through fathoms and fathoms. It has shape when it's in a waterfall, the shape of the rocks over which it rushes, a tall, mighty, ever-changing shape.

Water has smell too when it falls as rain, the cool, damp, fresh smell of wet earth and grass. And it has taste when you drink it from a tiny spring, newly discovered in deep woods.

Someplace I read that our bodies are something like 98 percent water. If that's true, a powdered form of me sure wouldn't take up much room. I think I prefer me the way I am, however, complete with water added.

Without water we would die. But even if we could figure out some way to do without it, I don't think I'd like the world very much. Colorless, shapeless, smell-less, tasteless thing that it is (or can be), I love it.

Thank You, God, for water.

220

HABITS

Today my mom pointed out a habit that I didn't even know I had. When I'm thinking hard about something, I pull on my earlobe. Mom said she used to worry that by the time I was 12 my whole head would look lopsided (apparently I always pull on the same earlobe), but since it hasn't happened yet, she's given up worrying about it.

Here I've been pulling on my own earlobe for years and years and years and didn't know a thing about it. Good grief, how many other habits do I have that are secrets from me? I asked mom, but she couldn't think of any others at the moment.

Of course I always get out of bed on the same side, and I always put on my right shoe first. I guess those are habits too. But they're just convenient habits. I'd hate to have to lie in bed every morning **thinking** about which side of the bed to get out of. I'd rather just do it and get on with my day.

I suspect there are other sorts of habits too, though, that don't have anything to do with convenience. For example, when I pass someone on the street, do I smile out of habit? Or do I frown? Or look down? I've never noticed. When I try something new—a new food or a new game or even a new person—do I have a habit of looking for all the good things I can find out about it? Or do I look for the bad things?

Habits like that could make a lot of difference in how I behave toward others and how I feel about the world. God, please help me get rid of any negative habits I may have and build some positive ones.

221

THINGS I CAN'T SEE

One of the questions my atheist friend likes to ask me is, "How can you believe in God when you can't even see Him?" I'm finally getting around to thinking about that question so that the next time she asks it I can come back with a snappy answer. I guess my snappy answer would go something like this:

There are a lot of things I can't see, and yet I still believe in them. There are countries on the other side of the world that I've never visited, never even seen pictures of. But I believe they exist. There are people whose faces I've never seen, whose names I've never heard. And yet I believe in them.

"But **somebody's** seen them," my friend would say. "So they don't count."

Well, nobody's ever seen the wind. And yet we all believe in it. We believe in it because we see what it does. It lifts things up, blows them around, cools them. Aha! I can't see God, but I can see what **He** does too.

I can't see vitamins or minerals or all the other chemical parts of my food that keep my body going. But I believe in them. I'd be in pretty bad shape if I didn't. Aha, again! I can't see God, but He nourishes me, keeps me going. I'd be in pretty bad shape without Him.

I can't see love, but I believe in it. I can feel it between me and other people. I can't even describe that feeling very well, but I know it's real all the same. One more aha! I can't see God, but I can feel His love, for me, and in me. That, too, is a hard feeling to describe, but it's as real as a rock—and will last longer.

Maybe you won't listen to my snappy answer, friend, or maybe you won't think it's so snappy. Maybe you'll just go on trusting your own eyes and nothing else. But I wish you wouldn't. You're missing so much!

222

I WISH I WERE WISE

Sometimes I feel so dumb. Not about facts either. Of course there are a lot of facts I don't know, but I'm learning those as fast as I can every day. It's putting the facts together and understanding something that's bigger than all of them that I want to be able to do. I think that's called wisdom. And I don't think I have very much of it.

My grandmother has wisdom. She can watch a person's

behavior for a while, notice all kinds of details, and then say something like, "That is a very insecure person. She needs to know that someone loves her."

After my grandmother's said something like that, I can see it plain as can be. But I can't come up with conclusions like that on my own.

My grandmother laughs when I complain about how dumb I am. She says I'm not dumb, just young. She says it takes some experience to be able to come to the sorts of conclusions she does—experiences with life and with people. She says that she's wrong sometimes too.

"Have patience," she tells me. "Keep your eyes open and your mind open too."

I guess that's a very wise thing she's telling me.

God, help me grow up to know more than facts. Give me wisdom too. I think it will help me a lot as I try to do Your work.

223

DON'T PUSH ME!

Yesterday I was all eager to grow up and be wise. Today I just want to be a kid, to mess around and to let other people handle the important stuff. I'm not ready to ask big questions, come up with big answers, cure the problems of the world. I **am** still a kid, so don't push me!

I think adults do push kids a lot more these days than they used to. Kids today are supposed to spend a lot of time and energy worrying about ecology and social problems and what college they'll get into. Sometimes I do that too. Most of the time. I try to be a very serious and responsible person.

But not today. Today I want to be a kid and drink a Coke and think about dogs and horses and look at comic books. I'm not ready to be completely grown up, and it's not fair to expect me to be.

What do You think, God? Is it okay for me to take a vacation and just be a kid sometimes?

224

I FEEL GOOD ABOUT THAT JOB

Today, for some totally unexplainable reason, I told mom that I felt like cleaning up the basement. After she felt my forehead and looked at my tongue, she said, "Well, all right, if you really want to," as if I might be losing my mind. I don't blame her. I thought I might be too. But I just wanted to **do** something.

Well, I cleaned that basement all right. I cleaned it to within an inch of its life. I sorted stuff that hadn't been touched for years, put it in boxes and labeled them, swept, scrubbed, and polished. I even cleaned up all the bug corpses and washed off the furnace. By the time I'd finished that basement was spotless. And I looked like a chimney sweep. Mom made me go out in the yard and hose myself off before she'd even let me take a shower.

But the amazing thing about this whole experience is how good I felt. I wanted to bring in the neighbors from miles around and show them that basement. It was the cleanest basement I'd ever seen. It was the best job I'd ever done. And I felt great!

God, I think people would be a lot happier if they could all feel that way about the jobs they do. I know I'd be happier. The key seems to be throwing yourself into what you're doing while you're doing it. Help me do that more often, God.

225

LOVE

Everybody's always talking about it, singing about it, dreaming about it. Love, love, love. Sometimes I can't stand the sound of the word.

I'm not talking about God's kind of love now. I'm talking about the mushy stuff between boys and girls, men and women. Moony, Juney, gooney old love. "Oh, darling, be mine!" "Forever, my sweet!" "Kiss me!" BLAH!

Of course, to be perfectly honest, I've never been in love. No one's ever made my insides feel all squishy or my heart all twittery. But I don't ever intend to fall in love that way either. I'm going to be sensible about the whole thing.

I'm going to fall in love with someone I like and admire, someone who shares common interests with me, someone who's fun to be with. This thing between us—love—will be very strong and powerful. It will keep us together, and it will help us both do more good in the world. But it's never going to be soppy or cuddly-cosy or sugar-sweetie. No way!

God, why do I get the feeling You're laughing at me? Why?

226

DIRTY JOKES

I went to the pool again today, and the big topic of conversation was dirty jokes. Several kids knew a bunch of them and told them to the rest of us. I think I got most of them, but frankly I didn't think they were very funny. Not because they were dirty, just because they were dumb. I got the feeling I was **supposed** to think these jokes were funny because they **were** dirty and not because anything really funny happened in them.

Well, I did laugh a polite little laugh once or twice, but the next time someone starts telling dirty jokes I think I'll just drift away. Sex is pretty important to me right now, and I don't like the idea of putting it down like that. In a way it reminds me of spitting on something beautiful that God has made. Maybe I'll change my mind when I get a little older, but I don't think so.

God, You did a wonderful job with sex. Forgive us for trying to make it dirty.

227

BUGS

There are times when I can't stand bugs. Not too long ago we got a flying red roach in our kitchen. Well, I blasted that little creep right out of existence in nothing flat.

On the other hand, I can't stand to step on a bug when I'm outside. (Yes, I know the proper word is "insects," but I happen to like the sound of "bugs." It sounds more like bugs.) Then it seems as if I'm destroying a life. I accidentally smashed a caterpillar once and I felt guilty all day.

Bugs really are remarkable when you stop to think about it. Such tiny little creatures, but perfect in their way. Those itty-bitty legs that work. Those eyes and feelers so small sometimes you can hardly see them.

And when you get to ants and bees and other bugs that live in communities, it just blows my mind. I understand that everything they do is instinctual, sort of programmed into them, but it sure doesn't look that way while I'm watching them. And even if it **is** instinct, what an incredible programming job God has done to make every part work just right.

God, I praise You for bugs!

228

COMFORT ME, PLEASE

Today I'm feeling down and not even for any particular reason. Nothing bad has happened to me or anyone I know. I just feel sad, deep down to the center of myself.

My grandmother calls this "world sadness" (there's a German word for it too, but I can never remember that). She says that sometimes it's just in the air and gets to her too.

When I feel like this, I want somebody else to be strong. I want to be very quiet myself and have someone put an arm around me and tell me that everything will be all right. I want to be able to cry and have someone else hand me the tissue. My folks are pretty good about that too. Maybe they've had days like this themselves.

God, I don't know why I should be sad when I know all that You've done for me. But I am and so I'm asking You to do one more thing. Comfort me, God, please.

229

THE MENTALLY ILL

My mom says that there used to be a time when no one would talk about mental illness. If someone had to go to a psychiatrist or be a patient in a mental hospital for a while, they felt terribly ashamed and wouldn't mention it to anyone outside the family. Mom says she thinks some people still feel that way. But I don't, and neither do most of my friends.

Oh, we make jokes about seeing a shrink and stuff like that, but I think that secretly we're all sort of glad to know that if things really got to us, there are people who can help.

I guess people used to feel that mental illness was something you should be able to control. If you had to go to a psychiatrist, you were admitting that your own willpower or self-discipline or even faith in God wasn't strong enough. You were admitting failure. But these same people didn't seem to feel that way about other illnesses. If they needed an operation, they probably told everyone they knew and hoped they'd get a lot of cards and presents.

Dad says that the treatment of mental illness is progressing in geometric proportions (that means very fast). I'm awfully glad it is because I do think it would be terrible to be mentally ill. I know I'd be terrified. But at least I wouldn't be ashamed and neither would my parents.

God, please be with the mentally ill. Let them know that You love them. Give them the courage and strength to work through their problems. Be with the people who treat them and care for them too. Make them understanding, and help them find more and more cures.

230

GOALS

I read someplace that your goals should exceed your reach. That means that you should want to be able to do more than you actually can do. That way you'll do as much as you possibly can and still go on trying. I guess it's good advice, but I don't want to follow it all the time.

I think I have goals of many different sizes. Some of my little goals are things like finishing the book I'm reading, making a good salad for dinner, washing the car for my dad this weekend. I'm pretty sure I can meet those goals, and I'll feel good when I do.

Then there are my medium-sized goals: getting better grades this year, trying to exercise every day, saving up enough money to buy a new bike. I can reach those goals too, but it will take longer. Of course I'll feel good when I do.

And then there are my really big goals: Helping to feed hungry people, helping to show the world God's love, growing into the kind of person God wants me to be. I don't know if I can reach those goals.

They're probably the ones that exceed my reach. But with God's help they **can** be reached. Maybe **I'll** never see it happen, but I think I'll feel good just for trying.

231

WILLPOWER

"I won't eat any more chocolate," I tell myself. "It's horrible for my complexion. And the same goes for pop, potato chips, and other junk food. Not another bite. Never."

And two minutes later my mouth is full of the stuff.

Why don't I have any willpower? Other people do. My mom's always on a diet. She can go without a potato chip for years. I've never seen my dad munching on a candy bar, and he doesn't seem to miss them in the least. But the minute I tell myself I can't have something, I go crazy until I've got it. What's the matter with me?

My mom laughed when I told her all this. She said she used to have the same trouble. It took her years to learn to really love lettuce. But she discovered a secret. She never says "never" to herself. She just says, "I won't have any potato chips today. I'm not making any promises for tomorrow." Then tomorrow she says the same thing to herself. And after a while she doesn't even want a potato chip anymore.

Maybe that's the way I'll have to learn willpower too, God. It seems sort of silly, but then so is this urge I have to stuff junk in my mouth. Help me, though, will You, the next time I come face to face with a bag of potato chips?

232

THEY TRUSTED ME

Some people up the street are painting several rooms in their house and decided they could use some help. So they asked me if I'd like the job.

"Well, sure," I said. "But I don't know very much about painting."

"That's okay," they said. "We'll show you."

And they did. They carefully explained just what I had to do. Then, after I'd painted a little, they came back to make sure I didn't have any questions. After that they left me alone. I painted that whole room by myself! I did a good job too. The people said so.

It was almost a surprise when I found out they meant to pay me too, although I was glad to get the money. But getting paid wasn't nearly as important as the fact that they trusted me with a whole room in their house. It made me feel so grown up and good about myself.

Thank You, God, for people who are willing to trust kids. And help me to be one of the kids people always can trust.

233

THE CAT

The lady next door has a cat. It's one of those friendly cats that just loves to be touched and played with. One time I even saw a little girl who lives on the other side of the lady next door put a doll dress and a bonnet on this cat. The cat just sat there, looking ridiculous. You could tell it was thinking, "Ho-hum. All in the line of duty, I suppose."

Today I spent some time with this cat. First I just looked at it. Cats have the most incredible eyes. After you've looked at them long enough you think you could travel into them for miles and miles to some mysterious world. Then I looked at the whiskers. They're very sensitive. That cat knew every time I touched a whisker, even when she was looking the other way.

Next I discovered this extra little flap of skin that cats have behind their ears. It forms a sort of pouch. I asked the lady next door about it, and she said it's where cats keep their secrets. Hmmm. I'm not so sure I believe that one.

At this point the cat flopped down on the porch and rolled over on her back. "You've looked long enough," she seemed to be saying. "It's time now for some serious tummy rubbing."

Well of course I obeyed. You don't argue with a cat who's presenting her tummy to be rubbed. And was it ever soft! I'm not sure who enjoyed the rub more, me or the cat.

I could go on forever about how this cat looks when she moves and the funny rusty-sounding meow she has and how she can sleep draped over almost anything. But I'm getting a little sleepy myself, so I'll just say . . .

I praise You, God, for cats!

234

WHAT ABOUT DRINKING?

One of the things my friends and I talk about when we're together is drinking. Some kids have tried it and others haven't, but everyone has an opinion. Of course some kids belong to churches that don't believe in drinking, and most of these kids say they'll never do it. I think that's neat too. My own church doesn't happen to feel that way, but I think it's important to go along with the beliefs of whatever church you do go to.

Right now I'm not really sure if I'll drink when I get older or not. My folks have let me take sips of their drinks just to see what they taste like, and, frankly, I think they're awful. They remind me of medicine, and I can't see why anyone would take medicine when it wasn't necessary.

The other thing that bothers me about drinking is alcoholism. I know that not everyone who drinks is an alcoholic, but on the other hand, if nobody drank then there wouldn't be any alcoholics.

I guess that sooner or later the day will come when someone offers me a drink, and at that point I'll have to decide whether to take it or not. Be with me, God, when I have to make that decision and help make it a good one.

235

ALL MY BOSSES

There are days—and this has been one of them—when it seems that everyone wants to boss me around. I can take a certain amount of that, especially from my parents, but after a certain point enough is enough.

Today mom and dad both had some rather firm ideas about what they wanted me to do.

"Sure," I said cheerfully. "Be glad to." And I could have patted myself on the back for being such a good kid.

But just a little later, the neighbor lady told me to run to the store and get her some milk. (Told, not asked.) Well, I did that too. I figured it was for the cat.

At the store the checkout lady told me to help an old lady out to her car with her groceries. (Told, not asked.) I did that too, even though it was the checkout lady's job. I don't mind helping old ladies.

I got home and my aunt called and told me to come over and help my cousin do some weeding. (Told, not asked.) "It's too big a job for one person," said my aunt. At that point I saw red.

"Just a minute, please," I said. "I'll have to ask my mother." And I stormed into the kitchen, explained to my mom everything that had happened, and told her I was sick of being **told** things.

"People would **ask** another adult," I said. "But they think they can just **tell** a kid. Everybody gets to boss a kid around."

"You're absolutely right," said my mom, and she went in to talk to my aunt. I didn't do any weeding either.

God, please help grown-ups understand that kids are human too. They like to be treated like humans. They like to be asked things, not told them. They'll do a lot more work that way too!

236

HURT FEELINGS

I have a friend who seems to get her feelings hurt just about every day. She called me this evening to tell me about the latest thing that happened to her. Honestly, it was the tiniest thing. I don't think the people involved had any intention of hurting her feelings. I doubt if

they even know they did it. I tried to explain this to my friend, but she wouldn't pay any attention to me.

"People should know I'm sensitive," she said. "They should know things like that hurt me."

Frankly, at that moment I wanted to hang up on her. I had the distinct impression that she **likes** to have her feelings hurt, so other people will feel sorry for her, and so she can feel sorry for herself. She's playing a game and using the people she knows as part of it. And I don't much like to be used.

I didn't tell this girl all that on the phone. **She** probably would have hung up on **me** if I had. Maybe I'll think of some other way to tell her, a nice way, when I see her. But I've really learned something from this.

It's easy to fall into that "poor sensitive me and my tender feelings" trap. Sometimes I've come pretty close to it myself. But it **is** a trap, and from now on I'm going to try to avoid it. It might get you a certain amount of attention from people, but it's the wrong kind of attention, and people don't like giving it one bit.

God, don't let me be that kind of sensitive. Don't let me worry about my own feelings all the time. Instead, let me be sensitive about the feelings of others. I think I'll be a lot happier that way!

237

THE MASKS I WEAR

Today I found myself in a lot of different situations. I was with my parents at breakfast. I was with my grandmother all morning. I was with kids my own age during the afternoon. And I was with friends of my parents this evening. The interesting thing is that with each of these people, or groups of people, I was a slightly different person. It was as if I put on a different mask for each situation.

With my parents I guess I was closest to being my real self. With my grandmother I was more gentle and in some ways more open. I can talk to my grandmother about a lot of stuff I don't talk to anyone else about. With the other kids I was a little bit of a clown, a little bit of a counselor, a little bit of a general good-time kid. And with my parents' friends I was on my best behavior.

When I first thought of all these changes in me and pictured them as masks, I got worried that I was being terribly phony. But that's not really so because the different ways I behaved were still all part of the person that is me. I simply showed the different people I was with the part I thought they'd like best or the part that feels most natural around them.

I think that's okay, don't You, God? Don't You make us sort of flexible like that so that we can adjust to different situations and make different people happy? Once again, God, I think You did a good job of making us. You thought of everything!

238

ANIMALS ALONG THE ROAD

There's one thing that bothers me so much I can hardly bear to think about it. That thing is the animals you see along the road that have been hit by cars. It's not just that some person has lost a pet that probably was very dear. I hurt for the animals themselves too, with their lives cut short like that.

It's as if our world has gone too fast, come up with highways and fast cars and things, and the poor animals haven't been able to keep up, so they get killed. It's not fair.

God, You say that You know every time a sparrow falls. That means You know each time one of these animals falls too. Make us a little more careful and more aware of Your gifts of creation.

239

EVERYBODY'S DOING IT

The best reason for doing almost anything you want these days is the line "everybody's doing it." Everybody's using bad words. Everybody's wearing a certain kind of shoe. Everybody's cheating on tests. Therefore, it's okay for me to do it too. In fact, I really **should** do it if I want to be part of the group. Right? Not right.

First of all "everybody's doing it" is usually a lie. What it really means is that some of the kids I think are cool or neat or somebodies are doing it. I want other people to think that I'm cool, neat, and somebody too, and that's why I want to do what they do.

But being cool, neat, and somebody is not the most important thing in the world, even though sometimes it **seems** that way to me. When I'm alone, though, and really thinking, what matters to me most is how **I** feel about myself. Am I proud of what I've done? Is it the sort of thing God would want me to do? After all, I'm **His** somebody, the person He **made** before I'm anything else. And when I know deep down that I'm not behaving the way He'd want me to, I feel terrible about myself, no matter what anybody else is doing.

God, make me strong enough to think about You first. Then I'll be all right. And maybe I can even work at getting "everybody" to do some of the things You want us to do.

240

TINY, TINY WORLDS

I can get excited about bugs and how incredible it is that they **work** in spite of their smallness. But what **really** turns me on is the tiny worlds you can only see through a microscope. We have some pretty good microscopes for science class at school. You can see a lot through them. But even the little one I have at home (I got it for Christmas a couple of years ago) is enough to show me entire worlds.

Take a drop of water from a creek. You can see critters swimming around in that drop that you never dreamed existed. (Actually it makes you pretty thankful for water purification systems.)

What I really love, though, are planarias. I got one once from the biology teacher at the high school. I'd read about them and wanted to see one myself, so I called him up and offered to buy one. He was so impressed by my scientific spirit that he gave it to me.

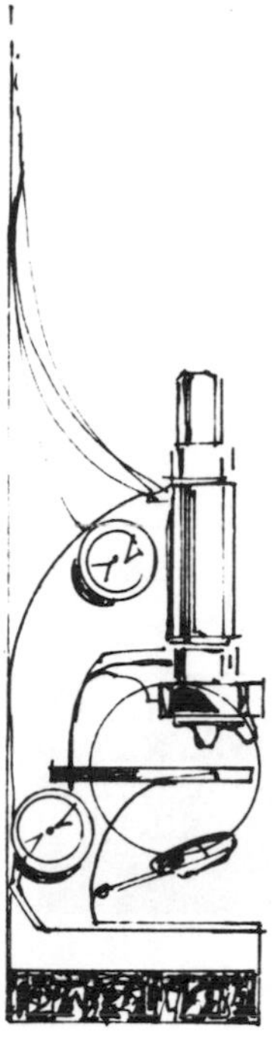

Planarias are little black flat worms about half an inch long. Actually you don't need a microscope to see one, but you can see it better that way. A planaria's mouth is in the middle of its body and it sticks its throat out through its mouth to eat. Planarias look like they have crossed eyes. That's the thing that gets you first, these little crossed eyes staring up at you. Actually they're not eyes in the same way ours are. But they are sense organs. I think they can tell the difference between dark and light.

The other neat thing about planarias is there aren't any males or females. Each planaria is both. But if you chop a planaria in half, the top half grows a new bottom and the bottom half grows a new top. I think that is absolutely amazing. And the scientists say it doesn't hurt the planaria at all (although I'm not sure how they know).

God, You have made some incredible things! How many more are there that I haven't even discovered yet?

241

NO PLACE IS SAFE

In some ways this is really a rotten world. You can't feel safe no matter where you go. There are robbers and murderers and rapists in the city, in the suburbs, and in the country. Perfectly innocent people are being hurt or even killed every day. In fact, it's to the point where people almost take it for granted. If there were one day without a single murder, rape, or robbery, that day would probably make headlines six feet tall.

I wonder what it was like when you could go out for a walk by yourself after dark. It must have been a neat feeling—just you and the moon and the stars. People probably came up with some good thoughts on walks like that. I've never been able to do it, though. It isn't safe anymore.

Does this mean there is more sin in the world or just more people? How do You feel about it, God? Sad? Angry? Do You sometimes wish You hadn't promised never to send another flood like Noah's?

There's one thing I know for sure. Today we need You more than ever. We need You to protect us. You're the only one we can really count on. And we need You to forgive us too. Because somehow I guess we're all responsible for the evil that's creeping across the face of our world.

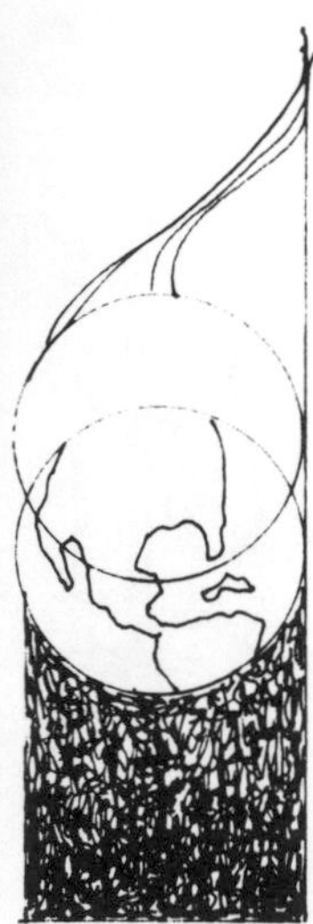

242

DON'T LET US MESS IT UP!

I've been thinking some more about what I wrote yesterday. It really bothers me, all the evil in the world. The evil of crime, the evil of poverty, the evil of pollution. Some kids want to blame it all on older people. They say older people have messed up the world, and now we kids are going to have to do something about it.. But I don't entirely agree with that.

I guess I don't think that kids are all that different from older people. I've seen evil in kids too. I've seen it in myself. The difference is that we haven't had a chance yet to spread our evil around on a worldwide level.

O God, this is a rotten world sometimes, but not because You made it that way. When I look at what You have done, it's so beautiful and so good that I want to cry. Please, God, don't let us mess it up any more than we already have. Show us how to work together—older people and kids too—to heal it, to stamp out the crime and the poverty and the pollution and all the other evils. You have us such a wonderful gift, God. That should be enough. But it isn't, not for us. Now we need You to show us how to love it.

243

THAT IRRITATING PERSON

I guess everyone knows someone like him. The irritating person. In my case it's a guy in my class at school. He has developed irritating other people to the level of a fine art. And nobody can stand him.

This guy is an interrupter. You know, everyone is having a big discussion about something and everyone has something to say. But this guy doesn't think that anything anyone else has to say is worth listening to. He just wants everyone to listen to him. He'll interrupt every time someone else starts to speak. And what **he** has to say usually isn't worth hearing, because he doesn't bother to think about it. He just pushes the button and lets his mouth go.

Obviously he doesn't worry about other people's feelings, or he wouldn't be such an interrupter. But he also says a lot of things that can hurt others. Like he'll talk about the "goofies on the funny farm" in front of a kid whose mom has just had a nervous breakdown. Or he'll mouth off about how badly our school is run right in front of the principal's kid. Fortunately most of us don't pay the slightest bit of attention to him, but that doesn't excuse what he does.

He's also a bragger. "We're going to Monte Carlo for our vacation this year," he says. "Only the best people go there." Well, that second statement won't be true for long. Not after he gets there.

I suppose, God, that I shouldn't feel like this about him. I should try to be more understanding and forgiving. But sometimes it's harder to forgive a whole bunch of little irritating sins than one big one. Have You ever noticed that?

244

IN A MINUTE I'M GOING TO **SCREAM**!

Today has been absolutely out of control. The little things have decided to fight me, and they're winning. It began when I got out of bed and stepped squarely on the rock I'd shaken out of my tennis shoes last night. Realizing that this was my own stupid fault did not make it hurt one bit less.

I poured too much milk on my cereal, and it erupted all around the edges. When I went to put the cereal away, the cabinet door swung back open and cracked me right on the back of the head. As I was putting the milk carton away, it developed a leak in the bottom and oozed out all over the floor.

And that was just the beginning. I'm not going to write down any more of it. The little things have declared war on me and that's that.

Funny, though, how it helps to write about them. To laugh at them too. Do I hear them whispering together? Do they sound scared? Do they know that with a few squiggles of ink and a couple of chuckles I've turned the tide of battle, that I'm winning now?

I don't think I'll scream after all, God. I think I'll try another chuckle. Thanks for such a good weapon.

245

MY BIKE

I've spent a lot of time on my bike this summer. In fact, I've spent a lot of time on my bike ever since I've had it. In many ways my bike has become almost a part of my body. I hardly even think about it anymore. But today I think I will.

For a kid, for me, having a bike is the closest thing there is to having wings. It means you don't have to be totally dependent on grown-ups to take you places (when they want to) and pick you up (when they want to). You're your own person to a certain extent. I'll bet the grown-ups are glad of that too.

Sometimes when you're on your bike, struggling up a steep hill, you can feel every muscle working. That's a good feeling. And when you're zooming down a steep hill, well, that feeling is indescribable. The closest I can come is to say that you feel you're a part of the wind.

If I could make three wishes for all the kids in the world, I'd wish first for enough to eat, second for a comfortable home, third for people to love them. Then I'd ask for a fourth wish and wish for a bike for every one of them.

I don't have any wishes, but I do have prayers—as many as I want. Let me tell You, God, about these four things I want for all the kids in the world . . .

246

SPORTS

Pretty soon it's going to be time for sports to start again. Team sports, I mean. I still do sports in the summer but they're mostly individual sports like swimming.

I'm not the best athlete in the world, but I sure do like sports. Most of all I guess I like the feeling of being on a team, of working with a bunch of other people to accomplish something. Of course I like to win too. I'm only human. But being on the team is definitely the best part.

I like to go to sporting events too. Football games, basketball games, stuff like that. It does bother me, though, when the spectators get too violent. I feel squirmy when someone yells, "Kill the creep!" I suppose they don't really mean it, but still I wonder . . .

I asked my dad once what he thought, and he said that everybody has a certain amount of violence in them. Being civilized means that we don't use that violence to harm someone else. We work it off in other ways. Maybe that's why some people have to yell, "Kill the creep!" at a game. Maybe they're just working off their violence.

God, I wish that violence weren't a part of us. It's part of sin, isn't it? But as long as we have it, please help us get rid of it in harmless ways, like through sports.

247

POP MUSIC

My folks definitely do not like the same kind of pop music I like. They like mushy stuff or else the kind of stuff that you can turn on and then ignore. Wallpaper music, my grandma calls it. Of course she doesn't like my kind of music either. I don't think my grandma's big on pop music period.

Me, I think it's great. The kind of music I like is the kind with a beat, a beat you can feel thudding all around you and through you. For me that beat is pure energy, and somehow it touches all the energy that's in me and makes me want to **move**.

I also like it when the musicians use electronic gadgets to make strange sounds. Swoops and slides and plinks and wails. Those sounds touch something inside me too, and all at once I'm part of that music, flying and wailing and wow!

Actually I don't pay much attention to the words, unless I'm listening to bluegrass or something like that. The words to pop music don't make a lot of sense. They're not supposed to. They're just supposed to be part of the flying and wailing and wow.

My folks say that one day I'm going to grow out of this, but I hope it isn't for a long while yet.

God, pop music may not be the most beautiful stuff in the world, but it certainly is alive. And that's okay, isn't it?

248

A NEW NOTEBOOK

There it is, sitting right in front of me, a new, untouched notebook. Next to it are sitting five new pens, the cheapie stick kind because I lose pens left and right. They're very nice pens, but it's the notebook that turns me on. I have a **thing** about new notebooks.

This one is red and fat, with those little divider things down the side. In it are 300 sheets of paper with light blue lines. And not one of those sheets of paper has been touched. **That's** what gets me about new notebooks.

What's going to end up on all those pages? Notes from a lecture that will help me understand something I've never understood before? A brilliant quote copied from some book that will change the course of my life? A bright idea of my own that will lead to some spectacular project or maybe a story? A poem that will capture a moment of life and hold it for me forever?

Whatever ends up on those pages is my decision. It's up to me whether I keep this notebook for the rest of my life or throw it away at the end of the school year. I can turn it into either something very precious or just a piece of junk.

A new notebook is like a new beginning, God. Help me approach all my new beginnings with the feelings of excitement and responsibility that I feel for this notebook.

249

WALLS

I had to go to school early the other day to talk to my counselor about a course change. It's strange being in an almost empty school building. It doesn't feel like school. It's more like a bunch of cubicles all separated by walls.

I had to wait for my counselor for a while, and so I got to thinking about those cubicles. Pretty soon I could picture a person in each of them, cut off from every other person, and then that began to seem like what life is like. Everyone in a separate little world and everyone

suffering from a horrible loneliness. An old person cut off from a young person. (And, of course, the young person cut off from the old person too.) A black person and a white person separated by walls. A male person and a female person. A married person and a single person. By the time I got in to see my counselor I was utterly depressed.

I decided to tell her what I'd been thinking, and she seemed really interested.

"But you know," she said, "we can use those same walls that separate us to help us communicate. We can tap messages to one another on them. Prisoners used to do that. And communicating might be the first step to tearing down the walls."

I'm not sure I completely understand what she said, but I think it's probably very wise and true.

I'd like to be wall-breaker, God. Isn't that part of Your work?

250

I WAS SO EMBARRASSED!

If there's one thing I hate and despise it's having to get up in front of a class at school and say something. You'd think teachers would understand what a horrible punishment this is for kids, but they go on doing it year after year just the same.

Last week we all had to get up and tell about our summer vacation. Now if **that** isn't cornball, I don't know what is. But I had to do it anyway. And of course I couldn't think of a thing to say.

It was easier for the kids who went away. They could describe the sea or the mountains or something. But the kind of stuff that happened to me this summer had to do mostly with my feelings, and I wasn't about to broadcast it to the whole class. So I just mumbled a couple sentences about going swimming and riding my bike and visiting my relatives and then I sat down. I could have died.

My mom always says that the best thing you can do when you're embarrassed is to laugh at yourself. She says other people are usually feeling embarrassed right along with you, and they're grateful if you give them a chance to laugh and break the tension. I wish I'd remembered that, but I didn't. I guess I was too busy thinking about myself to even consider the fact that the other kids might be feeling funny too.

God, **please** help me think of others a little more. It would make life so much easier!

251

PEOPLE DO SOME WEIRD THINGS

It's funny how for a short time after you get back to school in the fall you look at people a little differently. In a way it's like coming back from a vacation to the place you always live. You see things more clearly for a while. Then you get used to them again.

What I've been noticing is the weird things people do for no apparent reason. There's this one girl—I don't know her personally—who absolutely never looks up. She stares at the ground all day. It's surprising that she doesn't run into things, but she doesn't. Maybe she's developed a sense of radar.

Then there's this guy who always wears funny hats. He's got fishing hats, rain hats, sailor hats, and several other kinds of hats. He takes them off in class, but as soon as he's back in the hall, on goes his hat.

It's not just the kids who do weird things either. One of the teachers (a man) has a beard that he's always combing. Right in the middle of class, there he is, combing that beard and talking at the same time. I suppose he's trying to train it to grow the way he wants, but it sure looks strange.

Well, I probably do weird things too, don't I, God? Maybe we all do. It's a good thing You don't let that get in the way of Your loving us.

252

DRUGS

It really does happen and right in my own school. Kids use drugs. Some of them swipe pills from their parents, uppers or downers. Some buy their stuff from other kids. It you want drugs, you can get them, as much and as many kinds as you like. Of course they cost money, but the kids who buy them seem to come up with the money somehow. They probably tell their folks they're buying records or something.

I could get drugs with no trouble at all. But I certainly don't intend to. I understand **why** other kids want to try them. They want to see what it feels like. They want to have that adventure. Or they're under a lot of pressure at school or at home or both, and the drugs make them feel it less. I like adventures too. And sometimes I feel a lot of pressure. But I don't want to deal with either of those things through drugs.

There are a lot of reasons why I won't try drugs. First of all, my parents think it's wrong, and I'd hate to disappoint them. Secondly, I think it's wrong too. Thirdly, I know that drugs can be horrible for your body. They can turn you into an addict, and it's hard to get over being an addict. Fourthly, I can think of better ways to spend my money.

But the real reason I won't try drugs, the thing that would stop me even if all those other reasons didn't exist, is that I can't stand the thought of losing control. God gave me a good body and a good mind. I can see things and hear things and experience things just as they are, all on my own. I don't need drugs twisting my perceptions to make my experiences any better. They're super just the way they are!

253

MY TEACHERS

Well, I've got a mixed bag this year. Everybody says one of my teachers is absolutely super. They say one of my other teachers is a complete bore. Most of the others seem to be somewhere in the middle (according to the Kid Poll), and there is one teacher nobody knows at all. Well, that's how it usually goes. I guess I'll make it through. I always do.

I wonder if the teachers look at us kids the same way we look at them at the beginning of each year. I wonder if they have Teacher Polls and talk about who's got a winner and who's got a loser. Are they excited about confronting all those new classes, eager to teach them whatever it is they teach? Do most of them honestly care about kids or their subjects or both? I think they'd have to. From what I've heard, most teachers aren't into their professions because of the great pay.

I wonder how teachers feel when they find out I'm in their class. Am I classified a winner or a loser? Or am I part of that great gray mass in the middle?

I'd sure like this to be a good year for me, and I guess the teachers feel the same way about themselves. Help us both, God. Help all of us—winners, losers, gray-middlers, and unknowns. Help us make it a good year for each other.

254

I'M SO SCARED OF TESTS!

One of my teachers has done it already. A pop test. That is just about the dirtiest trick I can think of for a teacher to play. And I reacted in my usual way. I froze. That doesn't always mean I did badly on the test. Sometimes I thaw just enough to get by. But it's always sheer torture.

I don't know why I should be this way. I'm not a stupid kid. I do well on regular assignments and class discussions and stuff like that. But something about being put on the line, forced to show what I've learned under pressure, just does me in.

My dad says I should try to think of tests as a game, not take them so seriously. I asked him if he'd still feel that way after I brought home an F on a test paper, and he said yes, if it meant that sooner or later I'd get over this fear. Well, maybe I should take his advice then. I don't know many parents who would be that understanding.

God, would You help me get over my fear too? I know it must seem like a very little thing compared to all the other problems people bring to You, but it's important to me. And maybe if I could just remember that You're there with me all through the test, I could stop panicking. Do You think so?

255

THE SUBSTITUTE

We had a substitute in one of our classes this week. Oh, that poor lady! I don't know why it is that kids always pick on substitutes, but they do. And substitutes seem to fall for the oldest tricks every time.

First, someone near the front of the room wrote a note that said, "Look at the footprints on the ceiling." That note got passed around the whole class, and soon every pair of eyes was looking up and every mouth was grinning. All but the substitute's eyes and mouth. She looked ready to cry.

There's no way I can stand up to a whole class of kids and say, "Okay, now. This isn't fair. Let's be nice to substitutes. They're human too, after all." I'd be laughed out of the building.

But I did try to help a little. When I thought the substitute had as much as she could take, I asked what I thought was a very interesting and intelligent question about the subject we were studying, and soon the whole class was discussing it. Sorry, substitute, but that was the best I could do.

God, please do be with substitutes. They need Your help as much as anyone I can think of!

256

I'M WORN OUT ALREADY

I can't believe it. School has barely started and already I'm tired. Just the thought of all the assignments stretching ahead of me, all the textbooks we've barely cracked, makes me want to lie down and sleep for a hundred years.

I wonder if grown-ups remember what hard work school really is. It's not like having just one job and concentrating on it. It's like having six or seven jobs, one for each subject. And of course each teacher expects you to treat his or her subject as if it's the only one.

I suppose the only way to survive is to try to take the subjects (and the days) one at a time. Looking too far ahead is more than I can handle. It might help too if I made a real effort to get enough sleep. That might interfere slightly with my TV time, but it also might be worth it in the end.

In fact, I think I'll go to bed now. Good night, God.

257

GRADES

I have mixed feelings about grades. (My mother is always having mixed feelings about things. I probably get them from her.) Grades are great if you get As or Bs. They're terrible if you get anything else.

Another thing I don't like about grades is being forced to compete with everyone else in the class. I want to learn something because I want to learn it, not because I want a better grade than Emily Sue Schmidlapp. (Emily Sue Schmidlapp gets very good grades.) I don't even want to know what grades other kids get. It either depresses me or makes me feel superior—and for the wrong reasons. I don't want other kids to know what I get either. It's my business.

Usually when I begin working on a subject, I decide what grade I want to get in it. (That's not always an A either. There are a couple of subjects in which I'd be perfectly happy with a B.) If I meet my own goal, then I'm happy. If I don't, I'm unhappy. I'm competing with myself, and that's the only person I want to compete with.

This semester I know exactly what grades I want to get. I know exactly what I want to learn. I've set my goals high, but I think I can make them—with Your help, God.

258

CHEATING IS DUMB

Kids cheat. Lots of kids cheat. They do it by whispering or writing answers to each other. They do it by getting copies of old tests. They do it by writing answers on tiny pieces of paper and hiding these in their shoes or someplace. Personally I think cheating is dumb. Not to mention wrong.

If you cheat, all you do is make the teacher think that you know more than you really do. Actually you're missing all that learning. And the learning's the important part.

Of course you might get a better grade by cheating. A lot of the kids who cheat are the ones who worry about grades. They say their parents will be furious with them if they don't get good grades, and that's probably true. But why don't they just study harder instead of cheating? Or talk to the teacher about problems they're having? Or get a tutor? I'm just glad my parents don't pressure me about grades. Maybe they realize that I put enough pressure on myself.

When push comes to shove, though (another of my grandma's phrases), the real problem with cheating is that it's wrong. It's stealing knowledge from someone else, and it's lying about how much you really know. Help me, God, not to fall into those temptations, no matter how much I might want to someday.

259

THE FAVORITE? ME?

Good grief, I think the impossible has finally happened. I think I am the favorite pupil of one of my teachers; even more shocking, it's the teacher that everyone warned me was a loser.

She likes me. I can tell. Unfortunately, so can the other kids and they're going to give me a rough time about this. But I didn't **mean** for it to happen.

I think I've done two things to bring all this about. First I'm honestly interested in the subject this teacher teaches. So I've been working hard in that class. Naturally the teacher likes someone to be interested in her subject. I would if I were a teacher.

The second thing I've done is to be nice to this teacher. I suppose I felt a little sorry for her because so many of the kids think she's awful. So I smile and say hi to her in the halls. And I try to be cooperative in class.

Apparently, that's all it took for me to become the favorite. But now the tricky part begins. How can I go on being interested in that subject and nice to that teacher without getting all the other kids down on me.

Please help me figure out a good way to handle this, God. It's a problem I've never had before!

260

FIRE

It seems as if I've been thinking about school every day since it started, and I'm getting tired of the whole subject. So today I'm going to think about something entirely different. I'm going to think about fire.

I think fire is one of the most beautiful and mysterious things in the world. I love to watch candles burn. The tall, perfectly straight ones on the altar at church. Or the lumpy, waxy ones that mom puts on our coffee table. When I look at a candle, I find it hard to believe that fire is just burning gases. It's too pure, too magical for that.

The other place I love to look at fire is in the fireplace on a cold evening. We've had a couple of those already this year, and I don't know who was more eager to get that fire going—me or dad. Fireplace fires touch almost all of your senses. You can watch them and get lost in the flames. You can hear them crackling and hissing. You can smell them—there's no smell in the world like a fireplace fire. You can feel them, and there's something about their warmth that a radiator will never be able to compete with. About the only thing you can't do is taste them, not unless you burn your marshmallows as often as I do.

Of course fire can also be terrifying. Some people enjoy going to fires, but not me. It tears me apart to see something beautiful or something that someone loved being destroyed.

Thank You, God, for all the beauty and usefulness of fire. Help us use this gift wisely so that it won't become a force for destruction.

261

NEW KID

Every year it happens. I have a new kid in one of my classes. You can spot them a mile away, even if you don't already know all the kids in your school. The new kid as a different look, sort of panicked and defensive and beseeching all at the same time.

It's as if he or she were saying, "Please like me. I really **am** okay. You'd better like me!"

This year's new kid is different. She happens to be a girl. And she doesn't have any of that new-kid look about her. She seems perfectly relaxed and, well, **interested** in things. She's not afraid to ask questions about the stuff she doesn't know. She's not afraid to walk right up to the kids and talk to them. She doesn't seem to care which kids she talks to either—the somebodies, the nobodies, or all the kids in the middle. It's as if this girl is so positive she's okay that she doesn't worry about it. And you can just see people warm up to her, because everybody can't help liking someone who's interested in them.

God, I hope I don't ever have to be a new kid. But if I do, help me remember what this girl is like. Help me be so positive about myself (after all, I'm Your child) that I can afford to be interested in others—right away.

262

WE DROVE BY THIS FIELD

Today my parents and I drove out to the country to visit an old friend. On the way we drove past a field of grain. (I don't know much about agriculture, so I'm not sure what it was, but it might have been corn.) The sun was shining on the field and turning it to pure gold. And a little wind was blowing so that it looked like dancing gold. I think it was one of the most beautiful things I've ever seen.

Strangely enough, it made me think about the Bible. There are a lot of stories about fields and grain in the Bible. I guess a lot of people were farmers back then. I wonder if any of them ever felt the same way I did driving past that field. Did they sort of hold their breath at the sheer beauty of their crops?

I suppose they were mostly concerned about having good crops so there would be enough food. I don't usually think too much about that, although sometimes the announcers let you know what's happening on the news. I guess there are so many people and processes between that field and the food I buy in the store that I forget I have any connection with the field. But I do, and today I realized it and maybe felt a little like God's people did in Bible times.

I like these links with Your people, God. I like feeling close to them. It makes me feel even closer to You.

263

MY FRIENDS

I wouldn't say I have a huge mob of friends. But I have enough. Enough that I can spend time caring about all of them. And enough that I feel cared for by them. I guess that's all anyone can ask.

What's really neat, though, is when your friends do something unexpected for you, something to let you know they think you're kind of special. Last year on my birthday, a bunch of my friends picked me up at seven o'clock in the morning and took me to a pancake house (in my pajamas and robe, no less) for breakfast. They even had presents for me. That made me feel so good that I wanted to hug every one of them. In fact, I did.

Of course my friends and I don't always get along. We don't always feel the same about certain things. But nobody stays mad for long. The rest of us help them make up. And it's surprising how many things we do think alike about.

I don't plan to write a long essay here on friendship. More important and smarter people than I have already done that. But I do just want to say, God, thanks a lot for my friends.

264

PAINTERS

Today we took a field trip to the art museum. It's not the first time I've been there, but today I somehow managed to pay attention and notice things that I've never noticed before.

For example, I went up to this painting of a lake. At least it looked like a lake from a distance. But when I got very close, all I could see were thousands and thousands of little different-colored dots. Now I find that amazing. How did that artist know that from a distance all those dots would combine to form a lake? If I tried something like that, all I'd end up with would be a bunch of dots.

And for the first time I noticed how big some of the paintings are. Why, some are as big as the walls in my room! You'd have to stand on a ladder to do the top part, and then you wouldn't be able to see the bottom. I guess some painters worked like that too. In fact, I read somewhere that Michelangelo painted the ceiling of the Sistine Chapel while lying on his back on a scaffold. The paint kept dripping into his face—and probably into his lunch too.

Painters must be another one of those special breeds of people You've created, God. And today for the first time I'm really glad you did. They manage to show us Your creation in the most incredible ways!

265

HORSES

If I had to pick a favorite animal in the whole world, it would be the horse. I think horses are one of the most wonderful things God ever created. What I really wish is that I had a horse all my own and a ranch or someplace to ride him whenever I wanted. Sometimes I have this daydream.

In my dream I get up very early in the morning, before anyone else is awake. I go out to the stable and my horse whinnies as soon as he hears my footsteps. I give him a couple of lumps of sugar, lead him outside, and climb onto his back. I don't bother with a saddle. I don't want anything coming between me and my horse.

We walk out to the open country, me taking deep breaths of the fresh morning air and my horse shaking his mane and sometimes dancing a little with excitement. Then, once the fences and everything are behind us, I whisper very quietly, "Go, boy!" and my horse takes off.

For miles and miles we fly, and my horse and I move so perfectly together that we could be just one magic creature. Trees and bushes and flowers streak past us, and overhead the birds are shouting their glad morning songs. Finally I can't stand it anymore and I shout too, a shout of pure joy.

None of that has ever happened to me, God, except in my daydreams. But it could happen sometime, couldn't it? And in the meantime, I praise You, God, for making horses.

266

THAT LITTLE THING SHE DOES DRIVES ME MAD!

I care about my friends. I really do, including the friend I'm going to write about today. But I have to admit that she has this one tiny habit that absolutely drives me bananas. I feel silly even writing about it, it's such a little thing. But if I don't let off steam somehow, I'm likely to clobber her over the head. And that wouldn't do much for our friendship.

What this friend does is bite her fingers. Not just the nails. The skin too. All the while you're around her she's munching away on her hands. I'm surprised they're not down to stumps. They must grow back overnight.

Some of my other friends bite their nails, and that doesn't bother me too much. At least I don't think it's any great crime, even though it isn't the world's best habit either. But no one else goes at it quite as seriously as this girl does. You'd think she was getting **paid** by the nibble.

I wonder if we're good enough friends for me to say something to her about it. I'd hate to lose her friendship over such a silly little thing. Maybe I could make a joke about it . . .

Am I being petty, God, to get bothered by something as silly as a finger-biting friend? And, God, do You suppose **I** do anything that might be driving other people mad?

267

I MISS YOU

Something's different about school this year. A friend of mine isn't there anymore. His family moved to another town, and I haven't seen him since last June. You'd think I would have stopped missing him by now, but I haven't. Oh, I don't think about him every minute of every day. But now and then, in special situations, in places where we used to be together, I do think of him, and I miss him. A lot.

Of course I could always write him a letter. But letters aren't like seeing the person. Besides, we've probably both changed by now. A summer can change a person a lot when you're our age. And when two people aren't together while they're changing, they're almost like strangers to one another the next time they meet.

Hey, I'm really getting sort of depressed about this. I don't want that guy to go out of my life completely. He was a good friend, and friendship should be able to stand a summer's worth of time and changes.

I have a brilliant idea. I'm going to ask my parents if I can call this guy long-distance. I'll pay for the call out of my allowance. And I'll call at one of those times when the rates are cheaper, and we can talk long enough to feel close to one another again.

Thanks, God, for making people clever enough to invent things like telephones.

268

LEAVES

Everybody writes about leaves at this time of year, so why should I bother? On the other hand, why shouldn't I? I happen to get as excited about autumn leaves as anyone else, and I want to tell how I feel. Therefore, I will.

Leaves in the fall remind me of that painting I saw at the art museum, the one that looked like a lot of dots up close but like a lake from a distance. If I were a painter painting leaves, I'd make them a whole bunch of brightly colored dots. Red and yellow and orange and brown and some colors in between. I'd also throw in a few pine trees because I think autumn leaves look even more beautiful when you see them next to the dark green of pines.

Of course I feel like everyone else about walking through leaves on a crisp cool autumn day. There's nothing quite like it, especially if you come to a big pile and give it a good kick.

But I also like walking in leaves when it rains. Then they look like huge soggy cornflakes pasted all over the ground. If you work it right, sometimes you can slide for a long way on them, just like on ice.

Every year I pick up a few of the prettiest leaves and stick them between the pages near the middle of my textbooks. Then when winter comes and all the trees are bare, I come across one of those leaves and remember how neat autumn was.

God, if You have just a minute, I'd like to join with a lot of other people and praise You for autumn leaves.

269

SKY

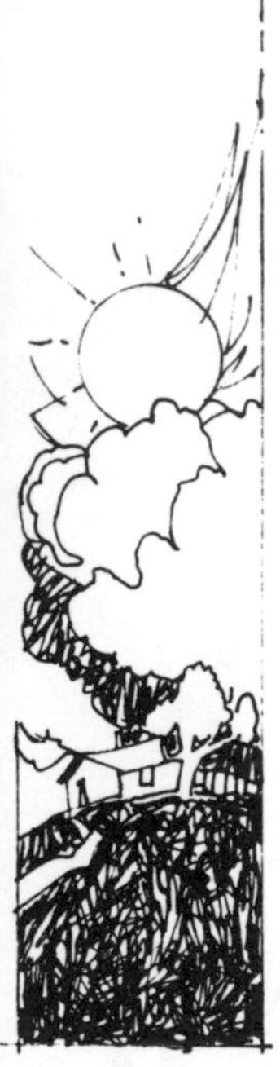

If you asked most people to describe the sky, they'd probably say "blue" and leave it at that. But blue is just one tiny part of what the sky's like, and today I'm going to try to say some more about it.

First of all, the sky can be many colors. A pale, pale blue that's almost white. A fierce turquoise blue that hurts your eyes to look at it. A cold, clean darker blue. An angry splotchy mass of grays that mean a storm is going to dump down on you at any moment. A quiet, sinister yellow gray that means something more than a storm might dump down on you. A mad splash of pinks, purples, and even greens at sunset. And, of course, a soft velvety black, prickled with tiny diamond stars.

Someone once described the sky as a bowl set down over the earth. Unscientific as it is, I can understand that feeling. But sometimes I don't see the sky as closing us in at all. I see it stretching wide and free and inviting us to be wild and free too. That's when I start getting jealous of birds.

I must be on a nature kick, God. Yesterday leaves and today the sky. I hope You don't get tired of hearing all this. But it's Your own fault if You do. You did such a super job, I just can't keep quiet!

270

SHADOW OF A BIRD

I had the eeriest, neatest experience this morning, I woke up and looked beside me and there on the wall was a rectangle of sunlight. Splitting the sunlight were the shadows of some branches, and right in the middle of them was the shadow of a bird.

I sat very still and watched it for several minutes. Then the bird moved, turned into a sort of blur, and flew away. I've awakened in this same bed in this same spot many times before. But I've never before seen anything like that.

I don't suppose it has any profound meaning. It was just a small perfect experience of beauty. And that's all it has to be. That's enough to make it a special gift from God to me.

Thank You, God.

271

OUR FATHER

I made the most amazing discovery today. We were saying the Lord's Prayer, and I suddenly realized that all the way through we use the first person plural pronoun, not the first person singular. In other words, we say "**Our** Father," not "**My** Father." Maybe everybody else noticed this a long time ago, but I hadn't. And I think it makes a lot of difference in how we think about that prayer.

The Lord's Prayer isn't a prayer we say just for ourselves. I mean, it's not a prayer I say just for myself or my mom says just for herself. It's a prayer we say for one another too. A congregation praying it might be saying it for every person in that congregation. A person praying it alone might be saying it for all of God's other children all over the world.

Jesus must have meant it to be that way, and that's why He worded it the way He did. He wanted us to feel free to pray for the things we need as individuals, but He wanted us to remember everybody else too. How very wise and wonderful He is!

272

I SAID TOO MUCH

I was talking to one of my friends today about another of my friends, and before I knew it I'd said too much and told the first friend a secret. Well, the second friend never really said it was a secret, but still I knew it was. And I blabbed it. Not on purpose. Not to make myself look big or important or anything. Just because I didn't think. My mouth was on go and my brain was on stop.

I remember how I felt when someone I trusted betrayed one of my secrets. I was so hurt I hardly knew what to do. I had a terrible time even figuring out how to forgive that person. And now I've done exactly the same thing.

Well, I guess there's only one way to handle it. I guess I'll have to go to that friend and confess what I did. This time I'll be the one asking for forgiveness. I hope my friend can give it.

Please help her, God. And please forgive me Yourself.

273

SICK

Today I had what is called the 24-hour flu. Personally I thought it was the bubonic plague or at least cholera. I was sure I was going to die. I even began to wonder whether a kid my age should have a will or not. You see, I don't get sick too often, and when I do it really hits me hard.

I will not write down the gory details. "Gory," in fact, doesn't even begin to describe them. But I will say that I felt like a whole colony of caterpillars was having a parade up and down my esophagus, that tiny people in golf shoes were jumping rope inside my stomach, and that somewhere below the stomach two cats were having a fight. Each of my teeth was wearing a fuzzy little sweater, my tongue was coated with sandpaper, and my eyes had been left out all day on the Sahara Desert. Does that give you the general picture?

I did not want to see one single person except my mother, who has a great way of whispering into the room with a glass of white soda and then whispering out again so you can die in peace. I cringed every time the phone rang. At least mom says it was the phone. I thought it was Big Ben. And when a delivery person knocked on the front door, I was convinced that the house was falling down on top of me.

Fortunately 24-hour flu only lasts 24 hours. I feel better already. But I've sure learned something from this. Health is one of the best gifts You give us, God. Please give it back to me fast!

274

BRAVE

I love to read stories about people who do really brave things—like rescuing a buddy on the battlefield or facing a pack of hungry lions rather than give up their faith in God or diving into ice-cold water to save a drowning child. Of course I always wonder if **I'd** be brave enough to do something like that. I guess you never know that about yourself, though, until you're actually faced with a situation where you have to be brave.

I think there's another kind of bravery too. It's a slow day-by-day sort of bravery. Some of the old missionaries had it, the ones who devoted their lives to working with people who had leprosy, for example. But people today have that sort of bravery too. A friend of my mother's has been taking care of her husband, who had a very bad stroke, for 10 years. She has to do practically everything for him. That takes bravery, and in a way I think it's a harder kind of bravery than the kind that is required when you can jump right in, save somebody, and get it over with. You're giving up your life for someone else, but you're doing it in a different, slower way.

God, if the time ever comes when I have to be brave—either all at once or over a long period—please give me some of Your strength. I'm pretty sure that's the only way I'll make it.

275

I DIDN'T CARE ENOUGH

A girl at school has had a mental breakdown, a bad one. In fact, I think she even tried to kill herself, although nobody has come right out and said that. I can't stop thinking about it, and I can't stop feeling guilty. Maybe, I keep telling myself, if I'd paid a little more attention to this girl, if I'd cared a little more about her, I could have somehow helped her before this happened.

But I didn't pay attention, and I didn't care enough, and it did happen. Oh, I know I can't go around helping **everybody** I meet. It's just too much for one person. And besides, I don't know enough. But shouldn't I have been able to see that this girl was **especially** in need of help?

Mom says I shouldn't feel guilty. She says this girl has had a problem for a long time and has been getting help, including some kind of drug therapy from a psychiatrist. But still, maybe she needed more than drugs. Maybe she needed another person to care.

I don't guess I'll ever know the answer, God. I don't guess there's much point worrying about it now either. The girl has had her breakdown, and I might as well concentrate on what I can do for her now. I can think of only one thing too, God. I'm handing her over to You. Please, God, take care of her.

276

MY IMAGINATION

My mother says I've always had a good imagination. She says that when I was a little kid I had a make-believe friend called Bubba Wubba who went everywhere and did everything with me. I also had four dogs, two cats, a monkey and a parrot—all make-believe—and I never forgot a single one of their names. I don't remember any of that too well, but I do remember that later I had a make-believe horse called Sunset. In fact, I won't tell you how long I had that horse. It's sort of embarrassing.

Now I use my imagination in different ways. Sometimes I write stories and poems. Sometimes I draw pictures of make-believe lands. Sometimes I even make up maps for those lands. But what I like to do most of all is sit around, stare off into space, and **see** things.

For example, there's this tree just outside the window where I'm writing. If I look at it and leave my eyes a little bit unfocused, I can see a tiny monkey sitting in that tree. (In reality it's only a branch, but when

I'm playing this game I forget about reality.) Now how, I ask myself, did a tiny monkey get in that tree? And I make up a whole story to go with the monkey.

Sometimes I don't even need to look at anything real to start seeing things with my imagination. I can close my eyes and there it is—a blue stork or purple rain or a country where the flowers grow big as trees.

I'm awfully glad You gave me an imagination, God. Maybe someday I'll even be able to share these wild things I imagine with others. There might be a whole lot of people in the world who'd enjoy hearing about purple rain!

277

EVENING

It's evening again. The air's turning cool, the sun's disappearing in a blaze of red, and purple mists are drifting across the sky. Somewhere in the distance a church carillon is playing hymns. It is a perfect moment.

It seems to me that perfect moments usually do come either in the evening or in the very early morning. I almost never feel a perfect moment at noon or at three o'clock. Of course the moments might be there, and I'm just too busy to notice them.

In the evening, though, I take time off from being busy, and then the quiet parts of the world, the gentle, beautiful parts wrap themselves around me. I hear sleepy birds muttering in their nests before they finally pop their heads under their wings. I hear orchestra after orchestra of night bugs tuning up for their evening concerts. I breathe air that is as cool and smooth as silk. And I feel very close to You, God.

278

I WENT TO A FUNERAL TODAY

A distant relative of mine has died, and today I went to the funeral. I hardly knew this person, but mom and dad thought they should go, and I asked if I could too. I've never been to a funeral before.

I don't know what I expected—maybe a lot of crying and moaning—but that's not what this funeral was like at all. All the hymns we sang were Easter hymns, great, joyous songs. The minister talked for a few moments about hope and said that this person who had died did not have to hope anymore because now she was seeing Christ face to face. Then all of us joined in a prayer, and asked God to comfort those who were grieving, and simply handed the person who had died over to His care.

When I left the service there were tears in my eyes and in the eyes of many of the people around me. But I don't think they were sad, despairing tears. In a way they were joyful tears, tears of gladness at this great and wonderful thing called resurrection that God has promised us and that we **know** is real.

I never dreamed I could leave a funeral feeling like that. It must be You, God. You sent Your Son to die on the cross. You raised Him from the dead. You forgive us when we do wrong. And You have promised us eternal life. You make all the difference.

279

A BABY WAS BORN

Another one of my distant relatives had a baby today, a little girl. Isn't that remarkable? The day after one relative dies, another is born. It's like God is saying, "Yes, I take people away when it is time for them to be with Me. But I give you people too."

In a way I wish we could have a special church service to celebrate births. We could sing more great, joyous hymns. The minister could talk about the hope that is God's gift to this child—and to all of us. And then we could pray together. We could ask God to bless the people that are rejoicing, and we could hand the new child over to His care.

I don't think we are going to have a church service, though, so I'll just do the prayer myself.

God, I praise and bless You for this new child. Be with her parents and all the other people who are so glad she's here. Help them love her, care for her, and teach her about You. Be close to her, God, through all her life and help her feel close to You.

280

CONTROLLING MYSELF

Today my mom and I were at the supermarket, and we watched a lady scolding a little kid who had taken some candy off a shelf.

"Why is she making such a big deal about it?" I asked my mom. "That kid's too little to know any better."

"But he's not too little to start learning," said my mom. "Pretty soon he'll stop taking things because he knows it upsets his mother, and he loves her and doesn't want to do that. Then, after a while, he won't take things because a little voice inside himself will tell him that stealing is wrong."

"You mean what his mother is really doing is teaching him to control himself?" I asked.

"Something like that."

Well, I just had to think about that for a while. It made me look at discipline in a whole new way. Discipline by others—like your parents—is just the first step toward learning self-discipline. And I guess when you've learned enough self-discipline, you're grown up. (Well, maybe there are a few other things you have to learn too.)

I wonder how I'm doing. I sort of like the idea of controlling myself, God. Would You please help me learn self-discipline?

281

I CAN'T DECIDE

I have to make this decision, and as far as I'm concerned, it's a pretty important decision. In fact, it's important enough that I'd like to be able to ask someone else to make it for me. But I can't. It's the kind of decision I have to make myself.

I've thought about it every way I can. I've made lists of what would happen if I decided one way and what would happen if I decided the other way. I've talked to people whose advice I trust, including my parents. Then I listed all the advice. I have five pages of lists in my notebook, and I still don't know what to decide.

Dumb me. It's taken me this long to realize that there's one person I haven't consulted. God. I'm going to spend a few moments now praying. Maybe God will tell me what I should decide.

I prayed. And God didn't come back with any clear-cut answers either. But He did help me remember something that makes all the difference in how I feel about my decision. He helped me remember that no matter **what** I decide, I can count on Him to turn what I do into the best possible thing for me and for His other children. Thanks, God! That's just what I needed.

282

THE CITY

Last night we rode through the city after dark. It was a strange experience. In a way it was beautiful seeing the warm coziness of lighted windows splattered against the dark sky. My dad said that when you fly over a city at night it looks like a huge collection of jewels spread over a piece of black velvet.

But in a way it wasn't so beautiful, that city at night. Because there was hardly a minute when you couldn't hear sirens—police sirens, ambulances, fire engines—and you couldn't help but wonder what all was going on to bring out all those sirens.

I wondered, too, how I'd feel if our car broke down, and I had to walk through those city streets. I'm sure my heart would have been in my throat, and I would have jumped at every shadow. And yet there are some people who have to walk through those streets all the time if they want to get anywhere. There are probably even some people out there who have nowhere to go.

God, be with the people in the city, especially in the poor parts.

Keep them safe. Walk the streets with them and protect them from loneliness and every kind of danger. And, God, help us to someday make our city streets places where we can notice just the beauty and not have to worry about the danger.

283

I'M GLAD HE WON—AREN'T I?

For the first time in my life I ran for a class office at school. And I lost. I lost to another kid who was running for a class office for the first time. And now I'm trying to convince myself that I'm glad he won.

Well, let's see. All the time I would have spent doing stuff for the class is now mine to spend in other ways. That doesn't make me feel glad at all. I **wanted** to spend some time doing stuff for the class.

Maybe this guy needed to be a class officer more than I did. I don't really know him well enough to know if that's true or not. But I do know that **I** needed to be a class officer pretty bad.

Hmmm. Maybe I should just be honest about the whole thing and admit that I'm **not** glad he won. Because I'm not. I wanted to win, and I can't pretend that I didn't.

Okay, I'm not glad he won. That doesn't mean I can't support him, though. I can ask other kids—the kids I know voted for me—to support him too. I won't have any trouble doing that. After all, it's what I would have wanted him to do if I'd won.

God, I feel bad about not winning that election. But I feel good about the way I've worked out what to do. And there's no reason I can't run again next time, is there?

284

MY FRIEND WITH A CONSCIENCE

One of my friends has suddenly become very religious. At least that's what she calls it. I'm not so sure, because ever since she's become religious she seems to be miserable all the time.

"My conscience is bothering me," she'll say to me. "I talked back to my mother last night." Or, "My conscience is bothering me. I forgot to send my aunt a birthday card."

Well, today I'd had enough.

"A conscience is a fine thing to have," I said. "But if it's all you've got, it's going to drive you crazy." (Not to mention the people around you, I thought, but I didn't say that out loud.)

"What do you mean?" said my friend.

"Well, doesn't your religion have any room in it for forgiveness? I asked. "All a conscience will do is make you feel guilty. It's God who forgives you. And being forgiven is the most important part of religion."

"You think you know everything," said my friend.

"Nope," I said. "But I **do** know how it feels to be forgiven after your conscience has made you feel guilty."

I hope I helped her, God. I hope I didn't just turn her off by sounding like a know-it-all. And if I did, would You please step in? Would You help her understand how great it feels to be forgiven?

285

GOOD AND BAD THINGS ABOUT ME

I don't know what's gotten into me lately, but I sure have been making a lot of lists. Somehow I keep hoping they'll help me understand things better. Today I made two more—one of good things about me and one of bad things about me. I suppose I thought they'd help me understand myself better. But they didn't. They just depressed me.

You see, before I put anything on the good list I had to feel sure that it was a good thing that was true of me most of the time. Like am I kind most of the time or only part of the time? Well, I didn't end up with much on that good list. And I found plenty to put on the bad one.

Before I began these lists, I thought I'd be able to take the stuff on the bad list and start working to improve myself, one item at a time. Well, the way that list turned out I'd be at least 180 before I'd worked my way through it.

God, I threw the lists away. The turning of me into a better person is just too big a job for me. From now on I'm going to leave it in Your hands. I need Your help.

286

EARNING MY WAY

Today I mentioned to my Sunday school teacher the lists I'd made about myself.

"Why did you make them?" she asked.

"Oh, so I'd understand myself a little better," I said, "and so I could work to become a better person."

"And why do you want to be a better person?" she asked.

"Why, because it's **better** to be a better person," I said. Then I thought for a minute and said the next thing very fast and low because I already realized what a terrible mistake I'd made. "And because I want to go to heaven when I die."

"Oh, no!" groaned my Sunday school teacher. "I thought I was a better teacher than that. I thought you understood a little more about God than that."

"I do," I mumbled. "I just forgot for a while."

"So tell me," she said, looking kind of nervous.

"Well, what I do doesn't have anything to do with forgiveness or going to heaven or any of that. If it were up to me I'd never make it. But forgiveness and heaven and all that is God's free gift to me—because of Jesus."

"That's better," sighed my teacher. "Please don't forget it again."

"I won't," I promised. And I won't.

287

I WANT TO **KNOW**

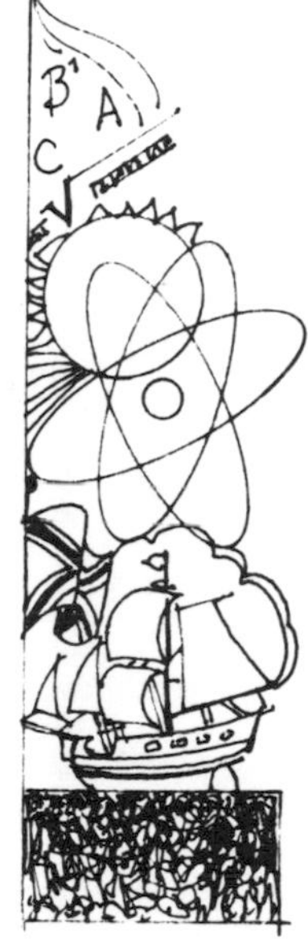

Today in school we learned about molecules. We also read a poem about ships, talked about the Civil War, worked some very complicated math problems, and practiced techniques of putting on makeup in drama class. (I got to do a beard!) Maybe I got all my essential vitamins and minerals at breakfast this morning. I'm not sure. But for some reason, I felt completely and totally alive during every one of those classes. I understood everything everyone said, and I wanted to know more.

I want to know if people will ever be able to control molecules with their minds so they can walk through walls and float through the air. I want to know how a poet thinks when he or she is putting a poem together. I want to know exactly why wars start so that I can figure out how to prevent them. I want to be able to toss math formulas around in my mind like a juggler. And I want to learn how to act.

There are so many things I want to know that I'll never be able to fit them into one life. And how will I ever decide on a career? Why, whatever I choose, there'll be hundreds and hundreds I don't choose. And the way I feel today, I want to try all of them.

Most of all, though, I want to **know** things. Please help me learn, God. And then please help me put my knowledge to good use.

288

WE CAN'T MOVE!

I think my world is coming to an end. Literally. Dad came home tonight and announced that his company might be transferring him to another city.

"Say you won't go," I told him right away.

"It's not as easy as that, Monkey," he said. (Sometimes he calls me Monkey when he's trying to be gentle with me.) "I'll spare you the gory details, but you can take my word for it that if they say I have to go, I'll have to go. Either that or find a new job."

"Couldn't you find a new job?" I suggested hopefully. "You're awfully smart."

"Thanks for the vote of confidence," said my dad. But he didn't say he'd look for another job if his company wants him to move.

So here I am, wide awake in the middle of the night and scared stiff that we might have to move. I **like** it here! I know people here. I like them too. I even love some of them. I have my special places, my school, my church. Sure, I could find new people and new places. But I don't want to. I want to keep the ones I have. What a crummy world this is!

No, it's not. I really do know better than that, God, no matter how scared and upset I may be feeling. It's Your world and You're all over it. You'd be with me in another place just as much as You are here. But, O God, I don't want to go! Please, please, help me make it through this.

289

TAKING FOR GRANTED

We aren't moving. My dad's company has decided to expand its facilities here instead of opening new ones in another city. I sure am glad they made up their minds so quickly. I couldn't have stood worrying about the possibility of moving for weeks and weeks. I'm so relieved!

And yet I've learned something too. I've learned how precious the people and places and things that play a part in my everyday life are to me. Most of the time I just take them for granted. Good old house. Good old school. Good old church. Good old Emily Sue Schmidlapp. Now that I almost lost them, I feel as if they're made of pure gold. Even Emily Sue Schmidlapp.

The scary thing is that someday my life **will** change. I'll grow up and move away. Or everybody else will move away and I'll be here without them. My life isn't going to stay the way it is forever. One thing's for sure though. God won't change. And His love won't change either. I can depend on that.

My family and friends? I won't take them for granted anymore. I don't think I'll ever forget the way I felt yesterday.

God, I thank You for Your never-changing love for me. And I thank You for my life just the way it is.

290

I CAN'T CONCENTRATE

I don't know what's the matter with me. I seem to have lost all control over my mind. No matter how hard I try, I can't get it to stick to any one thing. It's all over the place, thinking first about this, then that, then something else. Nothing important either. Just little stuff. I wonder if I'm going crazy.

No, I know what's wrong. I've been concentrating too much lately. My personal problems, my friends' problems, my schoolwork—it's all too much. I'm like a computer on overload. And in a minute I'm going to spit everything I know all over the floor.

Well, maybe I won't do that either. Actually what I need is a tiny vacation, just enough to get my brain functioning again. I think one day would do it. But my parents would never let me take a day off from school. It's unheard of. Isn't it?

I asked them. I told them how I was feeling and how I thought just one day off might really help. And would you believe they said yes? They really did!

Oh, I'm going to sleep and sleep and then eat a huge breakfast and lunch all at once and then go for a walk and then just lie around and **be**. I'm not going to even try to concentrate on anything.

Thank You, God, for such understanding parents. Please let my day off glue my concentration back together again.

291

THE BUM

This evening we went to a restaurant in the city for dinner. On the way we saw a bum. He was standing on a street corner (well, actually he was leaning against a building), and since we had to wait for a traffic light, I got a chance to take a close look at him.

I guess he must have been about 40 or 50 years old. It was hard to tell. His clothes were much too big for him and old and falling apart. He looked cold too, although it wasn't all that chilly. I don't think he'd shaved for days. And he just stood there, with nothing in his hands, staring off into space.

Then the traffic light changed, and we started to move. And just at that moment the bum looked up, right into my eyes, smiled a very small smile, and waved at me. Without even thinking I smiled and waved back. And that was all.

But was it, God? How long do You suppose it had been since anyone smiled or waved at that man? Couldn't it be just enough to give him the courage he needs to go someplace where people can help him? I really hope so, God. I hope that's how You work sometimes—through tiny things.

292

DISAPPOINTED

Tonight, by some strange coincidence, we drove past that same corner where I saw the bum last night. He was still there, and he didn't look one bit different. I just glanced at him and then turned my head. I was so disappointed. I thought You were going to **do** something about him, God. I thought You were going to use a smile and and wave to change his life.

Well, I guess that was my idea, wasn't it? Not Yours. Maybe You have a reason for him to stand there. Or maybe he's just not ready for

You to change his life yet. I don't pretend to understand. But I'm still disappointed.

Maybe I'm just being selfish. Maybe I wanted to be able to think of myself as some big hero or do-gooder who changed the life of some poor bum. Maybe I wasn't thinking of the bum at all. No, that's not true either. I was thinking of him. But maybe I was thinking of myself a lot too.

Hey, I just caught a little glimmer of something, God. Why do You have to do whatever it is You're going to do according to **my** time schedule? I mean, here I am, some kid (Your kid) demanding that You get busy and do what I want You to do exactly when I want You to do it—and that means overnight.

I'm **sorry** about that, God! I guess I just got carried away. Well, how would it be if I just sort of handed that bum over to You and left it up to You how You wanted to handle him? That's what I'm going to do, God. And I promise that this time I won't be disappointed!

293

WHAT TO PRAY FOR

I was talking to this girl in school the other day, and she told me a story about something that happened to her. I want to write it down so I won't forget it, because someday the same thing might happen to me.

This girl was in the hospital for an operation—a big one. Before the operation she prayed to God to keep her safe and to make the surgery go all right. He answered that prayer, and later in the day she was back in her own room. But she was in pretty much pain. The nurse told her she'd had a pain shot already and she'd have to wait at least another hour before she could have another one.

So the girl decided to pray about her pain. But then she couldn't think of what to say. She couldn't see much point in asking God to make the pain go away because she knew a certain amount of pain was part of having surgery. She didn't want to ask Him to help her bear the pain bravely because, frankly, she didn't feel like being brave.

Just at that moment her minister came in to see her, so she told him about her problem.

"You don't have to tell God what to do or ask Him for anything," said her minister. "Make it a simple prayer. Just say, 'God, I hurt.'"

So that's what the girl did, and almost immediately she fell asleep.

I think that's wonderful. I really do!

294

SHE'S NOT **ME**

There's a girl in my class at school who I think I could really help. She certainly needs **someone** to help her. First of all she wears the strangest clothes, different from what everyone else wears. They don't look like cheap clothes either, so I don't think she has a financial problem. I think she just doesn't know any better.

She wears her hair in a funny style too, sort of twisted around and up, but with part of it hanging down too. I've never seen anyone with a hairdo like that before.

And this girl is always hanging around the library. Before school, after school, and during free periods. I mean, libraries are neat and all, but too much is too much of anything.

I suppose this girl has some friends, but not nearly as many as I do. Maybe if I just talked to her I could give her some hints about how to change.

No. Wait a minute. I just read what I wrote, and I think I'm completely off base. What business is it of mine to try to change this girl just so she'll be more like me? Maybe she doesn't **want** to be like me. Or like any of the other girls or guys either. Maybe she's perfectly happy being herself.

I talked to my mom about it, and she says I **am** off base. She says one thing Christians have to be very careful about is not to become The Helping Hand That Strikes Again. That's someone who thinks he or she has all the answers and tries to force them on innocent victims. Please, God, don't let me fall into **that** trap!

295

MY VALUES

People talk a lot about values these days. There are even little tests or exercises we do in school to help find out what our values are and how much they mean to us. I guess you could define a value as something you believe in enough to make part of your life. And if that's the case, then my values are pretty much tied up with my religion.

That gets a little tricky in school because we aren't supposed to talk about religion. I haven't figured out a way yet to explain what I mean about forgiveness without bringing religion and Jesus into it. But then most kids know I'm a religious person, so I guess they have a general idea of what I'm talking about anyway.

One of the most important things I've learned about values is that they aren't real unless you are willing to stand up for them and live by them. They might be opinions or guesses or something, but they're not values.

Well, I **try** to live by my Christian values and sometimes, with God's help, I even manage to do it. But sometimes I don't. And that's why as a Christian I'm glad I have that special value thrown in—forgiveness. I couldn't get along without it!

296

INSIDE-NESS AND OUTSIDE-NESS

This happens to be a perfect time of year for inside-ness and outside-ness. And what are inside-ness and outside-ness, you may ask. Never fear. I will tell you.

Inside-ness is what you see when you're outside and it's just getting dark and you look through a lighted window. (It's best to do this at your own house. You can get in big trouble looking through other people's lighted windows.) Inside-ness is what you long for when your nose is red and your hands are blue and your legs feel like they're going to drop off your body. Inside-ness is what you feel when you walk through the door and know that you're home at last. Inside-ness is also what you feel when you're curled up in a chair with a good book and a cup of cocoa and the sleet is tapping outside the window.

Outside-ness is what you see when you wake up and pull back the curtain and the sky is as blue and clean as a brand-new mixing bowl. Outside-ness is what you long for when you've been doing homework too long and your head feels like a box of stale crackers. Outside-ness is what you feel when you step through the door and take a huge breath of air so cold and sharp that it makes your nose hurt. Outside-ness is also what you feel when you run races with October winds and slide through leaves and scare the squirrels busy burying that last nut.

I praise You, God, for inside-ness and outside-ness. I'm glad we've got them both.

297

MY COUNTRY

These days you don't see too many people running around waving flags and making speeches about their country being the best. I think we've realized that people in every country had better learn to get along if we don't want to end up one big mushroom-shaped cloud. (At least I **hope** we've realized that.) But I think most people still are proud of their own country and glad that they live there. I know I am.

I like the way government works in my country. It makes some bad mistakes at times (or the people in it do), but at least technically it's there to serve us and not the other way around. I'm glad that someday I'll have something to say about what people are in charge of it too.

I also like the way my country seems to care about people in other countries. Yeah, we get greedy at times and do some pretty rotten stuff for money. But when there's a disaster of any sort, we're usually right there, ready to help. That's something to be proud of.

Actually, God, I'm very thankful that You let me be born in my country. I don't know if it's the best one in the world, but I think it's the best one for me. Take care of it, God. Keep it strong, keep it honest, and keep it caring.

298

THAT PERSON WITHOUT A FAMILY

Up the street from us lives a lady all by herself. I don't know what she does for a living, but every morning she gets in her car and drives to her job, and every evening she comes home again to that little house where she lives all by herself. I almost never see anyone come to see her. I don't understand why either. She seems like a very nice lady. At least she always smiles and says hi to me when I see her.

Maybe she's shy. The world isn't such an easy place for shy people. Most of the time you have to go to other people instead of waiting for them to come to you.

Of course it could be that this lady is perfectly happy being by herself most of the time. (I do have to be careful not to act like The Helping Hand That Strikes Again.) But I think she might enjoy being with a family **sometimes.**

I think I'll ask my mom if we can have her over for dinner sometime. My mom's awfully good at making shy people feel at ease.

Do You think this is a good thing to do, God? Share my family a little bit with someone who doesn't have one?

299

HAIR

I once read a poem in which this guy said he felt despair whenever he thought about human hair. I can't understand why. I think hair is super (unless it's clogging the drain or in your food or waiting to be washed).

First of all, hair looks nice. Even scroungy hair looks better than no hair at all, especially on kids. I don't mean to insult bald people, but even they usually have a little nubbly of hair, at least around the eyebrows.

The next thing hair does is keep you warm, especially when you've just accidentally left that lovely purple cap your Aunt Henrietta knitted for you someplace under your bed.

Third, hair feels good. It feels good when you're running and the wind's streaking it out behind you. It feels good when you've waited too long to wash it and the first blast of hot water hits it. It feels good when it's all squeaky clean and you know you don't have to go through that again for a while.

On the whole, I think hair was a very good idea. Thank You, God.

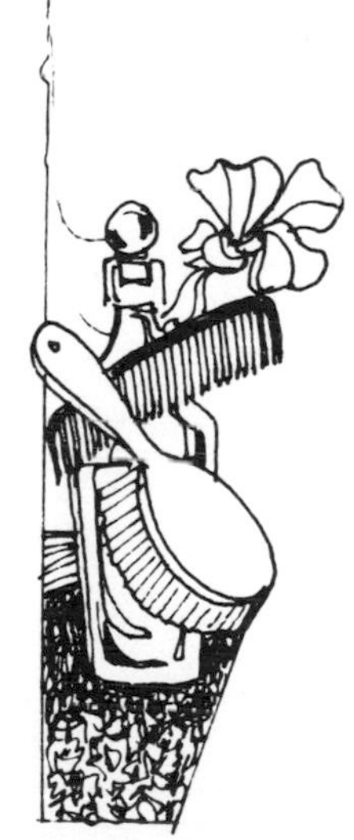

300

A LOST CHANCE

That lady up the street—the one who lives by herself and who I wanted mom to invite over for dinner—has moved. Apparently she got a better job in another city. And I guess she didn't have anything—or anyone—to keep her here.

In a way that makes me sort of sad. Now I'll never get to know her. She might have been a tremendously interesting person or a tremendously kind person or just an average nice person, but now I'll never know. I waited too long and lost my chance. She'll never know me either or what it's like to be with my family. She'll never know that those people down the street did care about her.

Well, what my grandma would say is "don't cry over spilt milk—but don't spill any more either." Wise old grandma! No, I won't cry, but I will keep my eyes open a little wider for other people who might be potential friends. And I'll do something else too.

God, please go with that lady. Help her make lots of friends in her new city. And even whe she **is** by herself, help her know that she's not alone, that You're with her.

301

MY WAY

Today a group of us were supposed to work together on a project at school. And I made the most dreadful discovery about myself. I didn't like working with those other people. I wanted to do the project **my** way. The thing is, I could just **see** how that project should turn out, what it should look like at the end. And the others weren't seeing that at all. They were still asking a bunch of dumb questions about the beginning.

Well, I think I handled it all right. I didn't act bossy and tell the others exactly what we should do. I didn't go off in a corner and sulk either. I just made gentle suggestions as we went along, and actually the project did turn out sort of the way I'd pictured it. Sort of, but not exactly. I think I could have done it better alone.

And maybe there's nothing wrong about my feeling that way. Some things **can** be done better by one person. I mean, who ever heard of a committee writing a poem? Or painting a picture? Maybe sometimes we should do things alone.

I think I understand myself, God. And I think my feelings are okay. But I know there are going to be times when I have to work with other people. Help me to forget about **my** way then. Help me think more about the others in the group than about the project. I guess that's what's called putting first things first.

302

TV

People say that kids these days are slaves to TV. They say that TV fills our heads with silly ideas and crazy commercials and turns us into zombies. They say that kids don't read anymore. Frankly, I think they talk too much!

Yeah, I do know some kids who are hooked to their TV sets. But most of those kids have bad problems that have nothing to do with TV. They use TV to get away from their problems. I'm not saying that's good, but it's not fair to blame TV for the problems either.

Furthermore, most kids know what's silly on TV and what isn't. If they watch the silly stuff, it's just because they feel like seeing something silly, not because they think the silly stuff is true. Most of us watch good stuff too, like the National Geographic programs. I just wish there were more good programs like that on.

I don't think the commercials influence us either, at least not any more than they influence adults. If I want a dirt bike, it's because a friend of mine has a dirt bike and it looks like a lot of fun. A TV commercial could tell me I **didn't** want a dirt bike, but I wouldn't believe it.

I also happen to know a lot of kids who read. Sometimes they even read to learn more about stuff they say on TV first. Of course many kids have problems with reading. But that's not TV's fault either.

After all, when you get right down to it, a TV set is nothing more than a box. You can turn it on, you can turn it off, and you can choose what channel you're going to watch. **You're** in charge, not the TV.

God, I'm glad we've got TV. You might help it get a little better but please don't get rid of it.

303

WHAT I READ

And now, just to prove to those people who say all kids watch TV too much, I'm going to write about some of the stuff I like to read.

Sometimes I like to read the problem books that people are writing for kids now. You know, they're the books about drugs or child abuse or stuff like that. Usually I try out one book by an author, and then, if I think he or she really has something to say, I read every book by him or her that I can get my hands on. (I sure wish we had a shorter way of saying he or she and him or her!)

The other kind of book that seems to be very big these days is fantasy. Judging by the people I know, you either love fantasy or hate it. I happen to love it. Most fantasy tells a story about good overcoming evil in some way. I find that very reassuring. I also like to see the tricky ways the author makes it happen. And I like to read about make-believe places and creatures.

I like to read old books too. Not too long ago I discovered the E. Nesbit books. In a way I guess they're fantasy too, but it's a different sort of fantasy. It sort of pops right into the middle of daily life and changes things around.

God, I'm glad You made some people to be writers, and I'm especially glad that You made some people to be writers for kids. I feel as if I really **know** some of those writers. So I guess I'm really saying thank You for friends!

304

MY PAST

Some people say that they're haunted by ghosts. Well, I never ran into one of those critters and I hope I never do. But sometimes I do feel haunted too. By my past.

I start thinking about all the things I've done and all the things I haven't done, and pretty soon I get depressed because it doesn't seem that I've made a very good job out of my life so far.

I tried explaining all this to my grandma one time, and she said I needed a good dose of cod-liver oil. Sometimes my grandma isn't too understanding.

On the other hand, maybe she understands too well. Maybe she's just trying to tell me that I'm being downright silly to spend perfectly good time worrying about what's in the past.

However, I don't really think I want to completely forget my past. I have some very good memories. And some of the bad things I remember taught me important lessons I don't want to forget. But maybe the good memories and the learning memories are the ones I should concentrate on.

God, please help me live my present in such a way that when it becomes my past I'll want to remember it. And please help me remember right now that all the messing up I did in the past is forgiven. And that forgiveness is final!

All Saints' Day

PEOPLE OF THE PAST

Today is a special day on the church calendar. It's called All Saints' Day, and it's the day we remember all those Christians who lived in the past and helped give us the church we have today. "They were faithful so that we might be faithful," somebody famous once said, and I think that sort of sums up what All Saints' Day is about.

There were the earliest Christians, of course, the ones who really struggled with the birth of a new church in spite of a hostile world, persecutions, and sometimes even death. Their faith must have been incredibly strong and powerful, and they must have felt very close to

Jesus. I think it must have been wonderful to be a Christian then, although I'm not sure I would have been brave enough. Anyway, I thank God for them.

Then there were the people who over the years gave us our great church music and prayers. People like Gregory and Bach, Martin Luther and Thomas Cranmer. I wish I knew more about them. All I really know is the gifts they've given us. But those are really special gifts, and I think they've done a lot to comfort us and keep our faith strong.

Then there were the great preachers, the scholars, the artists, and the poets. They turned their special gifts over to God too, and He used them in the building of His church.

And finally there were all the ordinary people, the ones who swept the church or kept the books or arranged the flowers or just told one other person about their faith. Most of the saints were ordinary people like that, I suppose. People like me. But God used their gifts too, and together they helped build this mighty church. I feel especially close to them today, God. And I thank You for every one of them.

306

I MISUNDERSTOOD

Today I got very angry with a friend of mine. We ended up practically screaming at each other and having a huge fight. Fortunately we went on fighting long enough for both of us to come to our senses and ask the simple questions, "What are we fighting about?" That's when we discovered that I had simply misunderstood something my friend said. He didn't mean at all what I thought he meant. But I hadn't taken time to really listen to what he said. I just got mad.

I apologized, and my friend said, "Oh, that's okay. I probably should have been a little clearer." But of course it wasn't his fault at all. It was mine. And the whole thing made me wonder how many other times I've gotten angry with people or felt hurt just because I misunderstood something they said or did.

God, You gave me ears and a brain for a very good reason. You expect me to use them. Help me to use them a little better. Help me really listen to what people are saying and really think about it before I fly off the handle. Then maybe I won't have to fly off the handle at all.

307

PSALMS

I'm still trying to read the whole Bible (sooner or later). My minister said that one of the books I could probably handle on my own is the Psalms. So for the past few days I've been reading them.

I'm getting a lot out of them too. It's amazing that people who lived so long ago could have feelings that are almost exactly like mine. Especially feelings of great praise and thankfulness. Or great sorrow and need for comfort.

What I've been wondering is why more people don't write psalms today. Psalms are such a good way (and such a beautiful way) to talk to God and about Him. I don't see why religious publishers don't put out more books of psalms written by people living now. Maybe when I get a little older I'll write a book like that.

In the meantime, though, I've been writing some psalms of my own. They're just kid-psalms, God, but they really do come from my heart. Do You like them?

308

GOOD SHEPHERDS

My pastor preached the neatest sermon recently about Jesus as the Good Shepherd. He said that when people think about Jesus as the Good Shepherd, they always picture themselves as the sheep, sort of dumb and helpless. And of course without Jesus we **are** sort of dumb and helpless.

But, said my pastor, once we become followers of Jesus and become part of His church, His body on earth, He calls us to be more than sheep. He wants us to be shepherds too. He wants us to go out and care for the people who don't yet know Him. He wants us to gently lead those people into His fold, like good shepherds would.

I really like that idea. It makes me feel as if I have a **purpose** or something. Thanks, God, for giving me such a wise pastor.

309

THE PHOTOGRAPH

The other day a photographer came to school to talk to our class and show us some of her work. She's not one of those photographers who takes pictures of current events or school classes or families all sitting together. She says she tries to take pictures that say more than just the picture itself.

I wasn't sure what she was talking about until she showed us some of the pictures she has taken. Then I understood very well. One of the pictures meant so much to me that I almost asked her if I could buy it—except it probably cost more money than I have.

It was a picture of an old woman. She looked like she was thinking. She certainly wasn't smiling one of those big cheesy smiles for the camera. But her face was covered with wrinkles, and every one of those wrinkles told me exactly the kind of person she was and the kind of life she had lived. Because every one of those wrinkles were smile wrinkles. They went up instead of down, and they were one of the most beautiful things I've ever seen. They made me want to try to be just like her so I'd have wrinkles like that when I was old.

Thank You, God, for putting such a beautiful person on this earth. And thank You for getting her together with a photographer who was smart enough to see how beautiful she was.

310

THE GAPER BLOCK

My folks and I were supposed to go to some friends' for dinner this evening. But we got stuck on the highway and were almost half an hour late. It seems there was a bad automobile accident up ahead of us. Several people were hurt. But it wasn't the accident itself that held up traffic. It was all the people who stopped or slowed down to **watch**. They call it a gaper block.

When my folks and I finally drove by the accident (we could only go about 10 miles an hour because of all the spectators who were still standing around), an ambulance had taken the victims away. But we could hear the spectators talking.

"Sure wasn't much blood."

"Yeah, but that one guy was hurt pretty bad. I bet he doesn't make it."

God, they were enjoying themselves! I don't think I'll ever understand human nature. No person should enjoy the sight of another person's pain. But judging from the size of that gaper block, there are a lot of people attracted to tragedy for the wrong reasons.

God, I'd like to think I was Christian enough to understand those kind of people. But I'm not. Maybe someday I'll understand how people can feed on the pain of others. For now, though, please don't let me become like them.

311

WE TOUCHED

A beautiful thing happened at school this week. The weather wasn't bad so we were outside playing games, boys and girls both. Another kid and I were sitting along the sidelines, waiting for our turn to play, when three things happened almost at once. A bird swooped down over the field, singing its little heart out. The sun came out in one of those bright bursts that seem so rare in November. And this other kid, whom I don't know very well, reached out at the same moment I did and we touched hands, just for an instant.

It didn't have any big significant meaning, that touch. Just that we were two human beings, sitting there on the ground and somehow related. That's all. And yet that's enough. I felt warm and somehow comforted for the rest of the day.

Thank You, God, for those rare and wonderful moments when we touch.

312

A GREAT TIME FOR FEET

This is it, world. I hope you're ready. Because I have decreed today National Feet Day. And when you start paying a little attention to feet, well, you never know what might happen.

My feet and I met quite early this morning. They were sticking out of one end of the bed. I was sticking out of the other.

"Hey, feet!" I said.

"Cold," said my feet.

So I quickly snuggled them into some woolly bedroom slippers.

"That's more like it," said my feet.

They stayed burrowed in those slippers all through breakfast. But then I gave them a real treat. A nice piping hot shower. Well, they got so pink and pleased and grateful looking that I felt sort of bad I didn't do that for them more often.

After they were dressed and the rest of me was too, I took them outside, and that's when they really knew it was National Feet Day. Ice. One puddle of ice after another.

"This is living!" yelled my feet.

"Think nothing of it," said I.

But I still had one more treat in mind for them. Soccer. Even my coach seemed to know it was National Feet Day and decided to cooperate.

"Hot ziggety!" shouted my feet as they hit the field. And those little rascals kicked three goals. They made me a hero. You can't help but have a warm, tender feeling for feet like that.

I thank You, God, for feet!

313

SHOULD I TELL?

There's something very wrong going on at school. I'm not directly involved in it, but I know the kids who are, and I have no idea how to handle the whole situation. You see, the principal should know. This thing should be stopped. But I don't want to be the one to tell.

Telling on other kids—no matter what they're doing—seems such a low thing to do. I don't think I'd be able to look myself—or them—in the eye if I did it. And yet they might hurt themselves or someone else by what they're doing. Oh, it's a mess!

I suppose I could talk to the kids themselves, tell them how wrong and dangerous I think their actions are. But, frankly, they'd probably just laugh at me. Kids don't listen to other kids very well.

I suppose I could talk to my parents too. But they might march right out and call the principal themselves. Adults have a way of sticking together like that. And that would make me feel the same as if I told the principal.

Maybe I'll talk to some of my friends, other kids I know don't approve of what's going on. Maybe together we'll be able to figure out something to do.

Help us with this problem, God. Help us know the right thing to do. Then give us the courage to do it.

314

THE DUMB KID

There's one kid in our class that everybody calls The Dumb Kid. He knows we call him that, and it doesn't seem to bother him at all. He just grins and says, "Yeah." "Yeah" is one of the two things he says. The other one is "I don't get it." (He says that one a lot.)

He's a nice kid, The Dumb Kid is, and everyone likes him. But he is just so incredibly **dumb**. It's hard to believe he's gotten this far in school. I think teacher after teacher has passed him along because none of them know what to do with him, and they feel sort of sorry for him.

I was talking to my mom about The Dumb Kid today, and she said we might not be doing him a favor by calling him that.

"I know he doesn't **mind**," she said. "But names can be pretty potent things. People start trying to live up to them. They **see** themselves as their names. And you sure haven't given this kid much to live up to."

"Yeah, I guess you're right," I said. I was thinking how I might act if all my life people had called me Big Mouth. Or The Klutz.

Names are potent, aren't they, God? Like the name Christian. That one means a lot to me. It means I am a follower of Christ, Your Son, the One who gave His life for me that I might have Your forgiveness. I sure try to live up to it. So maybe I'll start calling this kid by his real name. If I can just remember what it is.

315

JEALOUS

A friend of mine at school has been given a job—a position—that I wanted very much. The teachers made the decision, and they chose this girl instead of me. I'm not surprised that I feel terribly disappointed. I have every right to be disappointed because I really wanted that job. What does bother me is that I feel jealous, horribly jealous, of this girl. And I think jealousy is one of the worst feelings I have ever known.

Whenever I even see the girl, the words pop into my head, "Why not me? Why not me?" I tell myself that I deserved the job every bit as much as she did, maybe more. I even find myself hoping that she'll fail at it, just so everyone will know that they made the wrong decision.

I read somewhere that jealousy eats away at you. That's the perfect description. I can feel it gnawing at my insides.

O God, I don't **want** to feel like this! I don't want to be jealous of my friend. I wish I'd never even heard of the job. Please, God, help me get over this jealousy. Help me be honestly happy for her and content with the things I do have. Jealousy is a very destructive feeling, God. I want to be rid of it!

316

MOTHER, MAY I?

Sometimes I get so tired of having to ask my parents for permission to do something. It seems so humiliating. Sometimes I want to be able to make my own decisions and to do what I think is right without having to check with anyone else. After all, I'm **not** a little child anymore.

There. I feel better having got that all out of my system. Now maybe I can look at the whole thing more objectively. That's one thing I've learned recently—to look at things objectively (well, at least sometimes).

My parents are not tyrants. Actually they give me a lot of freedom to make my own decisions. It's just certain things they want me to ask permission for before I do them. And I can even see why. They aren't totally convinced that I'm ready to handle those things on my own yet. The problems start when I think I **am** ready.

Does there have to be a problem? Couldn't we just talk every so often about what I am and what I am not ready to handle on my own? And if I do disagree with them about something—well—does it have to be such a big deal? Couldn't I just do it their way for a while longer because I love them and know they love me?

Now that's what I call being objective. Don't You think so, God? But now that I figured out how I should handle these situations, please give me the patience and the wisdom to do it.

317

THE PARABLES ARE **HARD**

I've been reading the Bible again, this time parts of the gospels. I thought the parables would be fun to read. You know, nice, simple little stories? Well, they're not nice, simple little stories. They're hard.

Take the one in Matthew about the workers in the vineyard. Those guys that worked just a little bit of time got paid just as much as the ones who'd worked all day. Now to me that doesn't seem fair. I'd think the men who worked all day deserved more than those who worked just one hour. Surely they earned more than those who barely got started.

Hey, that rings a bell! Earned! God's kingdom is a gift. We don't **earn** it. By ourselves we aren't able to earn it. Christ has done that for us. My pastor says God distributes the gifts of His kingdom according to His good will. The thief on the cross was promised salvation just as all of God's faithful followers in the Old Testament had been promised salvation. Is that fair? No, not according to human standards. But I'm glad that's the way it is. I guess God's way of being "unfair" is better than human ways of being fair.

Anyway, the parables are hard. But I have a funny feeling that to understand them, what you have to do is look the hard part right in the eye. I think that might be where the real message is. And once you get to the real message, it's worth the hard part.

318

THEY CHOSE **ME** TO BE LEADER

It's amazing. It's unbelievable. It's scary. Some kids at school chose **me** to be the leader of our group. Me! What do I know about being a leader? Oh, sure, I've always dreamed about what a great thing it would be to have power and be able to order other people around and stuff like that. But now that I **am** a leader, I don't think it's going to be much like my dreams.

Leaders can't do whatever they want—at least not good leaders. They're responsible for all the people they're leading. They have to think over every decision they make and figure out what will be best for everybody. If they make a mistake, a lot of people will have to pay for it too. Good grief, that **is** scary.

I don't think I'll ever look at other leaders in quite the same way again. I mean leaders like the people in government. Or even the principal of our school. I never **dreamed** how much pressure there was!

Well, God, I'm one of them now. Not a big leader, but a leader all the same. And in a way, it's just like everything else in my life. I won't be able to do it without You. Please, God, help me be a good leader.

319

ACCIDENTS

I had an accident today. Just a little one. I slipped in the bathroom and banged my elbow against the basin. It hurt like fury for a while, but what bothered me more was what **could** have happened. I could have slipped a little further and hit my head instead of my elbow. I could have given myself a concussion. I could have . . . but it doesn't make much sense to go on thinking like this. I simply hit my elbow, and the next time I'll be more careful in the bathroom.

Maybe there is something else to think about, though. Accidents in general. Some of them we can prevent by being more careful. But some we can't do a thing about. They just happen to us because of what other people do or what's going on in nature or something. Those are the really scary kind of accidents because we don't have any control over them.

Maybe what I've got to learn is that I'll never be in control of everything. Only one person is that. God. So maybe I'd better just be careful in situations where I can prevent an accident and leave the rest up to Him.

Right, God?

320

WHO DO I WORSHIP?

It suddenly occurred to me that if somebody asked me to describe this God I worship—and didn't let me use any God words like "all-powerful" or "all-knowing"—I'd have a hard time saying what I meant. I don't really have any clear-cut picture of God in my mind. Instead I have a sort of collage of pictures, and I focus on the particular part of it that I need at a particular time.

For example. I don't think of God as some white-bearded old man in the sky. But I do think of Him as a father. I talk to Him the way a child would talk to a father. And yet sometimes I think of Him as a mother too.

I think of Him as a Spirit, but how do you describe a spirit? I could use words like "warm," "loving," "strong," "trustworthy." But those words don't exactly paint a picture. They describe feelings. And maybe that's part of my problem, part of the reason I can't describe God very well. A lot of the time I don't picture Him at all. I just feel Him.

Of course there's not a person on this earth who could really describe You, God. You're too big, too great, too **everything** for us to even imagine. But sometimes it's fun to try to describe just a little part of You.

321

MYSTERIES

Thinking about how I might describe God made me wonder how I might describe the way God works. I'm thinking about things like Holy Communion or Baptism or forgiveness or salvation. When I get right down to it, I have to admit that I don't completely understand how any of those things work. I might understand some parts of them, but never the whole thing.

My pastor calls things like that mysteries, and for a long time I thought that meant I wasn't even allowed to think about them, that God might get mad at me for being too curious. But that's not true. God doesn't purposely keep secrets from us. It's just that there are some things we aren't able to understand. We simply believe them.

It was like that in Bible times too. Jesus was no secret, at least not after a while. But a lot of people didn't understand Him or who He was. For one reason or another they weren't ready to understand. But that doesn't mean that God doesn't want them to.

So, God, I'll go on thinking about these mysteries of Yours. I may never understand any of them completely. But I will grow in faith in You as I learn more of You—with Your help.

322

MONEY

Someplace I heard that it says in the Bible, "Money is the root of all evil." I accepted that, but what I couldn't understand was why, if it was true, all the churches didn't get together and try to ban money. I also sort of wondered what we'd use in its place. Exchanging one thing for another might have been okay in the good old days, but I don't see how it could work now. What would you give to a hospital in exchange for an operation? Twenty years worth of free tomatoes you'd grown? In its way, money is definitely convenient.

Anyway, I found out recently that what the Bible (in 1 Timothy 6:10) really says is, "The **love** of money is the root of all evil." Now **that** makes sense. Loving money messes people up. Sometimes they get to love it so much that it means more to them than anything else—other people, their beliefs, anything. They make a god of money, and they'll do anything for that god.

I don't think you have to have a lot of money to make a god of it either. You can just love money in general, even the money you haven't got. You can wish too hard that you had more and think all your problems would be solved if you had it.

I don't know if I'll ever have a lot of money or not, God. But, please, don't ever let me love it. Love is too precious a thing to waste on money. Let me save it for people—and You.

323

MY SOUL

I am always hearing about my soul, reading about my soul, praying about my soul, even singing about my soul. And yet, when you come right down to it, I haven't the vaguest idea what my soul is.

Okay. My soul is that part of me that will go to heaven someday, even though the rest of me turns to dust. (Blah!) And yet it also says in the Bible that I will have a new and perfect body at the resurrection. My soul will get together with my body again, and I will live with Jesus because His resurrection has guaranteed eternal life.

You know, I **do** have a picture of my soul, but it's so silly that I've never told anyone about it. I don't know where I got this picture, but I see my soul as sort of a white filmy handkerchief. Isn't that **weird**?

Well, maybe it's no more weird than some of the other pictures people have come up with for souls. I saw a painting once that showed the soul as a little tiny version of the person—same clothes and all.

I guess we'd better face it, God, that You're the only one who knows very much about souls. Maybe we'd just better be content with the fact that we have them—and that they're Yours.

324

SNOW

It's here! The first snow of the year. When I woke up this morning and saw that gorgeous white stuff all over the ground, I wanted to run right outside in my pajamas, scoop up an armful, and yell, "Welcome back!" (I didn't.)

I sure wish everyone in the world could have snow—at least once a year. My mom has a friend who lives in southern Texas, and they hardly ever get snow. One night though they did get some, about an inch. At five o'clock in the morning my mother's friend and her husband were awakened by the doorbell. They opened the door and there stood all the kids in the neighborhood.

"Please," said one of the kids. "We want to make a snowman, but it's going to take all the snow on the block to do it. Could we have yours?"

I think that's really touching. Of course, one good thing about our modern world is that many people travel more, so more people that live in warm places can come up north and see snow now and then. But that's not the same as having your **own** snow.

To me, snow is like winter giving the earth a big, soft hug. It cleans everything up, quiets it down, and makes it beautiful. What more could you ask from a hug?

God, I praise You for snow!

325

THAT PERSON IN THE MIRROR

Have you ever been walking along, in a store or someplace like that, and all of a sudden you see someone who looks sort of neat or nice or strange. You look a little closer and suddenly you realize that that person you're looking at is **you** in a mirror. It's a very strange and unsettling feeling.

The first time that happened to me, I saw this person and thought, "Boy, does that kid have bad posture." You'd better believe I worked on my posture after that! But still, every time I catch an unexpected glimpse of myself in a mirror, I learn something new about me—sometimes good and sometimes bad.

I wish there were inside mirrors too, the kind that would show what you're **like** as well as how you look. I bet I'd learn a lot about myself from one of those too. I might also get pretty depressed.

In a way church acts like that kind of mirror. A sermon or a hymn or maybe even a prayer will touch on something that suddenly makes you think, "Hey, that's me!" And to tell the truth, it isn't always a bad thing that you see.

I'm not sure where all this is leading, God, except I guess I'm saying that I'm grateful for all the opportunities You give me to grow.

326

I'LL NEVER NAG

It is a sad but true fact that sometimes my mom nags. She will ask me or my dad to do something five times when both of us had every intention of doing it after the first time, although maybe not at that exact minute. I suspect mom doesn't mean to nag. Maybe she doesn't even realize she's doing it. But she does. And it's a habit I never intend to get.

Sure. I can remember when I was about seven and watching the older kids. "Boy, those kids are so dumb," I thought. "All they care about is clothes and dumb stuff like that. **I'm** never going to be like that. Not **me**!" And look at me. Saving my allowance just so I can get the right kind of tennis shoes, the kind everyone's wearing.

I have a feeling that it is very dangerous to say that you will never do something. Never is a big long word even though it has only five letters. Probably my mom used to listen to her mom nagging and say to herself, "**I'll** never do that."

Anyway, she doesn't nag **all** the time. Just now and then. Maybe she does it when she's tired. I hadn't thought of that before.

God, all of this reminds me of a sign I once saw. It was a sign with a prayer on it, and I think I'd better say that prayer right now: "God, please make my words sweet and tender today because tomorrow I may have to eat them."

327

CAN I LIVE UP TO THEIR DREAMS FOR ME?

Last night I made the big mistake of asking my parents what they thought when I was born. These are some of the things they told me:

"Well, we were awfully glad to see you, of course. And right away we started having dreams for you. We weren't sure if we wanted you to run the country or write a great novel or discover a cure for some awful disease. Most of all we wanted you to grow up to be a happy, loving, Christian person. We wanted you to have a good life, and we wanted your life to accomplish some good for others."

"Is that all?" I said. I mean, good grief! No kid can live up to dreams like that. Nobody's going to be happy all the time or loving or even Christian.

"I'm afraid you're in for a big disappointment," I said to my parents.

"I don't think so," said my dad. "You see, we did realize that we gave birth to a human kid, not an angel. We didn't expect you to be perfect and we still don't. You asked us our dreams, and so that's what we told you. But we had a prayer for you too. We prayed that God would do with you just exactly as He pleased. We turned you over to Him."

Well, my parents' dreams may not come true. But I'm pretty sure their prayer will be answered. And that, I think, is the important thing.

328

GREAT HOPPING HANGNAILS!

Last night I went for a ride with a friend and his parents. Her father has **got** to be one of the worst drivers I've ever met. It's not so much what he does with the car. It's what he does with his mouth. He's forever cursing other drivers. A couple times he got so mad, I was afraid he was going to have a heart attack. And to be perfectly truthful, all that cursing bothered me.

I can understand that sometimes people just have to say something to let off some of the steam building up inside them. I sure do. But my mom taught me a neat way to do that.

"Everybody always says the same old words. They're not only wrong—they're boring! Now a really creative person should be able to come up with other things to say. Don't you think?"

Well, I've been making up my own "steam-words" ever since. Words like "Toadguts!" And "Barbecued toenails!" And "Pumpkin-dust!"

The great thing about my steam-words is that they not only help me let off steam, but they keep me so busy thinking them up that I forget to stay mad.

I think, God, that You gave us imaginations for a good reason. I intend to use mine in all sorts of creative ways!

329

MY HOUSE

If I were a stranger and walked into my house, I'd say to myself, "Now what's so special about this?" Because my house doesn't look all that special. The furniture doesn't exactly go together, the rugs are pretty worn, and some of the rooms definitely need repainting.

Nevertheless, I would know exactly what to say to that stranger.

"This house is special," I would say, "because it's **my** house."

I'd show him the hole in the red chair where I used to hide pennies when I was a little kid. I'd show him the drawing I made of Oscar the Grouch behind the bathroom door. (I did it in permanent black Magic Marker. Unfortunately no one knows it's Oscar the Grouch unless I tell them.) I'd show him the spot on the kitchen ceiling where mom's tomato preserves exploded. I'd show him the cabinet door in the kitchen that still swings open and bonks you on the head even though my dad has tried to fix it a hundred times.

"I don't think those things are going to do much to increase your real estate value," the stranger might say. I'd have a snappy comeback for that too.

"So what?"

I love my house, God. Please, watch over it. You live there too!

330

SHE LIED

A girl at school said a very cruel thing about me recently—a lie. I just found out about it by chance. And in a way I wish I hadn't. It's ruined my whole day.

I don't know why she said that thing. I've never done anything to hurt her. Not that I know of. Maybe she doesn't like me on general principles. Or maybe she just likes to lie.

I talked to one of my friends about it and he said, "Oh, just forget it. Nobody who knows you is going to believe it anyway."

I guess that's true, but somehow it doesn't make me feel a whole lot better. I suppose what I'll have to do is confront this girl and ask her why she told that lie. Then she'll probably deny it and I'll feel like a fool. But at least she'll know I'm not a coward. And it might stop her from doing it again.

Yes, God, I can forgive this girl. It wasn't **that** big or **that** cruel a lie. But I sure wish I could understand why she did it.

331

THEY LOOK AT US SO STRANGELY

The other day after school a bunch of my friends and I went to a department store in the shopping center to buy a gift for one of our other friends. Now we aren't an especially bad-looking group of kids. We're all reasonably clean and everything. We're not rowdy. We just talk and laugh together like normal people. But the way some adults looked at us, you'd have thought Attila the Hun and all his fierce hordes were swooping down on the shopping center. I'm positive I saw one old lady grab her purse and clutch it to her front with both hands.

This sort of thing makes a kid feel pretty defensive.

Actually I wanted to go right up to that old lady—or any of the other adults who were staring at us—cross my eyes, wiggle my ears, and yell, "Bugga, bugga!"

I probably would have ended up in jail.

My mom laughed when I told her this whole incident. She says it's been going on for thousands of years, and in spite of my righteous indignation, she doesn't think I'll be able to change it.

"Kids in a group scare some adults," she said. "I think it's all that energy condensed in one small bit of space that frightens them."

Well, maybe. But someday, God, we're going to show them. We're going to use all that energy to do something about the problems of the world. Don't You think that's a good way of getting even?

332

I **LOVE** PEOPLE

The day after my little trip to the shopping center I saw three things that completely drove away all the bad feelings.

The first thing I saw was at the bank. A very old lady was standing in line behind a young man with a small baby. The man was holding the baby over his shoulder, and that baby and that old lady were carrying on the greatest conversation I ever saw. Neither one of them used real words, just gurgles and coos and little laughs. But you could feel the love flowing between them.

The next thing I saw involved two old people, a woman and a man. They were one of those couples who have obviously been married so long that they almost look like one another. And they were walking along the street holding hands. That one choked me up.

The third thing I saw was a policeman about to write a parking ticket and put it on a car. Then he glanced inside the car, and on the passenger side sat a young girl, crying as if her heart would break. She was so upset that she didn't even notice the policeman. And he just sighed, shrugged his shoulders, and walked away without leaving the ticket.

God, they are wonderful sometimes, these creatures called people that You made!

333

THE WORSHIP IS OVER

Lately our pastor has taken to putting a little saying at the end of our Sunday bulletins. "The worship is over!" it says. "The service begins!"I think that is **neat**. I'll bet that anyone who reads it will never talk about a "worship service" again without thinking of it in that way.

And yet the worship isn't exactly over either. Just the formal part. Because I have a feeling that everything we do to serve God's people is also a way of worshiping Him, especially if we ask Him to be with us as we do these things and bless what we do.

In fact, now that I really stop to think about it, I guess I'd change that saying. I'd say: "The worship isn't over, but the service is beginning." It doesn't sound quite as neat, but it says what I believe.

334

HOME SWEET HOME?

"Is all your homework done?"

"Have you fed the cat?"

"**When** are you going to clean up your room? I've asked you a million times."

All that they threw at me in one hour. One hour! And they call this home sweet home? Phooey!

And now that I've gotten that out of my system, I feel guilty. Because my homework isn't done, I haven't fed the cat, and my room is a mess.

Why couldn't I be perfect so my parents wouldn't yell at me? Why am I such a mess? Oh, rats, I'm going to cry.

I cried. And mom found me. She didn't say anything for a long time, just hugged me. Then she said she and dad didn't expect me to be perfect. They just wanted me to try a little harder. Sometimes **they** were scared about whether they were being good parents or not.

Then she helped me clean my room.

O God, I love them! I really do! And one of the things I love most about them is that they don't pretend that they're perfect. Some of my friends aren't so lucky. Thanks for my parents, God. Thanks a lot!

335

GOOD WAITING AND BAD WAITING

Sometimes I just hate to wait. Like at the store when 49 people are checking out in front of you. It's so **boring.** Or at the dentist's office when your insides crawl up inside your throat and your legs feel like two licorice whips. Even when I know it's not going to hurt I'm terrified.

But there's a good kind of waiting too. It's the kind you feel the day before your birthday when you know your family's planning something special for you but you don't know exactly what. You feel all quivery inside, and this silly smile keeps creeping across your face.

Why am I thinking about all this waiting? Advent. The beginning of the church year. We are waiting for the coming of God's Son. For me Advent is more like my second kind of waiting. After all, I know what God did that first Christmas and it's hard to pretend I don't. Oh, I know I'm supposed to think about other things during Advent too, like all that repentance stuff John the Baptist talked about and the end of the world. And sometimes I do.

But even when I'm being very solemn and thinking heavy thoughts like those, somewhere underneath is the quivery feeling and the silly smile ready to creep out. Because He **did** it! God sent His Son to that stable in Bethlehem and the whole world changed and that's Christmas.

336

A GREAT TIME FOR NOSES

Today I decided to pay particular attention to my nose. Normally I don't think about my nose too much. It's there and most of the time it works. But today I decreed National Nose Day for me. And I couldn't have picked a better time of year.

First of all my nose woke up to the smell of bacon. It practically **dragged** me into the kitchen.

Then it wandered into the living room and went straight to the table where we have our Advent wreath. Pine! Then it moseyed over to a bowl of candy. Peppermint!

"Enough of that, nose," I said. "Let's go outside."

We did and that nose almost went crazy. Air! Winter air—clean and sharp with just a touch of snow smell. My nose turned very cold and red before I got it inside again.

Hot turkey sandwiches. Wet soil where dad watered the plants. Mom's evening perfume. Cocoa. Soap. The cat's soft warm fur. Wood burning in the fireplace. My nose is exhausted.

Thank You, God, for noses.

337

NOT EVERYONE CAN KEEP A PROMISE

I remember when I was about five I was supposed to go to the ball game. It was going to be one of those special days when they give free caps to all the kids in the crowd. I could just **see** myself strutting around in that cap. My friends would know how important I was then!

But the day before the game I got the measles. **Millions** of measles all over me. I tried to hide them with mom's makeup but it didn't work.

"Sorry, sport," said my dad. "We'll go next time."

"But you **promised**!" I cried. "You PROMISED!"

Of course there was no way my dad could keep that promise. Measles were something he just couldn't control.

But God can. He can control measles and anything else He wants to. Those people who lived long ago in Old Testament times knew that. That's why they could count on God to keep the promise He'd made to them, the promise to send a Savior who would save them (and us) from sin and death forever.

Those people weren't disappointed either. God sent the Savior, His own Son. Not everyone can keep a promise. But God can. I can count on that!

338

WHAT SORT OF LIST SHALL I MAKE THIS YEAR?

About this time of year everyone I know starts making lists. My mom lists all the things she still has to do before Christmas. My dad lists all the money we've spent. My friends list all the presents they want, just in case someone should ask.

I've got a lot to do too. And I haven't saved up nearly enough money. There are plenty of presents I want, and I'd be glad to tell them to anybody who asks.

But I'd like my list to be different this year. I'd like to write down the things I want to give others—my parents, my friends, maybe even God. And I don't want those things to be things you can touch. I want them to be parts of **me.** Like kindness or cheerfulness—things like that.

The people I'd give them to (except for God) might not even know they were presents. But I'd like to give them anyway—all year. In fact, I might just hide my list somewhere and check it next year to see how I've done.

One thing though. I don't think I could go on giving presents like that for very long on my own. After all, I'm only human. Do You suppose You could help me, God? And while You're at it, pick out a good present for Yourself!

339

TWO WORLDS

I went to the shopping center with my parents this evening, and there it all was. My dad calls it schlock. Christmas schlock. Tinsel and trees, elves and reindeer, music (too loud) and flashing lights (too bright). There were mechanical Santa Clauses, live Santa Clauses, and a Santa Claus made entirely of feathers. (That was **weird**.)

And in church we're talking about repentance and waiting and a promise.

They're two entirely different worlds, and sometimes I feel as if I'm walking a tightrope stretched between them. One minute I lose my balance and lean a little toward one of them. The next minute I'm leaning back the other way.

To be perfectly honest, I **like** some of the Christmas schlock. It's fun. It makes me feel happy, and it makes the people around me feel happy too.

But deep inside I know what Christmas really is. That little Baby, crying in a cattle shed. God, stepping right into the middle of our lives. And that's so tremendous I can't even find words for it.

Maybe all this is part of what it means to be a Christian. Walking a tightrope between two worlds. Enjoying some of the good things of the one but not forgetting the tremendousness of the other. That's a tricky thing to do. I'm glad I don't have to do it alone, God.

340

SYMBOLS AND SONGS AND STUFF I DON'T UNDERSTAND

There's an awful lot about this Advent business that I don't understand. I think the wreath is neat, but I'm not sure what it means. And I love the eerie melody to "Oh, Come, Oh, Come, Emmanuel," but I don't really know what the words are about.

Well, I decided it was time I started learning. So I asked my Sunday school teacher about the word "Emmanuel." She said it means "God with us."

God with us. "Oh, come, oh, come, God with us, and ransom captive Israel."

Of course! It's an invitation, a sad, desperate sort of invitation. "We are captives, God. Please. Come be with us. Save us."

What a perfect song to sing during Advent when we're all acting out that time of waiting. But even in the song we can't pretend to be completely sad. We **know** what will happen and so at the end we sing, "Rejoice! God with us **will** come."

Obviously there is a lot more to the symbols and songs and stuff in Advent than I ever dreamed. They probably all mean something special. I think I'll just have to do a little more detective work.

341

A PRESENT FOR GOD

I've been thinking some more about this whole idea of giving a Christmas present to God. There's a poem by Christina Rosetti that talks about it:

"What can I give Him, poor as I am?
If I were a shepherd, I would bring a lamb;
If I were a wise man, I would do my part;
Yet what I can I give Him: give my heart."

Of course she's talking about Baby Jesus, but I don't think it makes any difference. I really like the poem, but I'm not sure about the meaning. How can you give God your heart? Does it just mean you love Him? I already do. I've loved God ever since I was a little kid in Sunday school. You're **supposed** to.

But when people talk about giving their hearts away in songs or movies, they're not talking about a "supposed to" kind of love. They're talking about this incredible force that shakes them up and turns them all around. They act as if they can't help themselves, as if their love for that person is the most important thing in the whole world.

Hey, maybe that's it! Shaken up, turned around. The most important thing in the world. Maybe that's how to feel when you give your heart to God. At least it's a place to start. And now, God, if You wouldn't mind helping . . .

342

THE END OF THE WORLD SCARES ME

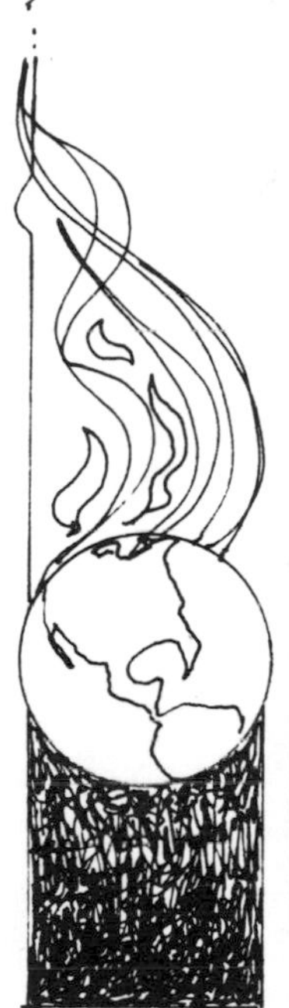

All right. I'm supposed to think about it during Advent and I will. The end of the world. But I'll tell you this: It scares me.

I don't **want** the world to end. It's full of problems, I know. But it's all we've got, and besides, I'm sort of used to it. And the thought of trumpets and fire and people gnashing their teeth, well . . .

Of course when you get right down to it, I don't know what the end of the world will be like, and I don't think anybody else does either. Everybody describes it differently, and even the Bible uses a lot of different pictures.

So what's the important thing? (I'm learning that that's a very good question to ask. It sort of clears your head.)

The important thing is that Jesus is coming again. Jesus. Why, I **trust** Him. He's loved and taken care of me ever since I can remember—and before that, I guess.

Why should I be so scared of Jesus' coming? Maybe I'll feel ashamed and guilty about some of the things I've thought and done. But He's not going to stop loving me because of those things. He proved that a long time ago.

If the end of the world is the same as Jesus' coming then I feel a whole lot better about it.

343

TRADITIONS

We have a tradition in my family. About this time of year we make a special cake. It's got raisins and nuts and all sorts of stuff in it and the whole family works on it together. My mom says the recipe goes back to her great-great-grandmother and maybe even before that.

We have traditions in our church too—traditions with candles and music and a special Advent banner that hangs across the whole balcony. I don't know how far back all of those traditions go, but some I think were being done hundreds of years ago.

I can just see this kid, someone about my age, dressed in funny clothes. (Yeah, I guess mine would look funny back then too.) He—or she—is singing the same song I sing and watching a candle being lit in the same ceremony. Is he—or she—thinking the same kind of thoughts? Maybe even thinking about some kid in the future—me?

It gives me chills to wonder about things like that. But they're good chills. They're part of feeling myself a member of something much bigger than I dreamed possible—the family of God. It's a family that stretches from the beginning of time till the end. And traditions? Well, they're something like holding hands with other family members across time. I'm glad we have them.

344

THE SONG INSIDE ME

Every so often it happens. I get a feeling inside me, right about where my heart is supposed to be. It's a hard feeling to describe. It's bubbly and ringing and excited and glad and very, very eager to get out. I call it my song.

This feeling doesn't have much to do with what's going on outside me. Sometimes it even comes when things aren't going too well—like in the middle of tests.

But once it comes, the feeling sure changes what's going on outside me. Or maybe it just makes me feel so good that everything out there looks better.

I don't think I'll ever sing that songlike feeling. I can't imagine it all tucked away in one song. It's too big, too alive.

But I do want to share it with other people someday. I think it's something God wants me to share. And I think He'll show me the best way to do that when the time comes.

Meanwhile, I feel **great.** Thanks, God!

345

COULDN'T IT BE A SIMPLE THING?

Well, we're really into Christmas at my house now. Everyone is running around like crazy, buying things, wrapping things, cooking things, cleaning things, mailing things. I don't think anyone is having a good time. Does it have to be like this?

Couldn't Christmas be more simple? Couldn't we give each other just one present apiece? (I can't believe I wrote that, but I think I mean it.) Couldn't we write to our friends throughout the year instead of trying to catch up with all of them at Christmas? Couldn't we have just a few special things to eat—like our traditional cake? Couldn't we take time just to be quiet together and wait for the Baby?

I decided that instead of sitting here in a sulk and writing all these thoughts, I should talk to my parents about them. It took a while to get their attention, but I finally did it.

And do you know what? They **agreed** with me. Dad even hugged me.

We won't be able to change too much this year anymore. But we all promised each other to have a much simpler Christmas next year. And I'm going to remember that promise!

346

A POSITIVE ATTITUDE

My teacher took me aside the other day and said I needed to develop a more positive attitude. She said I always look on the bad side of things, whether it's current events or a math assignment or a test. She also said that if I acted that way toward my friends I'd have trouble socially.

The first thing I wanted to do was punch her in the mouth. (How's that for positive?) The second thing I wanted to do was cry. Finally I just said a polite little "thank you" and walked away.

Do I need a more positive attitude? After all, current events **are** pretty rotten. And math **is** hard for me and I **am** scared of tests. I don't think my attitude can change any of that. Or can it?

If I really believe that God's in charge and that He cares about what happens to me and the rest of the world, doesn't that make everything look different? Sure, the world's in bad shape and math is hard and tests are scary, but I can work to change all that, even if just a little.

God, I really do believe You're in charge and You care. Please help my attitude show that.

347

FAIRY TALES

My mom bought a book of fairy tales as a Christmas present for my little cousin, and I made her let me read it before she wrapped it. It was really neat reading all those old stories again. I just loved them when I was younger.

I remember, though, that I had this Sunday school teacher who said we shouldn't read fairy tales because we'd get them all mixed up with Jesus. Boy, she sure underestimated little kids! **We** knew fairy tales were make-believe. And we knew Jesus was real.

The great thing about fairy tales is that evil is all there where you can see it—in a monster or some wicked person. Along comes a prince or princess and POOF! Evil is dead.

Real life isn't that simple. First of all you can't always tell what's evil and what isn't. And even when you can tell you can't just chop off its head once and forever. It keeps coming back.

No, in the real world you need help. You need Jesus. So it's a good thing that He's real and that God sent Him.

348

A TAKER OR A GIVER?

Tonight at dinner my dad was talking about some guy he works with. He said the world was divided into two types of people—takers and givers—and that this guy was a taker. He's always wanting everybody to do him favors and help him out. He never thinks about what he could do for other people.

I'd feel **terrible** if that's how people felt about me. I like to think of myself as a giver. But am I?

I **do** take things—favors and help—mostly from my family and friends. But I do mean to give things too.

Let's see. This week I brought the kid up the street his books because he's been sick and getting behind on his homework. And I listened while this girl told me about a problem she had. And I cleared off the table twice without waiting to be asked. I guess those count as giving things.

I think we all have to be takers sometimes. Nobody can make it alone. But maybe God works through us to make us givers too—when we let Him. I'm going to try to let Him do it a lot more from now on.

349

"REPENT!"

"Repent!"

That's what John the Baptist cried, and it's another one of those things I'm supposed to think about during Advent. I was having a tough time with it, though, until my Sunday school teacher said it just means "turn around." Then I saw another one of those movies in my mind.

Here I am, doing all these terrible things and not even caring one bit. All of a sudden I hear this voice:

"Repent!"

I open my eyes very wide, and I see the things I've been doing and how terrible they are. I want more than anything to turn around, to look away from them and toward God. But I can't do it. I'm not strong enough.

Then slowly and softly I feel someone pushing me, pushing till I'm all turned around and facing the right way again. It's God. **He** knew I couldn't do it alone. So He helped.

And that's repentance. I'm glad I thought about it.

350

DO MIRACLES STILL HAPPEN?

At this time of year everybody starts telling stories about miracles. The little juggler does his act and the statue of Jesus smiles at him. The poor girl wakes up and finds presents all over her bed. The mean old man hears a kid singing and becomes a changed person.

I wonder if miracles really do happen anymore or if they stopped at the end of the Bible. I asked my mom and she said she thought it was probably a very complicated issue. I said that answer didn't help me too much, and she laughed and said it didn't help her too much either.

Apparently there are very special sorts of things—like what Jesus did in the Bible—and those are the real miracles. But there are other things that can happen today that feel a lot like miracles because they help us remember that God is with us and working in our world. A cure for some dreadful disease would be that sort of miracle. So would a miser suddenly caring about the poor. Or, in a way, a flower opening.

That's what my mom says about miracles, and I like it.

351

A WISH FOR THE WORLD

Today I read the neatest thing on—of all places—a Christmas card. It said:

"Happiness depends on what happens.
Joy is a gift from God.
May joy be yours this Christmas."

Well, did **that** get me thinking! About how happy I am when I get a good grade or someone says something nice about me or I get invited to a party. When the right things **happen.**

But joy is different. It's part of that bubbly ringing feeling inside me that I call my song. It's what I feel in church when everybody's singing and light is pouring through the windows. It's what I feel when I see my family all together and know for sure that God is watching over us.

Sometimes I think our world is running like crazy after happiness. We try to make the right things happen to us and the people we love, but too often they just don't happen.

So if I could send a Christmas card to the world, it would say what that other card said:

"May joy be yours this Christmas."

352

BOOKS

I've been trying to decide on a Christmas present for my dad, and I finally settled on a book about the Middle Ages. He really likes reading about history, and the lady at the bookshop told me this was a new book, one he wouldn't have read yet.

Being in that bookshop gave me the neatest feeling. There were all these shelves and shelves of books, and every one of them was a trip to some other place, some other time, or some other person's mind. You could never visit all those places or know all those people without books.

And books are so **convenient.** I picked one up and held it. Just a little rectangle, something I could carry anywhere. But inside it was a world.

God, I've seen models and pictures of brains, and we even talked about them in science class. But none of that even begins to explain how a human person came up with the idea of "book." And none of it explains how a human person can squunch a whole world inside a book. **You** made us able to do those things, and sometimes what You did just takes my breath away.

Maybe I'll give everyone I know a book this Christmas.

353

EVERYBODY WANTS MY TIME!

I've written about how everybody else is running around like crazy this time of year. Well, I'm doing it too. It seems as if **everyone** wants my time. At school they keep piling on tests and homework. At home there are more chores than ever. Even the church is having Advent services and special choir rehearsals for our Christmas music. As my grandma sometimes says, "My time is not my own anymore."

Grandma was over for dinner tonight, and I told her how I was feeling. She smiled and nodded.

"Yes, I do say that," she said. "But even while I'm saying it I know my time was never mine to begin with. It all belongs to God. I just try to manage it so I can give as much of it back to Him as possible."

"How do you give time back to God?" I asked.

"By asking Him to use everything I do to show the world His love."

I'm not sure I completely understand that. At least I can't quite see what it has to do with homework and tests. But maybe I don't have to understand right now. Maybe I can trust God to do the understanding.

One thing I do know for sure: I have a neat grandma!

354

I THINK MY PARENTS ARE PEOPLE

Today I did a little pre-Christmas snooping. No, I didn't try to find out what my presents are like I used to when I was little. Instead I watched my parents. And I found out something all right, something that almost knocked me over.

I saw dad baking Christmas cookies. On his face was this worried frown that made him look kind of crabby. Normally I would have stayed out of his way. But somehow today I knew it wasn't crabbiness at all. He just wanted to do a good job and was afraid he might mess up. Boy, do I know that feeling!

Then I saw mom reading a Christmas card from an old friend of hers who's moved out of town. When mom looked up from the card she had tears in her eyes. I could almost feel the terrible missing, the loneliness she felt right then.

Later, in the kitchen, I saw them kissing. And suddenly I knew exactly what that kiss meant. Mom was saying, "You did a good job and I love you." Dad was saying, "It's okay. I'm still here and I love you."

My parents are people! They have the same sorts of feelings I have. They can feel unsure. They can be lonely. They need to be told sometimes that it's okay, that someone loves them.

O God, don't let me forget this discovery. It makes such a difference just to know. And maybe it will make a difference in how I act toward them too. Maybe I can help them have good feelings, the kind I want to have. Help me, God, please.

355

WHAT IN THE WORLD ARE ANGELS?

At the top of our Christmas tree is an angel. It's very pretty with long golden hair, a silvery robe, and outstretched wings. I've looked at it every Christmas for years, but today for the first time I began to wonder if that's what angels really are like.

I know in the Christmas story one of them talks to the shepherds and a lot of them sing. So I guess they have mouths—unless they used mental telepathy. Could a whole choir sing in mental telepathy?

In the Easter story Luke talks about two men in brilliant clothes. Does that mean angels look like men? Or did they just make themselves look that way so the women wouldn't be too scared?

And someplace in the Old Testament it talks about creatures with wings and wheels and hands and lots of eyes. **That** would scare me.

I don't think I'm going to find out what angels look like—at least not in this life. But the Bible does say that God made them. In fact, one of the psalms says He made **us** just a little lower than angels. God certainly knows what He's doing, so I guess I'll leave it at that.

Maybe after I die I'll meet an angel. That's something to look forward to.

356

THE LITTLE KIDS

It's more fun to watch the little kids when it gets close to Christmas. They're so excited and yet so serious at the same time.

For example: At church the nursery class is putting on a pageant of the stable scene. At one point all of the children playing animals are supposed to make noises like their animal would make. But at the last rehearsal one little girl—a sheep—wouldn't do it. She just stood there with her mouth shut tight, shaking her head.

"Come on, Nancy," said her teacher. "Say baa like the sheep does."

"No," whispered Nancy.

"But why not?" asked her teacher. "Does your throat hurt?"

"No," whispered Nancy. "I just don't want to wake the Baby."

I can remember feeling that way about Christmas—as if everything was so sacred and wonderful that I'd better tiptoe around so I wouldn't break it. I guess I still feel that way sometimes. In fact, I don't ever want to grow up so much that I forget that wonderful excited-serious feeling about Christmas.

Don't let me, God. Let some tiny part of me stay a child forever.

357

WHAT WAS IT REALLY LIKE THAT FIRST CHRISTMAS?

Were all the animals really clean and cuddly at the first Christmas? Did Mary really wear a beautiful blue dress without a wrinkle in it and her hair all in place? Did Joseph really stand there in the cosy stable with a warm, proud smile on his face?

It's a nice picture for Christmas cards, but I don't think that's the way it really was at all.

My Sunday school teacher said the stable was probably a cave in a hill behind the inn. That means it must have been dark and dingy. It must have smelled too. Animals do.

And I'll bet Mary and Joseph were both worn out from all that traveling and having a baby. They probably looked wrinkled and smudged and ready to fall asleep any minute.

No, Jesus didn't come to earth on a Christmas card. He came into the real world the way ordinary people do. He came with poor people in a smelly, dirty place.

I think God had a reason for sending Him that way. I think God was saying, "This Child won't be the kind of king you're used to. He'll be different, and His kingdom will be different. But I've kept My promise and here He is."

Christmas Eve

FEELINGS TOO DEEP FOR WORDS

It's Christmas Eve and I don't know what to write. I guess there are times when the feelings inside you are so deep and so strong that there are no words for them.

We went to church, we heard the Christmas story from Luke, and we sang the old songs. At home we each opened one present and mom made cocoa. That's what we **did,** but it doesn't begin to explain how I **felt.**

After a while I put on my coat and went outside by myself. For a long time I just stood there quietly looking at the stars. Then dad came out and stood there with me. We didn't say anything till we were back inside.

Right now that Advent hymn, "Oh, Come, Oh, Come, Emmanuel," keeps running through my head—even though it's Christmas now. And maybe that's the one word I'm looking for—Emmanuel. God with us.

God **is** with us and tonight I know it. And it is very good.

Christmas Day

WHAT WOULD THE BABY THINK?

If somehow they could be brought here—Mary and Joseph and Baby Jesus—to my living room this Christmas Day, what would they think? What would He think, the Baby?

Would He wonder why we had a tree in the house, with strange things hanging from it that He musn't eat or play with?

Would He cry because everybody get presents except Him? Or would He think that neckties and blenders and TV tennis games were pretty silly presents anyway?

Would His nose wrinkle at the smells coming from the kitchen, smells of foods He never tasted—like mince pie and sweet potatoes with melted marshmallows?

Would He be angry about all the things here that don't really have anything to do with the time and place He came to earth?

Or would He sense the love that's reaching out from each of us to all the others? Would that make Him feel at home? Would that love tell Him what we're really doing—having a birthday party for the most wonderful Baby that ever was born?

What **would** the Baby think?

360

DO I CARE TOO MUCH ABOUT "THINGS?"

I looked through my Christmas presents this evening and, boy, did I get some neat stuff. There's a watch that even tells the date. I can hardly bear to take it off. And there's a jacket with a lining that's so soft I just want to pet it. And there's . . .

Oh, no! Am I caring too much about **things**? What an awful trap to fall into at Christmas and after I've been writing all these religious thoughts too.

But I **do** like my watch and my jacket. That's why mom and dad gave them to me. Is it **wrong** to like them?

I finally asked Dad. He **laughed.**

"Look," he said, "how much do you like those presents? Would you hurt mom or me just to keep them? Would you betray one of your friends or stop going to church?"

"Of course not," I said. "I just **like** them a lot."

"Then I think you're okay," said dad. "You can forget about that guilt trip. Start feeling guilty about some of your real faults."

He grinned.

Now what did he mean by that?

361

I'M DEPRESSED!

I don't believe it. I'm depressed. Here I am in the middle of the Christmas holidays and I feel as if I could cry a bathtubful of tears. **Why**?

Well, for one thing I think I hate it because everything is beginning to end now instead of just beginning. I think I waited so hard for Christmas to come that when it got here I was sure it would go on forever. And now I'm afraid that nothing good will happen again till next Christmas.

What dumb feelings to have! But I've got them. And now that I stop to think about it, I'm pretty sure I had them last year too.

I've tried telling myself not to be depressed but that doesn't work. Being depressed is sort of like having a cold. You have to live through it. But it **does** help to know that I've lived through it in other years. And maybe I could do something about the symptoms, like you do for a cold. Maybe I could take a walk. It snowed last night. Yeah, I'd like that.

I guess I'll make it without overflowing the bathtub. But, God, could You help a little?

362

THE RELATIVES

Today they all came. The relatives. Aunts, uncles, cousins, grandparents, everyone who lives anywhere near. Mom and dad's bed was heaped with coats and right in the middle, like a bird in a nest, slept the littlest cousin who's only a baby.

We ate and talked and ate and exchanged presents and ate and sang songs. Everyone said how much I'd grown, and I pretended to hate it but I really didn't.

The relatives don't usually all get together except on holidays. So today I took a good long look at them. Some of them are really neat. I wish I saw them more often. Some are sort of weird, not like **my** family. And some are just—well—relatives.

That's what I saw when I looked at the relatives. But then I began to think. Each one of them is a person just as I am. Each one has feelings and plans and disappointments and dreams. And I don't know very much about that part of them at all.

Maybe this year I'll learn a little more. Maybe I'll try to talk to some of them like I talk to my friends. In the meantime, God, please take care of them. They're mine!

363

HAVE I BEEN A PIG?

I have gained weight. I just can't understand why. I'm just eating pies and cookies and cakes and candy. (I hope my dentist never reads this.) There's only one word to describe me: OINK!

Now, what does that mean? Should I feel guilty and hate myself for what I've done? The next time someone offers me a Christmas cookie should I ask for a carrot stick instead?

I don't like either of those ideas. Somehow I suspect God thinks it's okay for us to celebrate now and then—especially the birth of His Son. After all, Jesus Himself even celebrated, like at the wedding at Cana.

Maybe, as my mom likes to say, it's all a matter of **degree.** Maybe I should eat just two (or three) cookies instead of six. Maybe I should try to sit someplace besides in front of the cookie plate.

I'm going to go on celebrating, God, especially the birth of Your Son. But maybe I'll sing a little more and eat a little less!

364

ICE STORMS AND HIGHER AUTHORITIES

Boy, did we have an ice storm last night! This morning the trees and bushes and powerlines looked like crystal statues. People had to chisel their way into their cars. And the sidewalks and streets were like one huge skating rink.

I loved it. I went outside and slid and slid and slid. But it wasn't so much fun for the people who had to drive somewhere. They slid too—sometimes into each other. I personally heard four men say words they shouldn't have said and saw one lady cry.

The whole thing made me think about how carefully we plan—our days, our lives, our world. Then along comes one little ice storm and all our plans fall apart. We're practically helpless.

I wonder how that makes the people who don't believe in God feel. Do they get scared, depressed, mad? It must be awful to have those feelings and not even be able to talk to God about them. At least I can say, "I'm scared, God. Help!" Or "Could You please help me feel a little less depressed?" Or "**Why** did You let this happen?" It really makes a difference when you can talk to a Higher Authority.

About this ice storm, God: I thought it was neat!

New Year's Eve

PATTERNS

December is over. A new year is almost here. Everyone is shouting "Happy New Year." I'm beginning to feel like shouting it too.

The church year has already begun. Now the regular year begins. We have waited for Jesus and He has come. (That alone is reason for shouting and joy.) Soon we will learn from the Wise Men and go out to show God's light in a darkening world. We will struggle and stumble as we try to follow Jesus. We will follow Him to a cross. And we will burst with Him from a stone-blocked grave to new and unending life. We will celebrate the birthday of a church. And then we will do it all again.

They are all patterns—the church year, the calendar year, the seasons, even the school year—they are patterns that stretch across centuries. In fact, there are many patterns in our lives as Christians. Sin and forgiveness. Death and resurrection. Grief and joy. Over and over again the same things happen, and yet we never seem to get tired of them.

I guess, God, that is because they all come from You, and from them You have woven the very cloth of our lives.